WORLD BANK WORKING PAPER NO. 185

Enhancing Regional Trade Integration in Southeast Europe

Borko Handjiski
Robert Lucas
Philip Martin
Selen Sarisoy Guerin

THE WORLD BANK
Washington, D.C.

Printed on recycled paper

1 2 3 4   13 12 11 10

World Bank Working Papers are published to communicate the results of the Bank's work to the development community with the least possible delay. The manuscript of this paper therefore has not been prepared in accordance with the procedures appropriate to formally-edited texts. Some sources cited in this paper may be informal documents that are not readily available.

ISBN: 978-0-8213-8259-2
eISBN: 978-0-8213-8266-0
ISSN: 1726-5878   DOI: 10.1596/978-0-8213-8259-2

Library of Congress Cataloging-in-Publication Data has been requested.

Contents

Tables

Figures

Boxes

Acknowledgments

This paper consists of three reports. The first report, "Evolution of Intra-regional Trade in Southeast Europe: The Role of CEFTA for Enhancing Regional Trade Integration," was written by Borko Handjiski (World Bank). The second report, "Labor Mobility in Southeast Europe," was prepared by professors Robert Lucas (Boston University) and Philip Martin (UC Davis). The last report, "The Impact of Establishing a Virtual Customs Union between Southeast Europe and the European Union," was written by Selen Sarisoy Guerin (Vrije Universiteit Brussel and Centre for European Policy Studies). Peer reviewers for the first report were Leopoldo Rubinacci (European Commission, DG Trade), Juan Sebastaian Saez (World Bank, International Trade Department), and Renata Vitez (CEFTA Secretariat). Peer reviewers for the other two reports were Vladimir Gligorov (The Vienna Institute for International Economic Studies), Juan Sebastaian Saez (World Bank), and Trpe Stojanovski (MARRI Regional Centre). Their comments and suggestions are gratefully acknowledged. The paper also benefited from the comments of World Bank staff including Bernard Funck, Vesna Kostic, Matija Laco, and Sanja Madzarevic Sujster.

The work on the last two reports was initiated by Sanjay Kathuria and was financed by the governments of Finland, Norway, Sweden, and the United Kingdom through a contribution from the Multi-Donor Trust Fund for Trade and Development.

Foreword

The Southeast Europe (SEE) region comprises a group of countries at a relatively similar stage of economic development and with a common objective, and prospect, of becoming members of the European Union (EU). To achieve the goal of EU membership, the countries of the region have pursued closer integration with the EU as well as with each other. Numerous regional cooperation initiatives have been introduced in several areas, including aviation, energy, and railways, but the greatest progress has been made in trade integration. In December 2006, the SEE countries and Moldova signed the Central European Free Trade Agreement[1] (CEFTA), a comprehensive free trade agreement (FTA) that aims to fully liberalize trade in the region as well as to achieve greater cooperation in a number of trade-related areas, such as investment, services, public procurement, and intellectual property rights.

This paper is part of the World Bank's efforts to understand the impact of CEFTA on regional trade flows, as well as to put forward other, complementary, ideas that could enhance further regional trade integration. It builds on previous analytical work done by the World Bank in this area, and in particular on the book *"Western Balkan Integration and the EU: Agenda for Trade and Growth"* (Kathuria, 2008).

The paper includes three studies. The first one looks at intra-regional trade flows and the remaining nontariff barriers to trade in the region (in particular in those areas that are included in CEFTA). The other two studies introduce two ideas that have so far not received sufficient attention from policy makers in the region: (i) to allow free movement [of certain categories] of skilled labor within the region, and (ii) to adopt EU's Common External Tariff as a measure to prevent trade diversion and to prepare for EU integration.

We believe the findings merit close attention and provide solid arguments for policy action. Intra-regional trade has increased rapidly in recent years; however, the amount and content of trade flows do not signal significant trade integration, such as the countries of Central and Eastern Europe achieved in the past decade. Following the tariff liberalization, nontariff barriers have become the main obstacles for trade and, therefore, the focus should now shift to eliminating those barriers. Enhanced regional trade integration should not be confined only to free movement of goods. Increased labor mobility (a key pillar of the EU) could also have trade creation effects and could help create a regional market able to attract greater foreign investment. Last but not least, tariff structures in many countries of the region allow some scope for trade diversion in favor of EU and CEFTA countries at the expense of the rest of the world. Such trade diversion could be reduced by adopting the EU's Common External Tariff structure. This would also help the SEE countries to prepare for EU accession.

This paper comes at an important point of the region's development, and should guide policy makers in defining policy actions that will help their countries unleash their trade potential as well as prepare them for EU membership.

Bernard Funck,
Sector Manager, Europe and Central Asia
The World Bank

Notes

[1] Also called CEFTA 2006 (to differentiate from the original agreement signed by the Central European countries in the early 1990s).

Acronyms and Abbreviations

ABTC	Apec Business Travel Card
AFTA	Asean Free Trade Area
APEC	Asia-Pacific Economic Cooperation
BEEPS	Business Environment and Enterprise Performance Survey
BiH	Bosnia and Herzegovina
CARICOM	Caribbean Community
CEFTA	Central European Free Trade Agreement
CIS	Commonwealth of Independent States
COMESA	Common Market for Eastern and Southern Africa
CSME	Caricom Single Market and Economy
DCO	Diagonal cumulation of origin
EAC	East Africa Community
ECA	Europe and Central Asia
ECJ	European Court of Justice
ECOWAS	Economic Community of Western African States
EFTA	European Free Trade Area
EN	European Standard
EPL	Employment Protection Legislation
ETI	Enabling Trade Index
EU	European Union
FDI	foreign direct investment
FTA	free trade agreement
FYR	Former Yugoslav Republic
GDP	gross domestic product
ICMPD	International Centre for Migration Policy Development
ICT	information and communication technologies
IIT	Intra-Industry Trade
ILO	International Labour Organization
IOM	International Organization for Migration
MARRI	Migration, Asylum, Refugees, Regional Initiative
MERCOSUR	Mercado Comun del Sur
MFN	most favored nation
MOI	Croatian Ministry of Interior
NAFTA	North American Free Trade Agreement
NTB	nontariff barriers
OECD	Organization for Economic Cooperation and Development
SAA	Stabilization and Association Agreements
SEE	Southeast Europe
SITC	Standard International Trade Classification
SMART	Software for Market Analysis and Restrictions on Trade
SMEs	small and medium-sized enterprises

SPS	sanitary and phytosanitary
TBT	technical barriers to trade
UNCTAD	United Nations Conference on Trade and Development
UNHCR	United Nations High Commissioner for Refugees
U.S.	United States
VAT	value added tax
WEF	World Economic Forum
WTO	World Trade Organization

Executive Summary

The Southeast Europe (SEE) region comprises a group of countries at a relatively similar stage of economic development and with a common objective, and prospect, of becoming members of the European Union (EU). To achieve the goal of EU membership, the countries of the region have pursued closer integration with the EU as well as with each other. Regional cooperation has been focused on areas that aim to promote greater economic ties among the countries. A multilateral free trade agreement, CEFTA, was concluded in December 2006 to achieve the pursuit of economic integration. This agreement is very comprehensive and aims to enhance collaboration in several trade-related areas. In addition to the fulfilling the commitments of CEFTA, the SEE countries could consider additional policies to foster trade integration.

Intra-regional Trade Patterns and Constraints

As discussed in Part I of this paper, intra-regional trade performance in Southeast Europe has improved considerably in recent years. The increased trade flows have been a result of formal trade liberalization (first through bilateral FTAs and later through CEFTA) and of trade facilitation measures. The trade expansion in this decade had led to trade deepening with one fifth of the trade increase coming from new trade relationships. So far, trade liberalization has been by and large confined to manufactures, but these early successes should embolden CEFTA members to expand their efforts to agriculture and services.

Despite the significant increase in trade, its structure does not signal significant trade integration. Commodities continue to dominate, and intra-industry trade remains low compared to intra-industry trade performance in the EU-10 countries (now as well as in the period prior to joining the EU).

Growth in trade within the region was even stronger in 2008, following the entry of CEFTA into force, though of course this cannot be fully attributed to the Agreement. As a matter of fact, the most important novelty of the Agreement, in addition to the full liberalization of trade in manufactured goods, is the inclusion of other areas of cooperation such as technical barriers to trade, rules of origin, competition rules, public procurement, intellectual property rights, and so forth. CEFTA also establishes a well-defined dispute resolution mechanism and it is important to ensure that the Agreement is well implemented or that possible disputes could be efficiently resolved. Otherwise, disappointments are inevitable, as has happened under the bilateral FTAs, which are often not properly implemented for a number of reasons.

The report assesses the progress and challenges on some of the most important constraints to greater trade integration in the region. It finds that, with the abolishment of tariffs and quotas, technical regulations, and standards have become an important constraint on trade and greater collaboration is required to reduce these barriers. In this regard, the harmonization and international recognition of the quality of infrastructure in SEE is vital for further promoting regional trade.

The trade-related environment continues to include policy-induced barriers that prevent further development of intra-regional (and broader) trade. The report finds that most SEE countries have made significant progress on the trade facilitation agenda, but have yet to fully catch up with the more advanced European reformers on number of trade-related issues, as evidenced by global or regional surveys and reports such as the *Doing Business* report, the Business Environment and Enterprise Performance Survey (BEEPS), Enabling Trade Index, and the Logistics Performance Indicators. While no particular area can be identified as a binding constraint to trade per se, addressing these constraints could reduce the overall costs of trading and promote export growth. The case studies of two regional firms confirm the findings of the global surveys and report.

In this context, implementation first, then deepening of the CEFTA agreement will help the SEE countries' EU accession prospects. All countries in the region are strongly committed to becoming members of the European Union. Even though the timeframe for joining the EU is uncertain and probably varies among the countries, once the SEE countries join, their economies will be fully integrated into the EU's Single Market. Hence, creating a more unified regional economic space prior to becoming part of the EU will have multiple benefits: (i) firms will be better able to cope with the competitive pressures within the Union; (ii) national administrations will have gained experience in regional cooperation, which is essential for well-functioning within the EU; and (iii) by converging towards EU standards, the countries will sooner achieve alignment with the EU *acquis* in these areas.

The Benefits of Skilled Labor Mobility

Part II of this paper is motivated by World Bank recommendations (Kathuria, 2008, p. 22) that urge CEFTA member states to "negotiate an agreement on preferential liberalization of professional services that focuses on the movement of natural persons [beginning with] mutual recognition of professional qualifications [and extending] to all labor, skilled or unskilled…" to deepen economic integration.

The original CEFTA came into force in 1994, but all states that were members before 2003 exited CEFTA upon gaining accession to the EU. There are currently eight CEFTA members: the Republic of Albania, Bosnia and Herzegovina, Republic of Croatia, Kosovo, the Former Yugoslav Republic of Macedonia, Republic of Moldova, Montenegro, and the Republic of Serbia. All parties, except Moldova, aspire and expect to join the EU. Croatia and FYR Macedonia are most advanced in this process, while the others are considered potential EU candidates (Montenegro and Albania submitted membership applications in 2009). In 2003, EU leaders said that "the Western Balkan countries will become an integral part of the EU, once they meet the established criteria." (Thessaloniki European Council, June 19-20, 2003). It is important to see the issue of labor mobility among CEFTA members in the context of eventual EU membership and freedom of movement, a cornerstone of the EU.[1]

Many FTAs, including with the EU, allow and sometimes encourage labor mobility among member countries. A review of the mobility provisions of FTAs indicates a number of common features:

- Labor mobility often comes into force with considerable time lag, often several years after free trade in goods.
- Implementation of mobility provisions is generally far less complete among the developing countries; most lack institutions to which individuals who believe their mobility rights were violated can appeal.
- Labor mobility agreements, as with free trade agreements, can be bilateral or multilateral. Most FTAs are regional, involving neighboring countries. Countries that are members of more than one free-trade grouping often find progress toward labor mobility more complex. In any event, liberalizing freedom-of-movement between two countries requires consideration of so-called "third-country nationals."
- It is easier to negotiate agreements to liberalize skilled labor migration because the numbers are relatively small, the economic and public finance gains to receiving countries may be greater, and skilled workers may generate positive externalities such as innovation where they live.
- Some FTAs such as NAFTA limit free movement to highly skilled workers, while others encompass a wider range of skill categories. Movement toward mutual recognition of qualifications is important for mobility of skilled workers.
- The distribution of economic benefits from free labor mobility provisions are not equally spread across member countries or within each country.
- Lack of portability of pensions and health and similar benefits may discourage workers from working abroad and returning; portability is an issue in many labor mobility negotiations. Posted workers employed by a home-country employer abroad are less affected by portability issues because they remain covered by home-country benefit systems.
- There is sometimes less migration than anticipated under free labor mobility provisions, reflecting issues with information about jobs, language differences, credentials recognition, and lack of access to public sector employment.

All CEFTA member countries have substantial experience with labor migration. Most have diasporas that send home significant remittances. Estimates of migrant stocks and flows vary considerably reflecting different definitions, extensive irregular migration, and widespread dual nationality. Perhaps up to a third of the diaspora from Bosnia and Herzegovina is residing in other CEFTA states. The size of the diaspora is much lower and its distribution is different for the other CEFTA states, reflecting more migration to the EU. Moldova remains relatively isolated from this intra-CEFTA mobility, since most Moldovan migrants move to Commonwealth of Independent States (CIS) and EU countries. All of the CEFTA countries except FYR Macedonia and Montenegro require Albanians to obtain visas for visits.

The combined population of the eight CEFTA member countries is less than 28 million, slightly more than Romania. Enhancing labor mobility within the region can exploit scale economies, increasing productivity and attracting foreign investment. In turn, these factors can enhance the region's competitiveness in international trade.

Most of the CEFTA countries were part of the Socialist Federal Republic of Yugoslavia, which began disintegrating in the 1990s. Achieving freer labor mobility among the ex-Yugoslav republics should be expedited by similarities in education and credential systems and patterns of pre-independence migration, but may be slowed by high unemployment and under-employment (Iara and Vidovic, 2009; Fetsi, 2007), lingering hostilities from 1990s armed conflicts, and newly erected migration barriers in evolving migration systems and other changes.

Trying to formalize low-skilled irregular migration via guest worker programs, before labor markets are made more flexible and informal economies curbed, could reduce labor migration and reduce some of the flexibility that migrants currently provide.

Professionals and skilled workers are less likely to migrate to neighboring Balkan countries in an irregular status, justifying government efforts to foster skilled labor mobility. Specific steps to promote skilled labor migration might include:

- encouraging student migration, allowing foreign students to work while studying and graduates to seek employment with minimal bureaucracy, as in the EU
- allowing CEFTA employers to offer jobs to CEFTA nationals who have at least one university degree without a labor market test, as in NAFTA, where a job offer and proof of citizenship and credentials allows issuance of an indefinitely renewable work and residence visa
- promoting intra-company transfers by allowing firms with branches in several CEFTA countries to transfer workers between them with minimal formalities, the part of the GATS trade-in-services negotiations that has received the most liberalizing offers.[2]

Over time, guest worker programs may then be created and expanded that allow the admission of CEFTA workers to fill seasonal jobs in other CEFTA member states, extending such programs to encompass a wider range of workers and jobs.

EU accession will, in any case, eventually require development of such mechanisms. It may therefore behoove the CEFTA states to bring their migration and permit systems into line with the EU standards, implementing these among themselves initially, either on a multilateral or bilateral basis.

Reducing External Tariffs by Adopting EU's Common External Tariff

Even though SEE's exports have been increasing steadily, both intra- and extra-regional exports remain below potential. In addition to this they remain fragile as they heavily depend on a few items, mainly commodities. The aim of the final part of the paper is to establish the costs and benefits of adopting EU's CET in order to identify whether this can be the right policy option for SEE countries in order to encourage export-led growth.

First, the tariff structure of each SEE country is examined in detail and compared to that of EU. After such a reform, the region's simple average tariff would be reduced from 5.1 percent to 2.3 percent and the trade-weighted average tariff from 4.7 percent to 2.2 percent. Among the SEE countries, Serbia will go through the most ambitious adjustment process due to its higher average tariffs and tariff dispersions. On the other extreme, Croatia will require the least effort to adopt EU's CET thanks to its advanced status as an EU candidate country.

Second, the costs and benefits of adopting EU's CET are quantitatively estimated by making use of traditional concepts of trade diversion and creation. The estimation tools used include a partial equilibrium model of SMART developed by UNCTAD and the World Bank. The results indicate that the impact of this trade reform will be positive with net trade creation in the magnitude of US$998.9 million for the region, an increase of 4.3 percent from pre-reform import levels. Even though imports will increase significantly, the net effect of adopting the EU's CET will result in revenue loss roughly half of the gains from trade creation, that is,that is, US$459.7 million. The consumer surplus, which will result from reducing the deadweight loss from tariffs, is a modest US$51.7 million. The overall net effect of CET amounts thus to US$590.9 million, roughly 1 percent of SEE's combined GDP.

Another observation one can make based on the simulation results is that all countries will be able to diversify their trade to other countries outside the region. Although several EU member states are among the top 10 export partners, China, the Russian Federation, the United States, and Turkey are set to gain significant market share in the SEE market as a results of trade creation. The impact of adopting CET is going to have a negative effect on intra-regional exports. Nevertheless, the decrease in intra-regional exports (that is, trade diversion) is a re-adjustment and only amounts to 0.1 percent of GDP.

If the SEE countries decide to proceed with adopting the EU's CET unilaterally and individually, political resistance may arise against such a measure in those countries where the tariff revenue loss is the highest. A committee could be established to compensate those countries that are most dependent on customs import duties as revenue, for a temporary period of adjustment (for example, five years). Although it may be difficult for the SEE countries to pool their sovereignty over 'most' of their trade policy, it should be politically easier to adopt the EU's CET, an external benchmark. As all countries in the region have a clear EU vocation, adopting the EU's CET would bring them closer to EU membership.

Notes

[1] Moldova is not considered for EU membership and has limited economic inter-linkages with the remaining CEFTA states, and will be excluded from explicit discussion in the remainder of this report.

[2] Under GATS Mode 4, intra-company transfers are often limited to managers, workers with specialized skills, and sometimes trainees who have been employed by the multinational firm at least a year (Martin, Abella, and Kuptsch, 2005).

Part I

Evolution of Intra-regional Trade in Southeast Europe: The Role of CEFTA for Enhancing Regional Trade Integration

Borko Handjiski, World Bank

Abstract

The countries of Southeast Europe, and Moldova, signed the Central European Free Trade Agreement (CEFTA) in 2006. CEFTA 2006 is a comprehensive free trade agreement that aims to fully liberalize trade in the region as well as to address various nontariff barriers to trade. It also promotes cooperation in other trade-related areas, such as investment, services, public procurement, and intellectual property rights.

This study aims to assess the impact of CEFTA on regional trade integration, as well as to analyze the remaining, nontariff, impediments to trade in the region. Intra-regional trade performance in Southeast Europe has improved considerably in recent years. Growth in trade was particularly strong in 2008, though this is a result of numerous factors in addition to the entry of CEFTA in to force, such as trade facilitation measures. The trade expansion in recent years had led to trade deepening. However, despite the significant increase in trade, its structure does not signal significant trade integration. Commodities continue to dominate, and intra-industry trade remains low.

The report also finds that, with the abolishment of tariffs and quotas, technical regulations, and standards have become an important constraint on trade and greater collaboration is required to reduce these barriers. In this regard, the harmonization and international recognition of the quality of infrastructure in SEE is vital for further promoting regional trade. The trade-related environment continues to include policy-induced barriers that prevent further development of intra-regional (and broader) trade. The report finds that most SEE countries have made significant progress on the trade facilitation agenda, but are yet to fully catch up with the more advanced European reformers on number of trade-related issues. The case studies of two regional firms confirm the findings of the global surveys and report.

CHAPTER 1

Introduction

Countries of the Southeast Europe[1] (SEE) region have witnessed significant economic improvement since the beginning of their transition to market economies in the early 1990s. Growth has been particularly strong in the past six years, but still lower than in other fast-growing countries in the East Asia and Baltic regions, or some of the other new member states of the EU. So far, trade (exports) have contributed little to the growth story, and for small countries such as those in SEE, sustainable growth should be export-led as small countries gain more than larger ones from trade-induced expansion in market size (see Kathuria, 2008). For example, the Central and Eastern Europe countries, and other countries such as Chile, have successfully followed export-driven growth strategies.

The benefits of increased trade have been well acknowledged in the economic literature. The fastest-growing developing countries have also achieved impressive export performances. This is especially the case for small economies, which are able to take advantage of the economies of scale from accessing, or being part of, larger markets. In addition, greater trade generates gains from factor reallocations, reduces macro-volatility, and stimulates innovation through absorption of foreign technologies (see Hallaky and Sivadasanz, 2009). A study by Gorodnichenko, Svejnar, and Terrell (2009) on the transition economies confirms that exporting and importing induces innovation, which in turns improves productivity and competitiveness. Fernandes and Paunov (2009) show that trade can also benefit the non-exporting sector; they find that import competition has positive effects on product quality, especially for non-exporting producers. Last but not least, trade could improve consumer welfare by allowing for lower prices of imported products and lower firm costs by reducing the prices of imported inputs.

Deepening trade among the SEE economies would bring both economic and political benefits to the region. The region comprises seven small economies (with a population and nominal GDP lower than that of neighboring Romania) that could benefit from creating a larger economic space as this would create economies and scale for production and increase their attractiveness for foreign investment. The region, excluding Albania, was a single country for almost five decades and some of the legacy from this economic integration remains despite the negative economic and political shocks of the mid-1990s. Last but not least, all countries in the region aim to become part of the EU and its Single Market of goods, people, capital, and services. In this regard, by enhancing regional trade integration prior to EU membership, the economies would be better prepared to face the competitive pressures of the EU's Single Market.

Enhancing trade performance has three dimensions: greater presence in global trade, trade integration with the EU, and enhanced regional trade. This report aims to focus on the latter dimension, and will look at trade performance in SEE mostly through the prism of the CEFTA 2006 Agreement.[2]

The purpose of this study is twofold: (i) to present recent trends in intra-regional trade in SEE, in particular following the implementation of CEFTA; and (ii) to bring the attention of policy makers to some of the remaining impediments to enhanced intra-regional trade.

What this study shows is that intra-regional trade is important for stimulating export-led growth, and that greater trade integration could also bring indirect benefits, including more foreign investment. Trade flows have been increasing at a fast pace since the signing of the bilateral free trade agreements in the early 2000s. The increase in volume has been accompanied by trade deepening, with some 20 percent of new trade coming from new products. However, trade is largely concentrated (in commodity-based products) and the share of inter-industry trade, which is an indicator of economic integration, is quite low.

Moreover, with tariffs and quotas eliminated under CEFTA, nontariff barriers such as technical barriers to trade (TBTs) and sanitary and phytosanitary (SPS) measures become more prominent. In addition, the quality and efficiency of the trade-related environment can become an obstacle to trade as unjustified costs and poor quality of services serve add an implicit tax on trade. Hence, eliminating nontariff barriers (NTBs) becomes essential for boosting trade flows and regional trade integration.

The rest of the study is organized as follows. Chapter 2 describes intra-regional trade patterns, both prior and after the entry of CEFTA into force, including more detailed analysis of trade structure. Chapter 3 emphasizes the role of NTBs, such as technical regulations and standards, and their potential impact on trade enhancement, as well as the importance of the trade-related environment drawing on global surveys and reports (*Doing Business*, BEEPS, Logistics Performance Indicator and the Enabling Trade Index). It also looks at rules of origin and their role in trade creation. Chapter 4 aims to present the view of the private sector on CEFTA and on trade-related reforms in general through two case studies of regional firms. Chapter 5 concludes by summarizing the key recommendations of the study.

Notes

[1] The SEE region, also referred to as the Western Balkans, comprises Albania, Bosnia and Herzegovina, Croatia, the former Yugoslav Republic of Macedonia (FYR Macedonia), Kosovo, Montenegro, and Serbia.

[2] The original CEFTA was signed in December 1992 by Poland, Hungary, the Slovak Republic, and the Czech Republic. In December 2006, the countries of SEE (including Bulgaria and Romania) and Moldova signed the Agreement on amendment and accession to CEFTA, or the so-called CEFTA 2006. The CEFTA 2006 Agreement consolidated 32 previous bilateral free trade agreements in SEE and entered into force on 26 July 2007 for Albania, Kosovo, Montenegro, Macedonia, and Moldova, 22 August for Croatia, 24 October for Serbia, and 22 November for Bosnia and Herzegovina. Bulgaria and Romania, signatory parties to the Agreement, left CEFTA when they joined the EU on January 1, 2007.

CHAPTER 2

Trade Patterns in the SEE Region

Starting from 2000, the SEE region witnessed significant economic growth, up to the beginning of the global financial and economic crisis in 2008. Despite the improved economic performance, growth rates were lower compared to other fast-growing countries such as East Asia and many of the EU-10 countries. Domestic demand, stimulated by rise in credit, wages, and remittances, was the main source of growth for most of the SEE economies. In contrast, exports have not played a compelling role in the region's growth story, and have in fact been the weak link; despite the preferential trade regimes with the EU and within the region (see Kathuria, 2008). To sustain and increase growth rates, the region's export performance needs to be boosted, and enhancing intra-regional trade is an important pillar of its export performance.

Box 2.1. The "New" CEFTA

The new CEFTA, signed in 2006, is a comprehensive preferential trade agreement covering a range of areas. The Agreement replaced the network of 32 bilateral FTAs in the region, and introduced fully liberalized trade of manufacturing products (with transition periods for few products) and largely free trade of agriculture products. The objectives of CEFTA are to expand trade (and transit) in goods and services, and foster investment, including foreign investment. It also seeks to provide fair conditions of competition and appropriate protection of intellectual property rights.

To achieve these objectives, the Agreement goes far beyond the standards issues covered under an FTA. It includes areas such as sanitary and phytosanitary standards, which are important, technical, nontariff barriers to trade. It also covers competition rules (including state aid), investment, government procurement, and intellectual property rights, which are important for promoting trade in services and investment. For some of these areas, concrete deadlines for action are specified in the Agreement, while for some of the most contentious issues only a commitment for collaboration is given without a specific timetable.

Last but not least, the Agreement stipulates a framework for collaboration and arbitration system for efficient resolution of disputes.

Source: Author.

Intra-regional trade in SEE has evolved considerably since the low levels of the late 1990s. However, the regional trade integration varies significantly among countries. In the case of FYR Macedonia, exports to CEFTA represent 14 percent of GDP, while in Albania and Kosovo this ratio is about 2 percent. Some countries, such as Montenegro, have developed a one-sided trade relationship with the region; imports being almost 8 times larger than exports. For Albania's economy, the CEFTA region plays a marginal role, and exports almost entirely to the EU.

Table 2.1. Key Economic and Trade Indicators for SEE (2008)

	Population (in million)	Exports to CEFTA (in € mn)	Imports from CEFTA (in € mn)	GDP (in € mn)	CEFTA exports per capita (in €)	CEFTA imports per capita (in €)	CEFTA exports to GDP ratio (in %)
Albania	3.2	125	298	8,364	39	93	1.5
Bosnia and Herzegovina	3.8	1,529	2,916	12,649	406	774	12.1
Croatia	4.4	2,253	1,051	47,165	509	237	4.8
Macedonia, FYR	2.0	922	511	6,477	452	250	14.2
Montenegro	0.6	159	1,227	3,393	247	1,911	4.7
Serbia	7.4	2,458	1,216	34,055	334	165	7.2
Kosovo	2.1	93	705	3,804	45	341	2.4

Source: ECA regional tables, national authorities.

Despite the differences in the levels of trade integration, intra-regional trade picked up significantly in 2008, following the entry of CEFTA into force, across the region. Total intra-regional trade, measured through imports (as being more reliable than exports), rose from €6.2 bn in 2007 to €7.9 bn in 2008 (table 2.2). The regional trade growth outperformed the export growth to the EU by a wide margin. In 2008, exports to the EU rose by some 6, 8, 10 and 12 percent in Croatia, FYR Macedonia, Bosnia and Herzegovina, and Serbia, respectively. Bosnia and Herzegovina, the largest importer in the region, and Montenegro, the largest importer relative to the size of its economy, accounted for 70 percent of the increase in imports.

Table 2.2. Quarterly Imports from CEFTA Parties, in € Million

	2007				2008				2008/07
	Q1	Q2	Q3	Q4	Q1	Q2	Q3	Q4	change
Albania	43	56	58	57	53	72	92	81	84
Bosnia and Herzegovina	351	525	571	563	514	646	701	1,055	906
Croatia	216	243	243	243	228	273	279	270	106
Macedonia	83	103	112	148	122	132	131	126	66
Montenegro	131	223	264	276	276	398	386	167	334
Serbia	214	279	291	318	281	326	321	541	368
Kosovo	123	129	163	155	136	181	208	179	136
Total	1,160	1,559	1,700	1,759	1,611	2,027	2,119	2,419	1,999

Source: National authorities.

Patterns and Structure of Trade Flows in SEE

World trade, and investment, flows have expanded significantly over the past decade, and global exports and imports were rising continuously for over three decades until 2009. In SEE, in contrast, trade flows in the first decade of transition were largely constrained by political factors (including embargoes) and conflicts in the region. While the political and developments in the early and mid-1990s had a negative overall effect on trade performance, intra-regional trade was disproportionally affected. Prior to the dissolution of SFR Yugoslavia, all SEE countries except Albania traded heavily among each other as they were part of one economy. The conflicts which followed the break-up of SFR Yugoslavia led to sharp contraction of trade flows in most parts of the region. At the same time, SEE countries received preferential trade treatment from the European Union (EU) which shifted trade towards the EU market.

Intra-SEE trade began to rebound in this decade and in particular after 2003. The recent reversal in trade patterns could be explained by the signing of bilateral FTAs, as well as the post-conflict recovery of the region. Overall trade flows have steadily grown in SEE, and total trade [at least] doubled in each of the countries between 2004 and 2008. In the absence of available data on trade volumes, rise in international price indexes could be used to assess the real vs. nominal increase in trade. And while prices of certain product categories, such as oil and food rose tremendously in the first years of the decade (followed by a decline in recent years), prices of most export products were either stable or witnessed small increases.

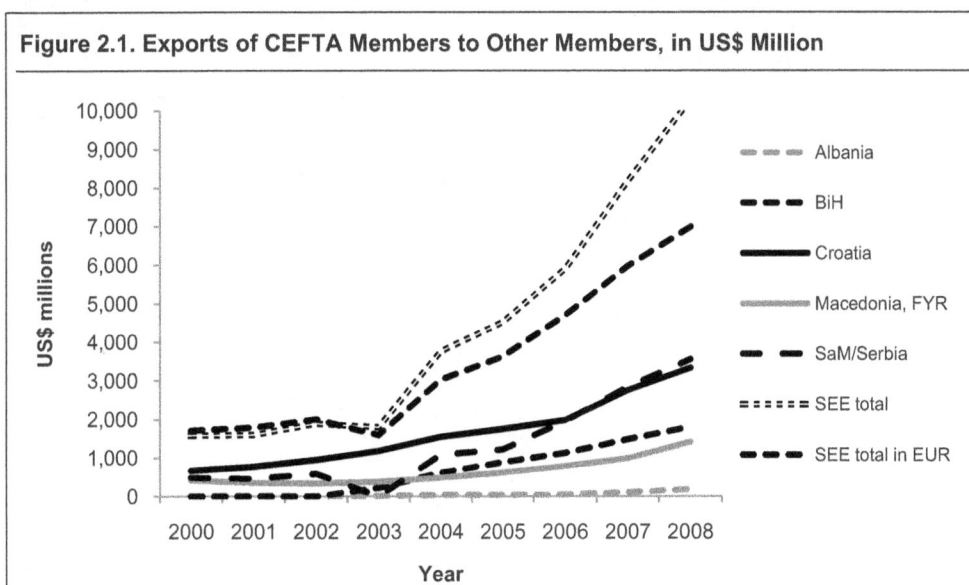

Figure 2.1. Exports of CEFTA Members to Other Members, in US$ Million

Source: COMTRADE, national statistical offices.

Tables 2.3 and 2.4 show intra-regional trade relationships in 2008, both in terms of exports and imports. Over 90 percent of trade flows go to neighboring countries, and the largest trade flows are between Bosnia and Herzegovina, and Croatia, and between Serbia and Bosnia and Herzegovina.

Serbia and Croatia, the two largest economies, were the largest exporters to the region. In contrast, the regional market seems to matter the least for Albania, Kosovo, and Montenegro, their exports account for some 5 percent of total exports. However, Kosovo's export base is very low, and exports to CEFTA account for almost a third of total exports. FYR Macedonia's exports are substantial relative to the size of its economy, and represent 36 percent of its total exports.

Table 2.3. Intra-Regional Exports in 2008, in € Million

Source/Destination	ALB	BiH	CRO	MAC	MON	SER	KOS	MOL	Total
Albania		2	2	26	19	16	60	0	125
BiH	10		730	41	97	602	51	0	1,529
Croatia	31	1,468		97	126	529	n/a*	1	2,253
Macedonia	70	69	152		25	606	n/a*	0	922
Montenegro	6	22	7	1		108	16	0	159
Serbia	52	907	294	334	866		n/a	4	2,458
Kosovo	15	4	1	16	7	46		3	93
Total	183	2,472	1,185	516	1,140	1,908	126	9	7,538

Source: National authorities.
* Kosovo data not published.

On the import side, Bosnia and Herzegovina is the largest importer, and the bulk of its imports come from Croatia (58 percent) and Serbia (38 percent). Kosovo and Montenegro are highly dependent on imports from the region. Kosovo's imports from the CEFTA region represent 38 percent of its total imports and are some 50 percent higher compared to imports from the EU.

Table 2.4. Intra-regional imports in 2008, in € Million

Destination/Source	ALB	BiH	CRO	MAC	MON	SER	KOS	MOL	Total
Albania		10	36	79	6	145	21	0	298
BiH	2		1,706	95	14	1,095	5	0	2,916
Croatia	3	556		190	5	291	n/a*	6	1,051
Macedonia	24	35	93		1	358	n/a*	3	514
Montenegro	20	165	170	30		839	3	0	1,227
Serbia	9	437	376	257	137		n/a	17	1,234
Kosovo	53	39	49	343	14	208		0	705
Total	111	1,242	2,429	993	177	2,936	30	27	7,945

Source: National authorities.
* Kosovo data not published.

Trade among the region is relatively concentrated with the top six HS 2-digit product categories[1] representing 40 percent of total imports (figure 2.2). Four of these six are commodity products: mineral fuels (27), iron and steel (72), steel products (73) and aluminum (76). The other two are beverages (22) and electrical machinery and equipment (85). Oil imports ranked among the top five product categories in each country, except Montenegro, and iron and steel is among the top five both import and export products, except Croatia (not a top five export).

Figure 2.2. Intra-regional Imports by HS 2-Digit Product Category

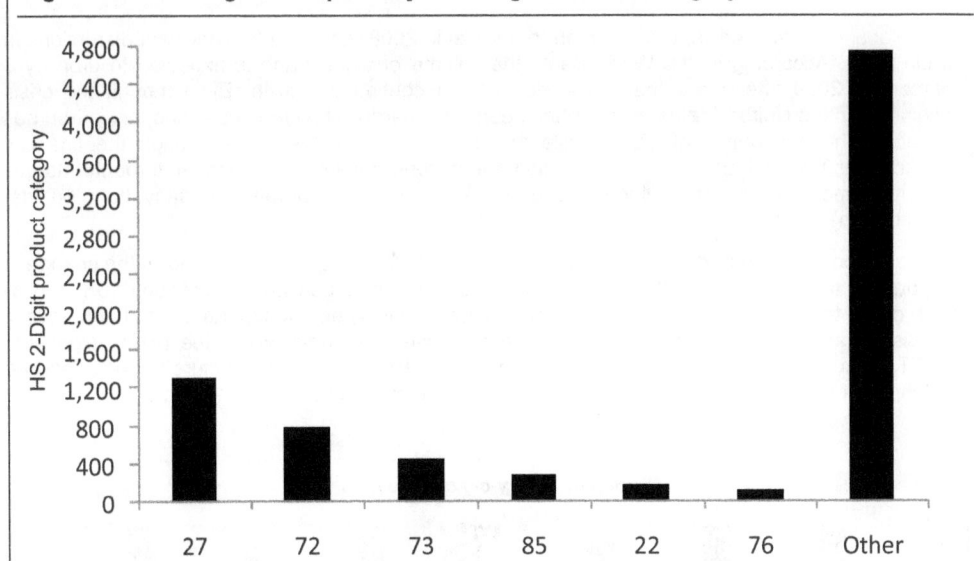

Source: National authorities.

Annexes I.A and I.B present the concentration of exports and imports (the top 5 HS-2 product categories) for each of the SEE countries in 2007 and 2008. The concentration varies among the countries. For example, the most import product category in Albania, Bosnia and Herzegovina, and Kosovo, mineral fuels, have a high share in their intra-regional imports. But apart from that, and maybe the second-largest import product, the concentration seems to be relatively low. In the case of Macedonia and Montenegro, the structure of imports is much more diversified, and most imported product accounts for around 10 percent of total imports.

In terms of the export structure, Albania, Croatia, Kosovo, Macedonia, and Montenegro have a high concentration of their most-exported product; steel for Albania, Kosovo, and Montenegro; oil for Croatia; and both in the case of Macedonia. Bosnia and Herzegovina and even more so Serbia, in contrast, have a quite diversified export structure. The concentration of trade in 2008 is very similar as in 2007, which is expected as trade flows do not change dramatically in short periods of time.

Last but not least, annex I.C shows the top five HS 2-digit product categories with largest trade surplus and deficit for each of the SEE countries. Croatia, for example, has a large intra-regional trade surplus in mineral fuels (oil), and significantly smaller surplus in other products (such as machinery). Serbia and Macedonia have more or less equal surpluses in their top five product categories. Bosnia and Herzegovina has only two products, aluminum and wood, with substantial trade surplus. Albania, Kosovo, and Montenegro have almost no products with positive net exports, and are on the other hand, significant net importers. Annex I.D lists the 2-digit HS categories.

Box 2.2. The Impact of the Crisis on Trade Flows in SEE

The global economic crisis, which began to unravel in 2008, has lead to significant disruptions in trade flows. According to the World Bank, the volume of world trade is expected to drop by 6 percent in 2009 after more than three decades of continued growth. Even though the crisis originated in the United States, Europe has been most hardly hit by the crisis, and this in turn has impacted the economies of SEE. While the transmission of the crisis through the financial markets has been so far limited in the region, the second transmission channel, through trade, is becoming more severe. The fall in demand from key European markets (Germany, Italy, Austria, and so forth) has harmed substantially SEE exports.

Overall exports and imports have sharply declined in 2009. The graph below shows the change in exports for the first four months of 2009, SEE's exports have declined by between 10 (Croatia) and close to 50 percent (Macedonia and Kosovo). Declines in exports have been mostly consistent among various markets, except in the case of Albania where the fall of exports to CEFTA has been much greater than to other markets. Exports for manufactured goods declined much faster than agriculture exports, except in the case of Albania and Montenegro.

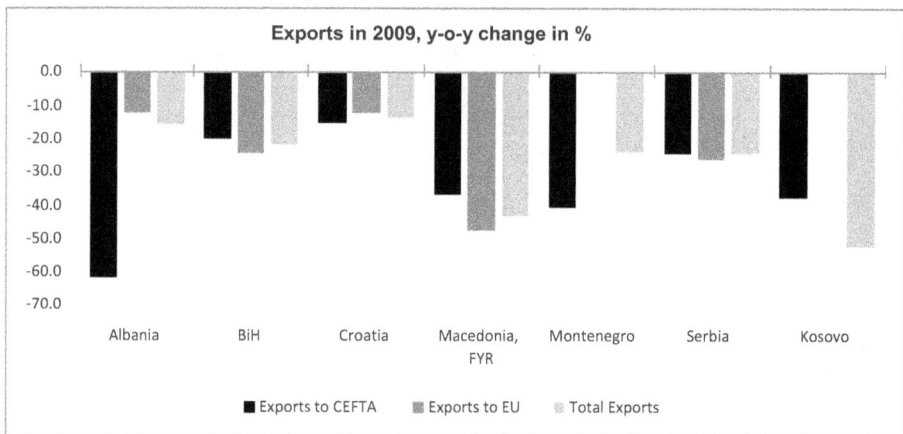

Exports in 2009, y-o-y change in %

Note: Data for Albania, Montenegro, and Kosovo are for January-March period, and data for Bosnia and Herzegovina, Croatia, FYR Macedonia, and Serbia for January-April period.

The crisis has fueled political pressures to protect domestic producers from import competition throughout the world. A study by the World Bank (see Gamberoni and Newfarmer, 2009) revealed that between October 2008 and February 2009, 47 trade protection measures have been implemented, and many more have been proposed. These actions, taken by both developed and developing countries, take the form of increased import duties, import bans, subsidies and nontariff measures.

While measures taken by developed countries comprise mostly subsidies and other types of support to exporters, measures in developing countries take a range of forms, including nontariff measures. The nontariff measures vary from increased standards and regulations to adding costly bureaucratic procedures. For example, Argentina has introduced additional licensing requirements for a variety of products (for example, auto parts, TVs, and toys), and Indonesia now requires certain goods to be imported only at five ports and airports.

Within CEFTA, several trade protectionism cases have been brought up in recent clear, but it is not clear to what extend these measures were a result of economic crisis. Most of the underlying issues precede the start of the crisis, and refer to nontariff barriers of various sorts. The sections on TBTs and SPS include more information on trade protectionism and box 3.3, for example, describes recently introduced trade protection measures by Bosnia and Herzegovina and Croatia.

Source: Author.

Decomposition of Intra-regional Trade

The marked increase in trade flows since 2000 led to some deepening in regional trade and integration, measured through the diversification of products exported to the region. As shown in figure 2.3, 86 percent of the exports' growth between 2000 and 2007 came from increase in exports of existing products (to existing markets), whereas 20 percent came from exports of new products. So in terms of export diversification, the SEE region compares slightly better compared to global trends, but worse compared to the ECA region. Brenton and Newfarmer (2007) find, in the case of 99 export countries, that increases of existing products to existing markets account for over 100 percent of total export growth, and new exports account for 19 percent. In ECA, however, the share of new exports was over 30 percent. The trade diversification in SEE could actually be higher as the above comparison is based on slightly different methodologies. Both studies use the same sources, COMTRADE and Standard International Trade Classification (SITC) methodology; however, Brenton and Newfarmer use more detailed 5-digit data, while this study uses more aggregated 4-digit data, because reliable 5-digit data were not available.

Figure 2.3. Decomposition of Export Growth of CEFTA Countries: 2000–07

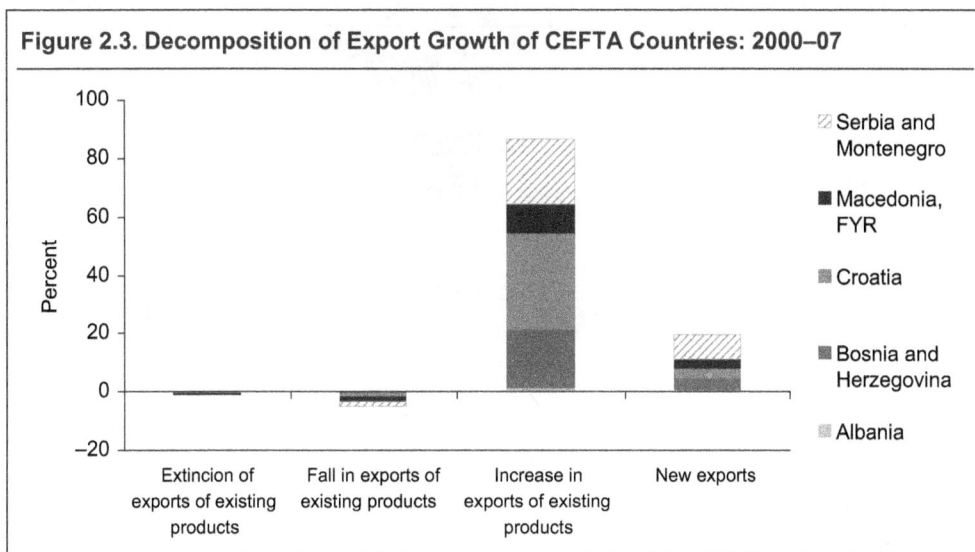

Source: UN COMTRADE database.
Note: The decomposition is done based on a dataset of 4 digit level products exported to SEE, based on the Standard International Trade Classification Revision 3. Data for Bosnia and Herzegovina are only available from 2003. Montenegro gained independence from Serbia and Montenegro in 2006, but to allow comparability with previous years, Serbia and Montenegro are considered as one economy.

A more detailed analysis of the export growth shows that new trade relationships have been created in most HS-2 product categories. However, the quantity of new trade flows is quite concentrated: the top 5 and top 10 product categories account over half and over two thirds of the value of the new trade relationships, respectively. Textiles, chemicals, and milk are in the top 5 list, followed by ceramic products, leather, meat, and wool.

The SEE economies diverge in terms of their export diversification. For example, 45 percent of the increase in Albania's exports to the region came from new products, while in Croatia the share was only 10 percent. However, this can be largely explained from the low starting point of Albania's exports, and the relatively large Croatian exports. Albania had 300 more export relationships[2] with the region in 2007 compared to 2000, while the other countries of the region managed to develop between 520 (Macedonia) and 1,100 (Serbia and Montenegro) new export relationships in the same period.

Decomposition of exports by sub-period shows that new exports had a higher share in the 2000–04 period, which was accompanied with a fall in exports of existing products (figure 2.4). During 2004–07, the share of new exports declined, and the fall of exports of existing products was reduced. In the entire period, the share of export products that were withdrawn from markets was negligible.

Figure 2.4. Decomposition of Export Growth in SEE by Sub-period, 2000–04 (Top) and 2004–07 (Bottom)

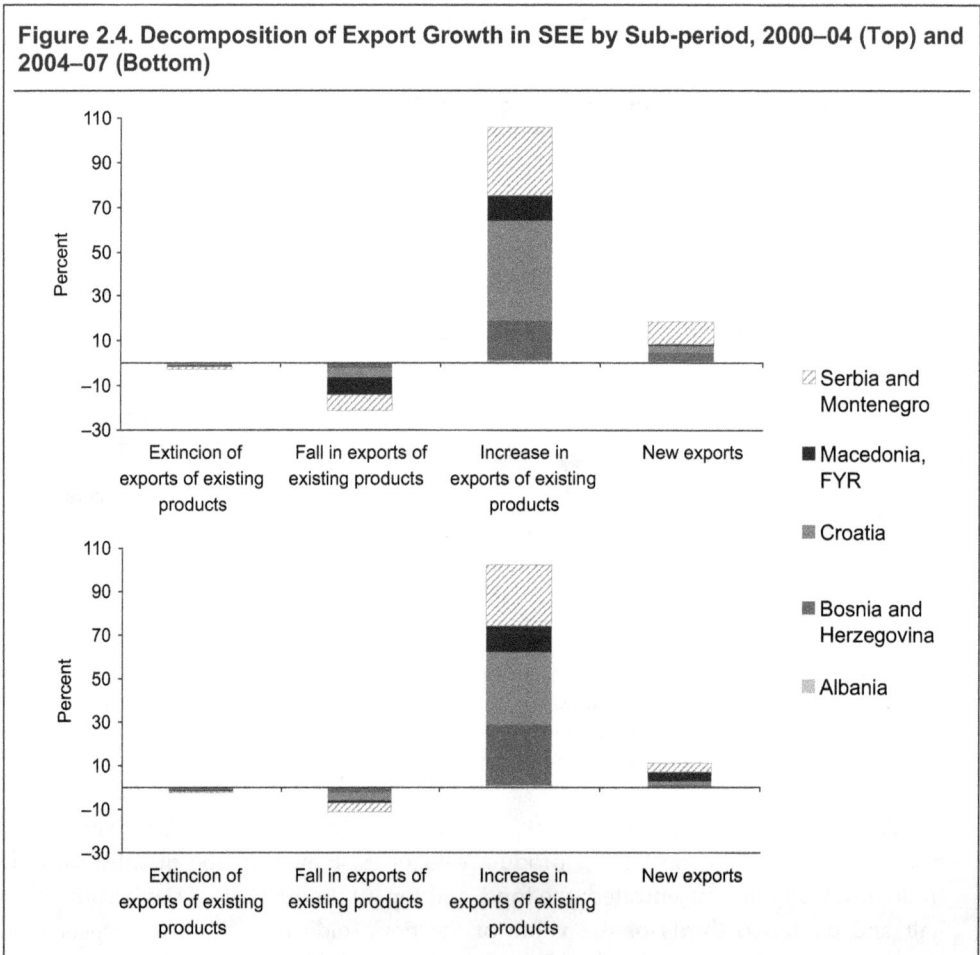

Source: UN COMTRADE database.

Table 2.5 shows that the concentration of exports in the region is relatively high, though with large variation among the economies. For example, Albania, which is the smallest exporter, has a very concentrated trade structure, measured by the share of the top five export products at 4-digit product level. On the other hand, the largest exporters, Croatia and Serbia[3] have relatively low concentration ratios. In addition, 4 out of the top 5 products in 2000 disappeared from the list by 2007 in the case of Serbia. The export decomposition graphs in the figure above show that Serbia had the largest fall in exports of existing products.

Table2.5. Top Five Export Products (4-digit SITC level), Share in Total

	2000	2007	Same "top 5 products" in both years
Albania	48.9	46.7	2
Bosnia and Herzegovina	33.6	31.8	3
Croatia	14.9	22.5	3
Macedonia, FYR	29.0	25.2	2
Serbia and Montenegro	14.2	17.6	1

Source: COMTRADE.

As detailed trade statistics per commodity are not yet available for 2008 and 2009, it is not possible to analyze the source of export growth after the entry of CEFTA into force in the second half of 2007. However, despite the lack of analysis, significant changes in trade patterns are unlikely to occur in a short-period of time. A study by Albornoz, Pardo, Corcos and Ornelas (2009) finds that exporters usually "start small" when entering new markets (by selling small quantities to neighboring countries). After this initial trial, they either withdraw or their exports rocket. The implication of this behavior is that reduction in trade barriers has delayed effects on export flows, which makes it difficult to assess the impact of trade liberalization, especially in the context of regional free trade areas. In any case, this "sequential exporting" theory suggests that large shifts in trade flows should not be expected in short periods of time following trade liberalization.

Last but not least, the study compares the structure of exports within the CEFTA bloc with SEE's exports to the EU, which accounts for the bulk of their total exports. Intra-regional trade patterns are slightly different compared to extra-CEFTA (EU) trade patterns. Differences between intra- and extra-regional trade are common in developing countries, which would imply that regional trade integration is complementary to, as well as an important pillar of, international trade integration. In the case of SEE, the differences in the composition of CEFTA and EU exports could be explained by the different trade regimes and the competitive advantages vis-à-vis the trading partners (table 2.6). For example, food, beverages, and tobacco account for one fifth of intra-SEE exports and less than 10 percent of SEE's exports to the EU. This is likely due to the tariff and quota restrictions on agriculture trade with the EU, but even more so from the strict requirements that EU puts on food products (such as sanitary and phytosanitary standards). On the other hand, SEE countries (in particular the former Yugoslav republics) have a long history in food trade and many national brands have a regional recognition. The second big difference is in trade of manufactured products. Miscellaneous manufactured parts (SITC category 8) account for almost a quarter of exports to the EU compared to 9 percent of CEFTA exports, and this is derived from textile exports which fall in this category. Textile exports are 13 percent of total exports to the EU, while their share in intra-CEFTA exports is only 2 percent, but the bulk of the exports to the EU come from "inward processing" whereas materials are imported from the EU for further processing and final products are shipped back to the originating country. In contrast, the textile trade within CEFTA mostly involves export of domestically produced products. Last but not least, SEE exporters trade much more high-value products such as machinery and transport equipment with EU firms. The share of machinery/transport equipment exports to the EU is double compared to intra-CEFTA exports.

Table 2.6. SEE's Export Structure to CEFTA and EU Partners in 2007

SITC	Description	CEFTA	EU
0	Food & live animals	15.2	7.6
1	Beverages and tobacco	5.4	0.9
2	Crude materials except food/fuel	5.7	7.8
3	Mineral fuel/lubricants	15.3	3.6
4	Animal/veg oil/fat/wax	1.1	0.3
5	Chemicals/products n.e.s	10.1	6.3
6	Manufactured goods	26.7	28.2
7	Machinery/transport equipment	11.8	21.1
8	Miscellaneous man. arts	8.7	23.9
9	Commodities n.e.s.	0.0	0.1

Source: UN COMTRADE database.
Note: SITC Revision 3, EU data is for EU-25.

Disaggregated data by country show no great differences among the countries, with one or two exceptions.[4] For each country, food (SITC 0 and 1) and mineral fuel (SITC 3) exports have a larger share in CEFTA compared to EU trade. On the other hand, SITC 8 products, which include textiles, are mostly exported to the EU. Exports in this category account for over 60 percent of Albania's total exports to the EU, while their share in exports to CEFTA is only 6 percent. In the case of FYR Macedonia, these products account for 37 percent of exports to the EU, and only 5 percent of exports to CEFTA. The differences are greatest in the manufactured goods (SITC 6) and machinery/transport equipment (SITC 7). Croatia's SITC 6 exports have an equal share, of 17 percent, in both CEFTA and EU trade. On the other hand, SITC 6 exports in the other countries have a larger share in total exports: 44 percent of CEFTA exports and 28 percent of EU exports for Bosnia and Herzegovina, 39 percent of CEFTA exports and 46 percent of EU exports for FYR Macedonia, and 23 percent of CEFTA exports and 42 percent of EU exports in the case of Serbia. In contrast, Croatia's machinery/transport equipment exports have a larger share then in the other countries, 33 and 15 percent of EU and CEFTA exports, respectively. Albania and FYR Macedonia have a modest share of SITC 7 exports, and in Serbia they account for 13 percent of both CEFTA and EU exports.

Intra- versus Inter-industry Trade

The following section looks at the role of inter-industry trade for regional integration and export performance. While traditional trade theory (of comparative advantages) was based on trade of homogenous products, new trade theory has focused on intra-industry trade. Intra-industry trade (IIT), that is trade of similar products, has been a key factor in trade growth in recent decades. These trends have mostly been attributed to the fragmentation of production (outsourcing and off-shoring) as a result of globalization and new technologies. Empirical research on intra-industry trade was first undertaken on the countries part of the European Economic Community in the early 1960s, and since then intra-industry trade continues to expand not only among developed but also in developing countries.

Box 2.3. Inter-industry and Intra-industry Trade

Inter-industry trade is defined as exchange of goods from different industries, for example, trading agricultural products for machinery and equipment. It is based on comparative advantages arising from different factor endowments and technology between countries.

Intra-industry trade is exchange of goods within the same industry, either similar products or products at different stages of production. IIT is explained largely by economies of scale, income levels, innovations, and demand for differentiated products, but also by comparative advantages (in the case of products along the value chain).

Intra-industry trade brings important benefits to trading partners. First of all, it allows for greater product variety, which is of benefit to both firms and consumers. Second, firms can benefit from economies of scale, and in case of vertical specialization, use comparative advantages. From a macroeconomic perspective, IIT stimulates innovation, and tends to be more stable and less prone to short-term fluctuations. Empirical studies show that intra-industry trade can improve export performance. Hoekman and Djankov (1996) find a strong relationship between export performance and growth in (vertical) IIT between the CEEC and the EU. In the early 1990s, the Czech and Slovak Republics achieved the highest export growth with the EU (among the CEEC) and had the highest level and rate of growth in IIT with the EU.

Export performance and regional integration prospects in SEE strongly depend on the structure of trade, that is, whether countries engage more in one-way (inter-industry) or two-way (intra-industry) trade. Neighboring countries which are at similar level of development and belong to a free trade area tend to have more intensive intra-trade relationships.[5]

Unfortunately, intra-industry trade in SEE is surprisingly low by any standards (table 2.7). Although there is great variation, share of IIT in total trade among SEE's economies was less than 22 percent in 2007. Albania and Montenegro are the outliers in the group with ITT accounting for less than 10 percent of total trade, while the rest of the region's IIT share ranges between 22 and 25 percent. On the other hand, IIT has increased in all countries between 2000 and 2007, Croatia making the largest leap. Nonetheless, even Croatia's share is about half of the IIT share for the EU-10[6] countries (see Kawecka-Wyrykowska, 2009). The share of IIT among the EU-15, which is expectedly higher, stood at 59 percent in 2007.

Table 2.7. Share of Intra-industry Trade for the SEE Countries

	IIT with CEFTA		IIT with EU-25	
	2000	2007	2000	2007
Albania	2.9	6.2	22.8	23.9
Bosnia and Herzegovina	14.2	23.6	n.a.	28.6
Croatia	11.6	25.0	37.5	36.0
Macedonia, FYR	18.1	24.6	8.3	10.7
Montenegro	n.a.	9.5	n.a.	n.a.
Serbia (SaM in 2000)	17.8	21.9	22.7	24.6

Source: UN COMTRADE database.

Note: Author's own calculations based on SITC Rev. 3 at 4-digit product level. The share of IIT has been calculated using the Gruber-Lloyd index (see Gruber et al., 1975). The index is sensitive to the level of aggregation of the data, the higher the grouping of products the larger is the value of IIT. For SEE, 4-digit disaggregation level is used (due to lack of reliable data at more disaggregated levels), while studies quoted use 5-digit level.

Intra-industry trade is also low between SEE and the EU. Despite the free-trade arrangements with the EU,[7] the share of IIT is below 30 percent for each country apart from Croatia, which is far less compared to the share of EU-10 prior to accession (40 percent in 2002) (figure 2.5). It is important to note that intra-industry trade accelerated for the EU-10 following accession in 2004 and in many EU-10 countries reached above 50 percent, which is higher than several EU-15 countries (Greece, Portugal, Finland, and so forth). The above results confirm earlier findings that export performance in SEE has been largely disappointing as these economies have commodity-based structure and have not been successful in integrating into global supplies chains (see Kathuria, 2008).

Figure 2.5. EU-10's IIT Share

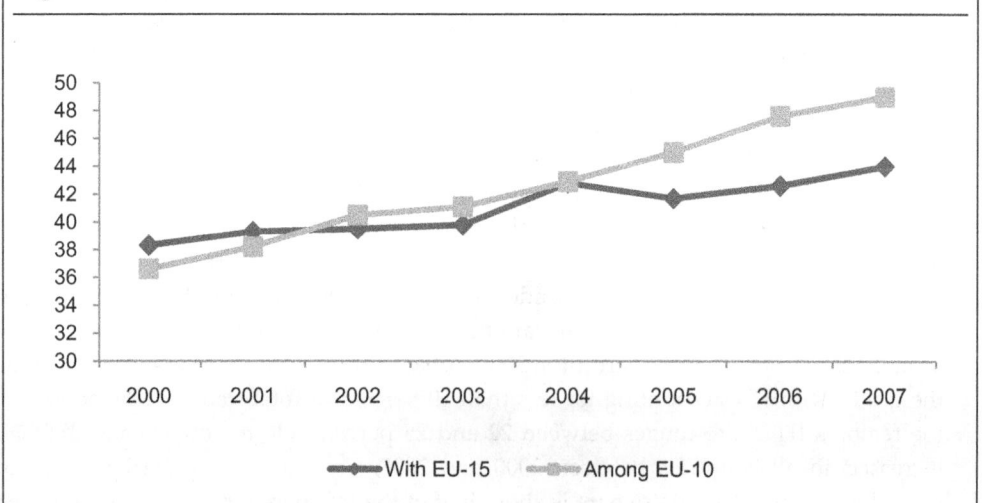

Source: Kawecka-Wyrykowska Elzbieta (2009).

There are several reasons why intra-industry trade should be higher among the SEE countries. First of all, all countries are small and immediate neighbors which should lead to greater integration among firms and production processes. Second, even prior to CEFTA, all countries had signed bilateral free-trade agreements among each other. In some cases, intra-industry trade has developed as a result of foreign investment, and so far there have been little intra-regional FDI inflows in SEE, particularly in the tradable sector. However, FDI was not the major force driving the growth of IIT in the CEEC in the early 1990s, except for in the automotive sector (see Hoekman and Djankov, 1996). The preconditions in SEE have been very similar to those in the "original" CEFTA group, yet regional integration has not occurred at the pace witnessed in CEEC.

Intra-industry trade in SEE is concentrated in few heavy industries and the structure is very similar for all countries of the region (table 2.8). The top four industries account for over a third of total IIT; iron and steel comes first in all countries except Croatia, followed by metal and non-metal manufactured products and electrical equipment. Throughout the region, these industries have a significant share in total industrial output, and trade in these products had been largely liberalized prior to CEFTA.

Table 2.8. Industries (at 2-Digit Product Level) with Largest Share of Intra-industry Trade in SEE

	Iron and steel (67)	Metal manufactures (69)	Non-metal mineral manufactures (66)	Electrical equipment (77)
Albania	12.6	0.5	3.0	1.7
BiH	5.4	4.9	2.6	2.3
Croatia	4.2	4.2	2.0	1.8
Macedonia, FYR	5.2	2.5	3.1	3.5
Montenegro				
Serbia	2.2	2.9	3.2	3.4

Source: UN COMTRADE database.

Intra-industry trade in agriculture products, on the other hand, is marginal despite the strong agricultural and food processing sector in each of these countries. Agricultural output accounts for over 10 percent of GDP in each country apart from Croatia. However, only two agriculture categories, vegetables and fruits (SITC 05) and beverages (SITC 11) are in (the bottom of) the top 10 categories of IIT. The low IIT share in agriculture products could be explained by the remaining tariff and nontariff barriers (sanitary standards and border crossings) to trade in agriculture products.

The CEFTA Agreement could facilitate greater intra-industry trade in the region. In addition to the full tariff liberalization, the commitment to harmonize standards and regulations and to ensure investment and intellectual property right protection, could lead to more regional investment. And the possibility to have diagonal cumulation of origin (see "Rules of Origin," chapter 3) with the EU, as well as EFTA and Turkey, could attract foreign investment in production facilities that would export products to the EU.

Quality of Foreign Trade Statistics for the Region

Trade statistics in the SEE region reveal significant deficiencies in registering exports and imports by customs authorities, which is a serious handicap for conducting analysis as well as for policy making. Mirror statistics, that is, statistics derived from the source and foreign trading partners, point to significant differences between imports and exports in each of the countries (see table 2.9). The differences could come from the fact that imports are recorded based on product origin and exports based on the source country from which the goods are being shipped, but could also imply data recording issues both on the exporting and the importing side. Unregistered trade is quite common for all countries and the efficiency in capturing all trade largely depends on the quality of the customs authorities. The differences in mirror statistics among the SEE countries are quite significant and deserve a greater attention by the authorities.

A mismatch in mirror statistics can be found for all SEE countries without any clear pattern as to which countries are under or over-reporting (table 2.9). Mirror statistics from trading country should not completely match, this would imply costless transport between destinations since exports are reported as f.o.b. (free on board) and imports as c.i.f. (cost, insurance, freight). Hence, imports of country A from country B should be slightly higher than country B's recorded exports to country A. However, trading between SEE countries shows a negative import-export ratio, which raises serious data quality concerns. For example, Croatia's imports from Bosnia and Herzegovina (recorded c.i.f. in Croatian statistics) in 2007 were recorded at €536 million, but exports to Croatia in Bosnian statistics (recorded f.o.b.), which should be lower because of the c.i.f.-f.o.b. difference, were €557 million. On the other hand, Albania's imports from Montenegro were €14.5 million, while Montenegro's exports to Albania were only €9.5 million, which implies unimaginably high freight costs of over 50 percent of the value of the goods. There are also large differences between other pairs of countries, actually, half of the "trading relationships" show a negative import to export ratio, which raises suspicion of possible duties and tax evasion.

Table 2.9. SEE Mirror Gap Statistics: Difference between Imports and Exports (in Percent)

Exporter/importer	Albania	Bosnia and Herzegovina	Croatia	Macedonia	Montenegro	Serbia
Albania		20.7	417.8	3.2	46.4	1,262.4
Bosnia and Herzegovina	15.7		−3.8	1.4	28.7	−3.9
Croatia	−5.0	−3.4		−5.8	8.1	−19.5
Macedonia	3.7	10.1	34.7			−51.7
Montenegro	54.2	−28.8	−21.9	−14.2		−28.1
Serbia	30.1	−5.5	−0.9	2.6	−6.2	

Source: National authorities.
Note: Fields in italic and underline denote total trade volumes below €10 million.

Historical data do not indicate positive trends in terms of improving the quality of statistics. Table 2.10 shows import/export ratios for several country pairs, excluding those with small trade values as well trade with Serbia and Montenegro as the data on SaM's exports and imports do not include Kosovo. With the exception of one or two country pairs, there are no particular trends in the mirror gaps of the selected pairs, and some such as Bosnia and Herzegovina's exports to FYR Macedonia show deterioration in quality.

Table 2.10. Difference between Imports and Exports (in Percent) for 2000–06 Period for Selected Trade Relationships

Exporter	Importer	2000	2001	2002	2003	2004	2005	2006	2007
AL	MK	27.7	−79.7	−77.3	29.4	−14.9	−12.0	−7.3	−20.0
MK	AL	84.8	50.7	19.4	−68.6	0.7	16.2	20.3	11.9
BiH	HR				11.0	5.9	−7.4	−6.3	−3.7
HR	BiH				−28.0	−21.8	−5.3	−1.4	−3.9
MK	HR	15.0	7.8	13.3	12.7	45.4	78.4	44.9	35.3
HR	MK	−1.9	−11.6	−6.5	−9.8	−11.8	−7.6	−5.2	−6.1
MK	BiH				−43.0	−11.0	15.3	15.3	10.1
BiH	MK				25.6	20.8	5.2	−2.5	1.4

Source: UN COMTRADE database.

As fully comparable data on mirror exports and imports (by origin) are not available, one way to assess the possible unregistered trade is to disaggregate mirror statistics by product to seek possible patterns. Figure 2.6 shows mirror trade statistics, by HS-2 category, between Bosnia and Herzegovina and Croatia, for the 20 categories with the largest mirror gaps. In the case where Croatia is the source and Bosnia and Herzegovina the destination (left graph), imports as expected are larger than exports in all but two product categories. However, for some product categories, such as 10 or 86, the difference is too large, and is probably unlikely that Bosnia and Herzegovina imported Croatian products in these categories from other countries. In contrast, Croatia's imports from Bosnia and Herzegovina are almost uniformly lower than Bosnia and Herzegovina's exports to Croatia, which deserves some greater investigation.

The gap in mirror statistics, beyond the expected c.i.f./f.o.b. difference and the differentiation in recording based on the origin of goods, could come from various reasons: smuggling of goods, under-invoicing and misclassification (to categories with lower duties/VAT), but also from exchange rate differences. And it is not uncommon to have trade statistics gaps even in developed countries. For example, intra-OECD exports are slightly lower (by around 1 percent) than intra-imports, according to UN COMTRADE database. In any case, the gaps bear further investigation by policy makers to determine whether there is possible misreporting, and if yes what are the causes.

Identifying the real causes would then allow for improving the efficiency of trade reporting, through strengthening the customs administrations or realigning incentives to ensure proper recording of trade. The implications of the misreporting are both financial and intangible. Under-reporting of imports means foregone revenues for the importing authorities. CEFTA has eliminated customs duties, so unregistered imports imply uncollected VAT (which is the largest revenue category collected by customs authorities). This, then, leads to unfair competition between illegally imported and domestic products. Inadequate statistics quality diminishes the perception and integrity of national institutions, which among other things, worsens EU prospects (including joining the Pan-Euro-Mediterranean Area of diagonal cumulation of origin).

Figure 2.6. Trade between Bosnia and Herzegovina and Croatia

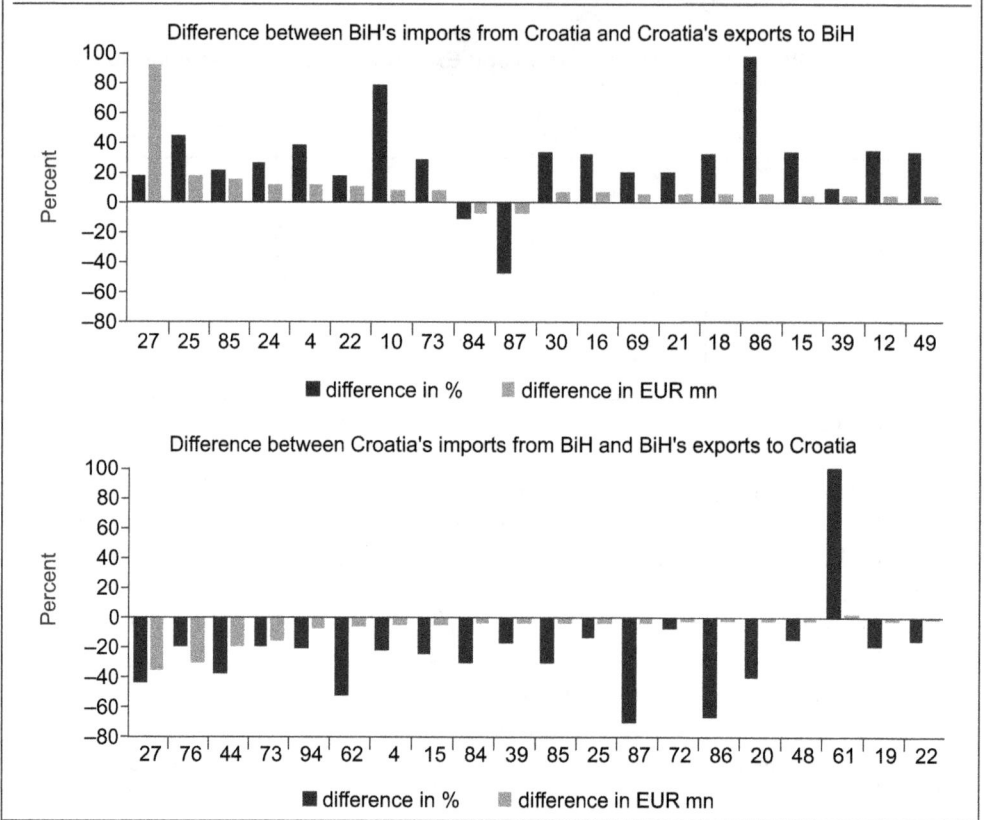

Difference between BiH's imports from Croatia and Croatia's exports to BiH

■ difference in %   ▓ difference in EUR mn

Difference between Croatia's imports from BiH and BiH's exports to Croatia

■ difference in %   ▓ difference in EUR mn

Source: national authorities.

Another, but much less relevant, issue concerning trade statistics in the region is their reporting and public availability. CEFTA is of course the only multilateral free trade area that the countries are members of, yet trade statistics with this region are not fully publicly available. Statistical offices of all CEFTA parties publish regular (monthly) trade statistics, by product and trading partners, however, Croatia and Kosovo are the only ones which report trade with CEFTA as a distinct category. Others report only trade with top trading partners and in most cases one or two countries are missing (for example, Moldova and Albania).[8] The Macedonian statistics office has a category "Western Balkans," and Bosnian statistics shows all CEFTA parties under "European countries in development." The Serbian statistics office shows Serbia's trade with the EU and 13 other economic areas (including MERCOSUR to which there are no exports), but does not include trade with CEFTA. It seems that trade statistics within CEFTA deserve greater attention and visibility in order for exporters and importers to assess better the trade potential in the region.

Last but not least, some countries continue to publish trade data in U.S. dollars (and in national currency) despite the fact that the bulk of their trade is conducted in euro. In addition, monetary (exchange-rate) policy in all of these countries is also anchored to the euro with de facto euro pegs in some countries (and euro use as official currency in Montenegro and Kosovo). Hence, trade data can be significantly distorted by the fluctuation in the euro-dollar exchange rate, which has been extremely volatile in recent years. In this regard, euro-based trade statistics would be of clear demand both among policy makers and analysts as well as among businesses.

Notes

[1] List of all HS 2-digit product categories can be found in Annex 4.

[2] Each export of a product at 4 digit (SITC Rev. 3) level to a country counts as an export relationship. If a country exports 100 products at 4 digit level to 5 countries, the number of export relationships would be between 100 (each product is exported to only one market) and 500 (each product is exported to each market).

[3] Serbia's exports in COMTRADE for 2007 are listed as Serbia and Montenegro.

[4] Disaggregated data in WITS were not available for Kosovo and Montenegro.

[5] See Helpman and Krugman (1985) and Helpman (1987).

[6] In Kawecka-Wyrykowska's paper EU-10 refers to the 10 countries that joined the EU in 2004 (CEEC, the Baltics, and Cyprus and Malta)

[7] In accordance with the EC's Autonomous Trade Preference mechanism and later the Stabilization and Association Agreements.

[8] None of the countries publish trade statistics with Kosovo.

CHAPTER 3

The Role of Trade Regulations, Trade-related Business Environment, and Rules of Origin in Trade Expansion and Integration

Technical Regulations and Standards

As the impact of tariffs and quotas diminishes within CEFTA, the impact of technical barriers to trade[1] (TBTs) and sanitary and phytosanitary (SPS) measures[2] becomes more prominent. TBTs and SPS, by their very nature, may result in restrictions on trade, even though that in most cases is not the purpose of their existence. They put additional costs on exporters to adjust their products to comply with the different market requirements of countries, and countries may use them as an excuse to protect domestic producers. So, as trade between countries expands as a result of reduced/eliminated tariff barriers, more opportunities for disputes on the TBT and SPS issues may arise.

Regulations and standards on industrial and agriculture products can facilitate or impede trade depending on the overall institutional setup. The empirical literature confirms that conforming to shared standards is generally considered to promote trade. To prevent technical requirements and SPS from becoming unnecessary barriers to trade, WTO members are obliged to apply the SBS and TBT Agreements. The CEFTA countries, while not all WTO members,[3] have agreed to apply WTO rules in their trade, including the SBS and TBTs Agreements. This is very important as around two thirds of intra-CEFTA trade involves non-WTO members. The countries in the region could take further steps to ensure full implementation of their commitments and to achieve a more ambitious progress towards minimizing the trade distorting effects of TBTs and SPS.

Technical barriers to trade (TBTs)

TBTs are used by governments to regulate markets, protect consumers, and preserve natural resources, and encompass most product categories, from automobile safety standards to pharmaceutical or food packaging regulations. TBTs, by their very nature, may result in restrictions on trade, even though that in most cases is not the purpose of their existence. As a matter of fact, recent empirical evidence shows that under the right conditions standards and technical regulations encourage trade. For example, strict standards and regulations can increase the confidence of consumers in the imported products (having had to meet these standards). Another benefit for exporters is that standards and regulations convey information on consumer preferences which reduces the costs for gathering such information. However, TBTs most often hamper trade through the diversity of standards among trading partners and the inadequate, public and private, infrastructure for standardization, accreditation and metrology. In such cases, they put additional costs on exporters to adjust their products to comply with the different market requirements of countries, and countries may use them as an excuse to protect domestic production. For example, empirical research shows that testing procedures, standards, and inspection lower developing countries' exports by 9, 7, and 3 percent, respectively (Taylor and Wilson, 2008). In addition, over 80 percent of surveyed firms in Eastern Europe have stated design, testing, and certification costs as a reason for not exporting.

The impact of technical regulations and standards on trade depends on the existence of appropriate national quality infrastructure system (box 3.1).[4] This includes standardization, accreditation, metrology, testing, certification, inspection, and supervision services to ensure that products meet the defined requirements. The absence of such well-functioning system is damaging to both exports and imports. Exports are hampered because firms cannot meet the requirements that foreign partners have set, and low quality imports can enter the market because of inappropriate quality control systems.

Box 3.1. How Technical Standards and Regulations Can Be an Obstacle to Trade

---

Technical standards and regulations encompass a wide range of rules and procedures, and in many ways some of these can be used as a TBT. In the context of CEFTA, firms from most countries have raised complaints about TBT in some of the CEFTA markets, though it remains to be seen how many of these complaints are in fact TBTs as often TBTs are mixed up with other types of NTBs. There seems to be, for example, great dissatisfaction among trading firms with the lack of progress on mutual recognition of certifications. In some cases, exporters from a country which has adopted certain EU standards (for example, on labeling) are facing difficulties when exporting to CEFTA parties which have not yet adopted those EU standards. Then, firms in some countries object that market inspection bodies in some countries take an additional sample for inspection, in addition to the one already given to other inspection bodies, for example, sanitary. Last but not least, it is often heard that exporters do not have sufficient information about import requirements and procedures. Moreover, regulations are frequently changed without prior notification.

Source: Author.

The national quality systems in SEE are still at a development stage, and this hampers trade between the bloc and key partners such as the EU as well among the bloc itself. There is of course a large discrepancy in this area within this group, but nonetheless, firms in the region are unable to fully penetrate the regional market created with the CEFTA agreement. Anecdotal evidence confirm that standards are an important obstacle to trade in the region; exporting firms often claim that standards are used as TBTs to prevent trade, and domestic firms claim that insufficient standards (or implementation of quality control) allows low quality products to enter the market and create unfair competition.

All countries have made some progress on improving their quality infrastructure systems as this is a key requirement for EU accession. Free movement of goods, which includes technical regulations and standards, is one of the four freedoms of the Single Market, and all countries will have to fully adopt EU's standards before joining the Union. However, the systems in all countries in the region were outdated, infrastructure obsolete and standards not internationally recognized, so substantial institutional and legislative reform as well as investment is necessary to bring the systems to EU levels.

The fact that all countries in the region are adopting European standards means that their systems are converging and this will in the long-run eliminate TBTs among the bloc. Despite the substantive progress achieved in 2009, most countries are still lagging behind in transposing the EU *acquis* in this area, so full alignment (and convergence) requires intensified and sustained efforts in this complex area. Croatia is, expectedly, most advanced in transforming its quality infrastructure; it has adopted most European Standards (ENs) and has a relatively well developed infrastructure with over 140 conformity assessment bodies. Albania and Bosnia and Herzegovina have also adopted substantial share of ENs (mostly by endorsement); however the number of bodies remains relatively low (table 3.1). According to the European Commission, despite the various degrees of progress, all countries need to further align their legislation in the area of free movement of goods with the EU *acquis*. In many of the countries, the institutional set up is well in place, but administrative capacities need to be strengthened to ensure proper implementation and enforcement.

Table 3.1. Progress in Convergence to EU Standards

	European Standards (ENs) adopted		Conformity assessment bodies	
	2008	2009	2008	2009
Albania	14,424	15,029	n/a	16
Bosnia and Herzegovina	8,000	9,653	32	35
Croatia	10,695	21,368	123	145
FYR Macedonia	3,674	6,011	20	36
Montenegro	500	1,530	n/a	0
Serbia	2,805	5,072	325	347
Kosovo	665	1,200	0	4

Source: European Commission progress reports 2008 and 2009.

In addition to mandatory standards, international voluntary standards are also important for facilitating trade. Thousands of firms choose to get certification for ISO developed standards because they perceive an added value in showing conformity with these standards. Clougherty and Grajek (2006) find that ISO 9000 diffusion has boosted trade, in particular in developing countries, as it eases the costs of trade through the quality signal it sends and the "common language." The authors also find positive links to FDI, again more in developing countries, as international standards allow for easier integration of production processes. The perceived value of international certification is much greater for firms in developing countries, whereas firms in developed countries do not necessarily feel a strong need for international recognition of their systems. That is why for example Germany has less ISO 9001 certified firms per population than Slovenia and twice less certified firms than Italy.

SEE firms have not engaged very strongly in adopting international standards. According to ISO's latest survey, the number of firms which have adopted ISO 9001, that covers quality management systems, is extremely low in Albania and Montenegro, but also in Macedonia (table 3.2). Even Serbia and Croatia have far less ISO 9001 certified firms compared to some of the neighboring EU-10 countries. The situation is similar concerning the diffusion of ISO 14001, the second most widely implemented, standard that covers environmental management systems. And only a few dozen firms in the entire region (most of which in Croatia) have introduced the ISO 16949 standard for quality management systems for automotive production and relevant service part organizations, despite the willingness and potential of several SEE countries to develop their automotive sector. The Slovak Republic, on the other hand, which is the leader in the automotive industry among the EU-10, had 151 firms implementing this standard.

Table 3.2. Number of Firms Using ISO Standards at the End of 2007

	ISO 9001	ISO 14001	ISO 16949
Albania	23	0	0
Bosnia and Herzegovina	652	44	6
Croatia	2,073	258	20
FYR Macedonia	255	13	3
Montenegro	136	12	0
Serbia	1,987	149	6
Bulgaria	4,663	214	14
Slovak Republic	2,840	437	151
Slovenia	1,886	438	80

Source: ISO Survey 2007 (www.iso.org).

The chapter on TBTs in the CEFTA Agreement states that parties shall identify and eliminate unnecessary TBTs and shall not introduce new such barriers. To achieve these goals the parties will cooperate within the CEFTA institutional framework to harmonize technical regulations, standards, and conformity assessment procedures. However, the legal language in this area is quite weak and requires only that parties enter into negotiations on harmonization and mutual recognition before the end of 2010.

Harmonization of standards and mutual recognition of conformity assessment can be a long process which requires close coordination between the public sector and the industry, including negotiating bodies, standards and conformity assessment bodies, and the regulatory bodies. For example, the Asia-PacificPacific Economic Cooperation (APEC) Mutual Recognition Arrangement for Conformity Assessment of Telecommunications Equipment (only), in which 18 countries participate, took almost three years to negotiate and more than a year to enter into effect.[5]

It is difficult to estimate the foregone trade due to TBTs arising from incompatible standards, high certification costs, and so forth It is to be expected that small and medium-sized enterprises (SMEs) are affected disproportionately more by the certification requirements as these processes involve fixed costs, so for small exporters this constitutes a significant barrier to trade. While no precise data on the structure of trading firms within CEFTA can be found for any of the countries, the BEEPS 2008[6] results show that the sharing of exporting SMEs is significant, especially in the three largest SEE economies. In Serbia, 41 percent of small (1–19 employees) and 58 percent of medium-sized firms (20–99 employees) are exporters. The respective figures are 24 and 44 percent for Bosnia and Herzegovina, and 20 and 34 percent for Croatia. The most traded products within CEFTA, such as oil, steel, and other commodities, are exported by large firms, but SMEs probably have a nontrivial share in exporting some other product categories.

In preparation of implementation of CEFTA, all SEE countries prepared reports on identifying and eliminating NTBs. The assessment of these reports,[7] prepared in May 2007, showed that SEE countries had made little progress in addressing NTBs. The assessment found there was insufficient coordination among the parties and under-emphasis on TBTs, and SPS, issues (and over-emphasis on improving border and customs procedures). To improve the collaboration and progress in addressing NTBs, CEFTA parties have established a subcommittee on NTBs, which has met on few occasions. While no major agreements have been made so far, an expert study[8] has been commissioned by the EC that would assess the progress made with regard to TBTs and provide recommendations (box 3.2). Concerning harmonization of standards and mutual recognition of conformity assessment, the study urges CEFTA countries to achieve full European, and international, recognition of their national quality infrastructure. At the same time, the countries should establish effective mechanisms for regulatory cooperation and implementation of CEFTA clauses on transparency with regard to TBTs. Technical cooperation on the progress made in upgrading the quality infrastructure need also be improved.

Box 3.2. CEFTA on Technical Barriers to Trade

TBTs are regulated in chapter IV of the Agreement, which obliges all parties to apply the WTO Agreement on TBTs. Article 13 requires that "the Parties undertake to identify and eliminate unnecessary existing technical barriers to trade within the meaning of the WTO Agreement on TBTs". In addition, the Parties "undertake not to introduce new unnecessary technical barriers to trade" and "shall inform ... of any draft text for a new technical regulation or standard".

Moreover, "the Parties are strongly encouraged ... to harmonize their technical regulations, standards and procedures for assessment of conformity with those in the European Community". The Agreement specifies a concrete deadline for action on this issue: "the Parties undertake to enter into negotiations to conclude plurilateral agreements on harmonization of their technical regulations and standards, and the mutual recognition of conformity assessment procedures... before 31 December 2010."

Source: CEFTA.

The small size of their economies and their close proximity allow for much greater cooperation at regional level. SEE countries could benefit from economies of scale by sharing their quality infrastructure, since the number of potential users might not justify having every service provided in each of the countries. Furthermore, some of the small countries might lack the necessary specific technical expertise and the financial resources to offer all services related to accreditation and metrology domestically.

Sanitary and Phytosanitary Standards

Sanitary and phytosanitary standards (SPS) are receiving increasing attention in the international trade context. The use of food safety, animal and plant health rules as a barrier to trade has increased considerably in recent years throughout the world. While the aim of these rules is to protect the health of domestic consumers, governments frequently use SPS to shield domestic producers of agricultural products from imports. As tariffs and quotas on agriculture products in CEFTA are largely abolished, and full liberalization is likely to be achieved by the end of 2009, SPS are likely to become more common barrier to trade.

Agriculture trade features prominently in intra-regional trade, hence SPS issues are of great relevance for improving trade potential. Most SEE economies have a significant agriculture sector, and agriculture products (HS categories 1 to 24) account for over a fifth of intra-regional trade (though not all products in these categories are subject to SPS measures). Agriculture exports account for over a quarter of total exports to CEFTA in the case of Kosovo, Serbia, and Macedonia, while they are only 5 percent for Albania (figure 3.1). Serbia is the largest next exporter of agriculture products, followed by Croatia. In contrast, Bosnia and Herzegovina, Montenegro, and Kosovo are significant net importers. Even though it is difficult to estimate the forgone exports arising from the possible use of SPS measures as a barrier to trade, exporters should strongly benefit from having more transparent rules of the game.

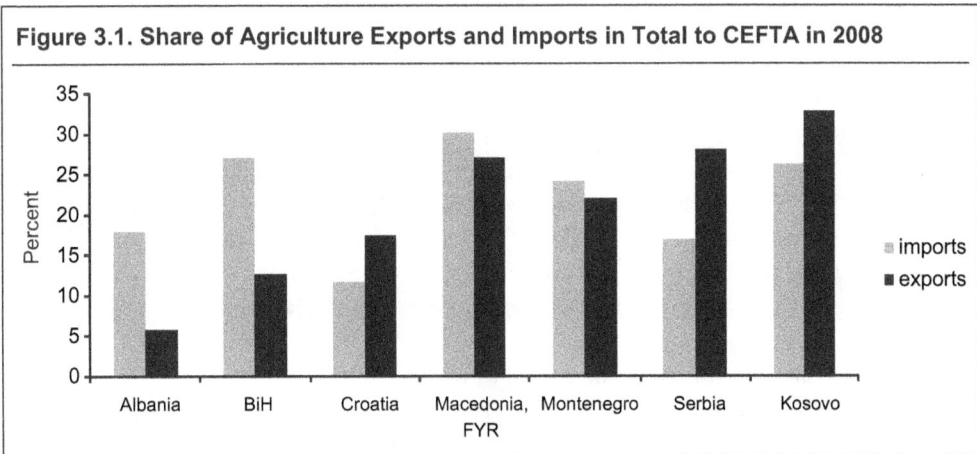

Figure 3.1. Share of Agriculture Exports and Imports in Total to CEFTA in 2008

Source: National Authorities.
Note: Data for Montenegro are for January-October period.

The CEFTA Agreement and the EU accession process should help reduce the distorting effects of SPS on trade within the region. The Agreement obliges all parties to adhere to the WTO Agreement on SPS, which of great importance as over 80 percent of agriculture trade in CEFTA goes to non-WTO members. In addition, all parties have committed to cooperate in the sanitary and phytosanitary field and to apply regulations in a nondiscriminatory manner. The parties also envisage concluding agreements on harmonization or mutual recognition in these matters, though, the Agreement does not specify any deadlines for this.

The EU accession process could also facilitate the convergence of sanitary and phytosanitary measures in the SEE region. As the countries progress on their EU accession path, they will have to increasingly comply with the EU rules in the area of food safety, veterinary and phytosanitary standards (chapter 12 of the *acquis*). So in the long run each of the countries will have adopted EU comprehensive set of standards in this area, and exporters will not have to meet requirements different from their domestic ones. This part of the EU *acquis*, however, is among the most difficult to comply with, so the convergence process will be a long one. For example, Croatia, which is by far most advanced in the negotiations process, has yet to make substantial progress in the area of food safety (European Commission progress report 2008).

It is important to note that when it comes to food products, large retail/supermarket chains often set their own standards (for example, fruits to be of same/similar size and shape) which go beyond the SPS import rules. While this is more the case with European retailers, retailers in the region are likely to follow similar trends (especially if they are bought by larger global retailers). So, agriculture producers will increasingly need to deal with these market-imposed standards in order to be able to access large suppliers (both in the CEFTA market and domestically).

The CEFTA Agreement introduces several novelties that aim to limit the use of SPS measures as a barrier to trade. SPS measures are regulated in the chapter on agriculture products (III) and article 12 of the Agreement obliges all parties to apply the WTO Agreement on the application of SPS measures. The same article requires that "the Parties shall co-operate in the field of sanitary and phytosanitary measures, including veterinary matters, with the aim of applying relevant regulations in a non-discriminatory manner." In addition, it obliges parties to provide information on SPS measures upon request of another party. Moreover, "The Parties shall enter, where appropriate, into negotiations to conclude agreements on harmonization or mutual recognition in threes matters...." However, a deadline for such action is not specified.

The collaboration on these matters is fostered by the CEFTA Subcommittee on NTBs. However, since the Agreement entered into force, firms from several SEE countries have voiced complaints about cases of SPS measures being used as a barrier to trade. Moreover, several countries introduced at some point measures (of SPS nature) that limit or prohibit imports from other CEFTA parties. Some of these have been resolved within the CEFTA framework, but others continue to be applied. For example, Croatia, FYR Macedonia, and Serbia have bans on import of some meet products (some of these bans precede the CEFTA Agreement). The business community in Bosnia and Herzegovina and Montenegro has complained that excessive inspection procedures and sampling of certain food products constitute discriminatory SPS measures.

Many of these arise from the non-acceptance of standards and certifications of the exporting party (box 3.3.). Faster progress on harmonization or mutual recognition should significantly reduce the complaints, that is, barriers to trade in this area.

Box 3.3. Import-Restricting Measures between Bosnia and Herzegovina, Croatia, and Serbia

---

Import-restricting measures between Bosnia and Herzegovina and Croatia for certain product groups, such as live bovine and milk, have existed for many years. For example, for some 9 years live bovine exports from Bosnia and Herzegovina to Croatia have been banned. In 2009, Bosnia and Herzegovina introduced a counter measures banning imports of live bovine from Croatia. Following this decision, Croatia introduced a ban on fish from Bosnia and Herzegovina. The escalation of trade protectionism measures on agriculture and food products finally led to negotiations between both sides at which most issues were resolved. Agreement had been reached to remove discriminatory measures for most products, for example, milk products (see http://www.dw-world.de/dw/article/0,4292323,00.html). Negotiations on removing bans on live bovine and fish remain to be finalized.

In June 2009, Bosnia and Herzegovina's Parliament made a major precedent in the trade relationship by enacting a law on protection of domestic production (*Official Gazette* issue 49/09). This law introduced MFN duties for imports of some 900 products from Croatia and Serbia, and presented a direct breach of the CEFTA Agreement. Following the enactment, the constitutionality of the law was challenged and on July 3 2009, the Constitutional Court of Bosnia and Herzegovina brought a decision annulling the implementation of the law.

Sources: http://www.dw-world.de/dw/article/0,4292323,00.html; *Official Gazette* issue 49/09.

The national reports on identifying and eliminating NTBs, as well as their assessments, included also SPS issues. The recommendation in the assessment of these reports was to improve coordination on SPS issues. The EC has commissioned another study[9] which would provide recommendations on harmonization and/or mutual recognition of SPS measures under CEFTA. As it has been found that most of the NTBs actually arise from SPS measures, it would be essential for the countries to assess carefully the proposals given in this study, and to make swift progress towards greater collaboration in this area.

Trade-Related Business Environment

The following section examines the trade-related environment in SEE through the prism of several global surveys and reports (the *Doing Business* report, BEEPS, and the Enabling Trade Index). The analysis derived from these reports does not necessarily relate to intra-regional trade; however, the findings should be considered valid for intra-regional trade as it captures a significant share of total trade. In addition, several pieces of country-specific and anecdotal evidence are included to reflect more specifically the impact of the trade-related business environment on intra-regional trade.

Tariffs and quotas are only one part of the overall costs of trade, so even when those are eliminated, trade performance can be impeded by high costs to transport and get goods across borders. The literature undoubtedly shows the negative correlation between trade costs and trade performance. Other aspects of the business environment, such as regulatory environment, telecommunications cost, and infrastructure are also strong determinants of trade as they impact the costs of production in addition to the trade cost.[10] Njinkeu, Wilson, and Foss (2008) undertake a review of literature on trade facilitation and find that improvements in the customs system, regulatory environment (including quality of institutions), and telecommunications have positive improvements on trade.

Hence, improving markets by establishing friendly business and trade-related policies is complementary to the formal liberalization of trade policy via FTAs. Aminian, Fung, and Ng (2008) compare two regions, East Asia and Latin America, which have followed different integration paths; integration was driven by market conditions in East Asia and by trade agreements in Latin America. The study finds that integration via the markets has been much more effective and East Asian economies have integrated much more despite the absence of a regional trade agreement until the mid-1990s.[11] For example, in 2005 half of East Asian exports went to the region, compared to only 13 percent in the case of Latin America (even though Latin American economies began introducing trade treaties in the 1960s). The conclusion is that two instruments of integration are complementary, and the benefits of trade can be maximized by improving the market conditions for trade in addition to the formal trade liberalization. Structural weaknesses and impediments arising from the business environment are equally important for unleashing the trade and growth potential.

To understand better the relative importance of trade costs, Anderson and Van Wincoop (2004) estimate that for developed countries trade costs, including distribution costs, are roughly about 170 percent of the production costs. Retail and wholesale distribution costs account for the bulk of total trade costs, followed by border-related costs and transport costs. Despite the obvious large variations in costs across countries and products, the importance of trade costs is indisputably large, and for developing countries these costs are probably larger as they often face higher transport and border costs (due to poor infrastructure and cumbersome procedures).

CEFTA opens up the potential to greater intra-regional trade and integration, but trade liberalization agreement is not the end of the story. Indeed, the SEE countries need to make progress on trade facilitation to ensure that they benefit to the maximum possible extent from their multilateral trade liberalization. Moving forward on trade facilitation will further lower trade costs and promote regional trade and integration.

Data from the World Bank's Doing Business database show that the overall cost of exporting and importing in SEE is higher than in OECD and well-performing EU-10 countries.[12] Last year, most of the SEE countries made progress in the "Trading Across Borders" area of the *Doing Business* report, however, most are lagging behind the top performers in the region. The cost to export and import in Kosovo are three times higher than in Estonia, and Serbia is over 40 percent more expensive than the Czech Republic. Unfortunately, no data is available as to the specific costs to export and import within CEFTA. However, the structure of these costs has a fixed component (related to licenses, other documentation, crossing the border, and so forth), so the data could be considered representative for intra-regional trade. Moreover, the documents and time for export/import are more or less the same irrespective of the final destination of the products.

The procedures for exporting and importing also seem to be unnecessary burdensome, according to the *Doing Business* 2010 report which results in extended time and cost to export and import (table 3.3). Moreover, policy-induced measures rather than infrastructure capacity and quality seem to be large contributors to the time and cost needed to cross borders. Exporters and importers need between 6 and 9 documents to move their product across the border, compared to 5 documents in OECD countries and less than that in Estonia.

Table 3.3. Doing Business 2010 Rankings in the Area of Trade

Region or Economy	Documents for export (number)	Time for export (days)	Cost to export (US$ per container)	Documents for import (number)	Time for import (days)	Cost to import (US$ per container)
Albania	7	19	725	9	18	710
Bosnia and Herzegovina	6	16	1,125	7	16	1,090
Croatia	7	20	1,281	8	16	1,141
Macedonia, FYR	6	12	1,436	6	11	1,420
Montenegro	7	14	775	7	14	890
Serbia	6	12	1,398	6	14	1,559
Kosovo	8	17	2,270	8	16	2,330
SEE average	*7*	*16*	*1,287*	*7*	*15*	*1,306*
Bulgaria	5	23	1,551	7	21	1,666
Czech Republic*	4	17	985	7	20	1,087
Estonia	3	5	730	4	5	740
The Slovak Republic	6	20	1,445	8*	25*	1,445*
ECA	7	27	1,582	8	28	1,773
EU	5	12	1,039	5	13	1,103

Source: www.doingbusiness.org.
* Doing Business 2009 data

The time to export and import in the region, 16 days on average, is longer than in the EU countries, but less than in many of the EU-10. And while the costs of shipping containers depend on many factors beyond customs legislation, the procedures (and time) for crossing borders could be greatly reduced through trade facilitation measures. For example, Georgia and Estonia have succeeded to reduce the time to export to five days. In addition, maritime shipping costs have declined significantly in the past several decades, so SEE firms face increased competition from abroad, so reducing unnecessary trade costs could help maintain the advantage of short distances among the economies in the region.

These long times to export and import can be a major obstacle for many firms, and for perishable products, such as fresh fruits and vegetables, are simply prohibitive. The array among the countries is quite large, 12 days to export in FYR Macedonia and Serbia, and 20 days in Croatia, which also causes great uncertainty among traders and hence limits trade opportunities. The longer time to move goods across the border imply not only higher opportunity costs but also additional expenditures for storage and wages (truck drivers). For example, some fruit exporters in Serbia have complained about the additional costs they face because the customs authority is closed on Saturday afternoon and Sunday.[13] Djankov, Freund, and Pham (2006) find that a day of delay at the border is equivalent to a country distancing itself from its trading partner by additional 85 kilometers. So, using this rough estimate, an eight-day unnecessary delay at borders between Croatia and Macedonia, places Skopje further than Istanbul in terms of transport costs for Croatian exporters. In addition, the long duration and high uncertainty force firms to keep higher inventories which raise their operational costs. The World Bank's Country Economic Memorandum for Albania (forthcoming) finds the cost of the tied-up capital in higher inventories to be quite substantial for importers but also significant for exporters.

Most of the SEE countries have undertaken deep reforms to ease doing trade by streamlining customs procedures and have achieved huge progress in recent years. Inspection of goods at borders has been identified as one of the biggest causes for delay in transport of goods, and each country has introduced some risk management techniques. However, the approach of customs authorities remains to be focused on trade control rather than trade facilitation. In most SEE countries, between 15 and 20 percent of shipments are physically inspected by customs officers, compared to 5 percent in the EU. In addition, other inspections, such as market, phytosanitary, and veterinary, often rely on 100 percent checking of all goods. Improving the efficiency of inspections, as well as removing other superfluous procedures could greatly reduce the waiting times for goods to cross borders (box 3.4). The World Bank's Country Economic Memoranda for Albania, Bosnia and Herzegovina, and FYR Macedonia (forthcoming), and its Croatia's EU Convergence Report (2009), provide more information on the remaining constraints to export in these countries.

Box 3.4. Single Customs Window in FYR Macedonia

The Macedonian Customs Administration introduced in November 2008 an electronic "Single Window" for trade facilitation. The new system simplifies the process of exporting, importing, and transit of goods, and is a first step towards achieving a fully paperless trade system. The electronic single window allows for most of the certificates and licenses for export, transit, or import to be submitted electronically, which relieves traders, as well as the Customs Administration, from burdensome and time-consuming tasks.

The "single window", once fully developed, would bring numerous benefits to trading firms and ultimately lowers the costs of imports and exports. For example, traders have now fast and efficient access to customs rules (for example, can get information online about all the customs requirements by tariff heading), information on requests submitted (for example, tracking of the current status of license applications online) and availability of tariff quotas. Some licenses are issued electronically and the system also provides information on the status of the license application, which takes away some of the uncertainty for traders. The new system also eliminates several procedures such as the obligation to submit evidence that the firm has been registered and that administrative fees for license application have been paid (fees can now be paid any time prior to receiving the license). Finally, the system is available 24/7 (www.exim.gov.mk), free of charge, hence the duration of the entire process is reduced.

The public authorities also greatly benefit from the new system which brings together 16 state institutions which are part of the trading process. The authorities now deal with electronic files which eliminates the time (and risk of errors) for entering data manually in the system. Also, they are able to monitor the payment of administrative fees as well as the distribution of quotas. The system allows for interlinking with other IT systems, so the access and flow of information is much more efficient.

Traders are increasingly showing interest in the new system. Almost 200 companies registered in the system by May 2009, and some 8,000 requests have been submitted electronically.

Source: Macedonian Customs Administration.

The Enabling Trade Index (ETI) prepared by the World Economic Forum (WEF) confirms the findings of the *Doing Business* report. The ETI measures the factors, policies, and services facilitating international trade of goods. The index[14] is based on hard data from various sources and survey data from the World Economic Forum's Executive Opinion Survey. Croatia stands out from the rest of the region (data for Serbia and Montenegro are not available), and even there the gap with well-performing EU-10 countries is significant in areas such as border administration (figure 3.2). The other three countries of the region rank lower than Estonia and Slovenia on all four sub-indicators, except on market access which is a result of EU's common trade policy. Between 2008 and 2009, Albania, Croatia, and FYR Macedonia had made progress in the ranking, while Bosnia and Herzegovina's position significantly deteriorated from 89th in 2008 to 102th in 2009. Again, the index relates to overall trade, but most of the indicators used, such as the domestic infrastructure, the border administration, and the business environment, are same for all trade irrespective of destination.

Figure 3.2. WEF's Enabling Trade Index 2009

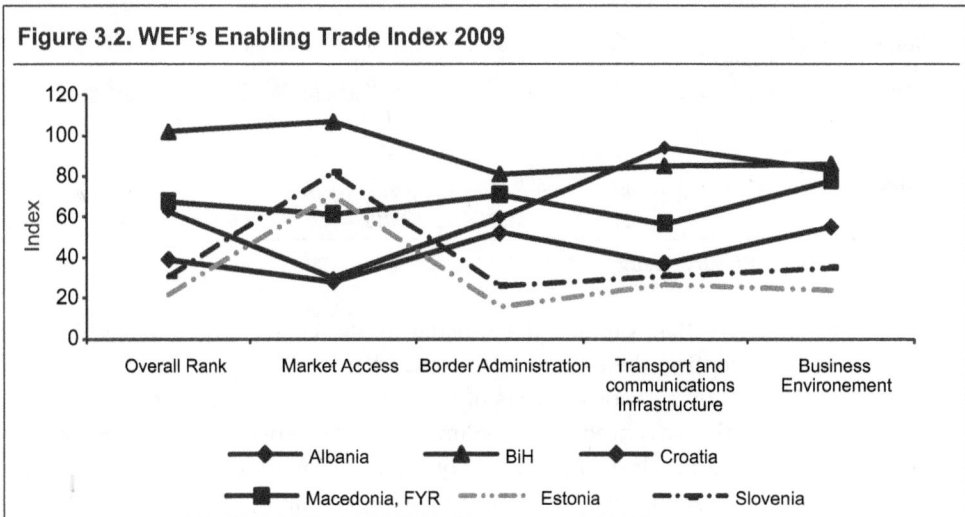

Source: WEF's Global Enabling Trade Report 2009.

The BEEPS 2008 depicts a less harsh trade-related environment as perceived by firms that trade, though there is much room for improvements on various aspects (table 3.4). For example, this survey suggests that in most SEE countries, it takes less time to clear exports and imports from customs than in some of the EU-10 countries. The time to obtain an import license, in contrast, is much longer in SEE (except Montenegro) than in the better performing EU-10 countries. The perception of the trade-related environment also varies among the countries, only 5 percent of trading firms in Montenegro list customs and trade regulations as a major constraint, compared to 18 percent in Serbia. At the same time, however, Montenegro has very few exporting firms, whereas almost half of the interviewed firms in Serbia were exporters.

Table 3.4. BEEPS 2008 Results

	% of exporter firms	% of firms that use material inputs and/or supplies of foreign origin	% of Firms Expected to Give Gifts to Get an Import License	Average time to clear direct exports through customs (days)	Average time to clear imports from customs (days)	Time to obtain import license (days)
Albania	21	94	6	1.9	2.6	27.5
Bosnia and Herzegovina	34	72	9	1.5	1.9	14.3
Croatia	28	81	1	1.5	1.6	13.4
Macedonia, FYR	38	80	4	2.5	3.7	18.8
Montenegro	9	75	0	2.6	2.7	4.4
Serbia	47	63	9	1.9	4.5	16.1
Kosovo	13	81	1	1.7	8.5	14.9
Bulgaria	17	50	8	4.2	5.4	24
Estonia	31	82	0	1.8	4.7	5.9
The Slovak Republic	20	57	30	2.5	4.8	2.5
Slovenia	58	88	7	2.9	3	7.3
ECA	22	62	16	4.5	8.8	15.2

Source: www.enterprisesurveys.org.

Other indicators that capture the broader trade-related environment (beyond border crossings) confirm the constrains to trade identified by the *Doing Business* and the WEF. SEE firms find various aspects of the business environment to be much less favorable than in the advanced EU-10 countries. Also, most trading firms rely on foreign supplies, and the days of inventory of the most important input are relatively high in the region: over 30 days in each country except Croatia (53 days in Macedonia). It would be useful to have information on the use of foreign supplies from SEE, as this would also give an indication of the use of production networks as well as the potential for cumulation of origin.

Improving the trade-related environment within the CEFTA framework

Chapter V of the Agreement refers to co-operation in customs administration, and article 14 stipulates that "the Parties shall simplify and facilitate customs procedures and reduce, as far as possible, the formalities imposed on trade". Article 15 prohibits fiscal discrimination: "the Parties shall refrain from any measure or practice establishing ... discrimination between the products originating in the Parties."

Several articles address services, which has both direct and indirect impact on trade flows. According to article 27, "the Parties will gradually develop and broaden their co-operation with the aim of achieving a progressive liberalization and mutual opening of their service markets, in the context of European integration...." Action on these matters could help reduce the costs of trade-related services including logistics, transport, and so forth. The following article stipulates that "the Parties, recognizing that the use of electronic means increases trade opportunities in many sectors, agree to promote the development of electronic commerce between them, in particular by cooperating on the market access and regulatory issues." Last but not least, the Agreement commits Parties to grant and ensure adequate and effective protection of intellectual property rights.

Any difficulties arising from the application of these provisions shall be resolved in accordance with the dispute resolution mechanism established in Article 42. This article establishes a Joint Committee (comprising representatives of all Parties) as a first mechanism for resolving disputes concerning the interpretation and application of the Agreement. The consultations in the Joint Committee could be done in the presence of a mediator. If a dispute is not resolved through consultations in the Joint Committee, a dispute may be referred to arbitration.

Cost and Quality of Trade Logistics

Cost and quality of trade-related services play an important role in trade expansion, and an inefficient logistics environment presents an implicit tax on trading. The logistics services encompass an array of actions, from transportation, consolidating of cargo, warehousing, and border clearance to in-country distribution and payment systems. These activities require solid physical infrastructure, ICTs and most importantly well-developed trade legislation (customs rules and procedures). High logistics costs and low service quality can be a barrier to both exports and imports.

The performance of customs, trade-related infrastructure, inland transit, logistics services, and information systems, are all critical to whether SEE countries can trade goods and services on time and at low cost, within the region and with the rest of the world. SEE's logistics performance is quite diverse, with Croatia being the best performer and Albania on the bottom of the list, but at the same time relatively poor compared to other European countries (table 3.5). All countries in the region, except for Croatia, have a lower score than the ECA average of 2.6 (5 being the highest score). All EU countries are ranked higher than the region's best performer Croatia (ranked 63 globally). Albania on the other hand ranks 139th out of 150 countries; its score is well below the average for low income countries. As with the previous indicators, these are based on overall trade performance, but again most of them are equally relevant for any trade.

Unnecessary costs and time delays arising from the logistics environment give a competitive advantage to traders from countries with more favorable conditions. Looking at figure 3.3, which compares trade logistics performance between SEE and the EU-10 countries, the latter outrank the SEE group on all aspects of trade logistics, apart from domestic logistics costs (which is to be expected as the average price levels in the EU-10 are higher than in SEE). This implies that goods can be imported faster and cheaper from neighboring EU countries than from CEFTA countries. The biggest gap between the two groups is in the timeliness of shipments in reaching destination, which is a key concern for traders, as well as in the ability to track and trace shipments (this largely depends on having the necessary ICTs in place).

Table 3.5. Logistics Performance Index

Country	LPI	Customs	Infrastructure	International shipments	Logistics competence	Tracking & tracing	Domestic logistics costs	Timeliness
Croatia	2.71	2.4	2.5	2.7	2.8	2.5	3.1	3.5
Bosnia and Herzegovina	2.46	2.3	2.3	2.5	2.4	2.3	3.4	3.0
Macedonia, FYR	2.43	2.0	2.3	2.7	2.3	2.5	3.0	2.8
Serbia and Montenegro	2.28	2.3	2.2	2.3	2.3	2.1	3.1	2.5
Albania	2.08	2.0	2.3	2.3	2.0	1.7	2.8	2.1
The Slovak Republic	2.92	2.6	2.7	3.1	3.0	2.9	3.1	3.3
Romania	2.91	2.6	2.7	3.2	2.9	2.9	2.6	3.2
Bulgaria	2.87	2.5	2.5	2.8	2.9	3.1	2.9	3.6
ECA (average)	2.59	2.4	2.4	2.6	2.5	2.6	3.0	3.0
EU-10 (average)	3.0	2.7	2.8	3.0	3.0	3.0	3.1	3.5
SEE average	2.4	2.2	2.3	2.5	2.4	2.2	3.1	2.8

Source: www.worldbank.org/lpi.

Note: The seven areas of performance are: (1) Efficiency of the clearance process by customs and other border agencies, (2) Quality of transport and information technology infrastructure for logistics, (3) Ease and affordability of arranging international shipments, (4) Competence of the local logistics industry, (5) Ability to track and trace international shipments, (6) Domestic logistics costs, and (7) Timeliness of shipments in reaching destination.

Figure 3.3. Trade Logistics Performance, SEE and EU-10 Countries

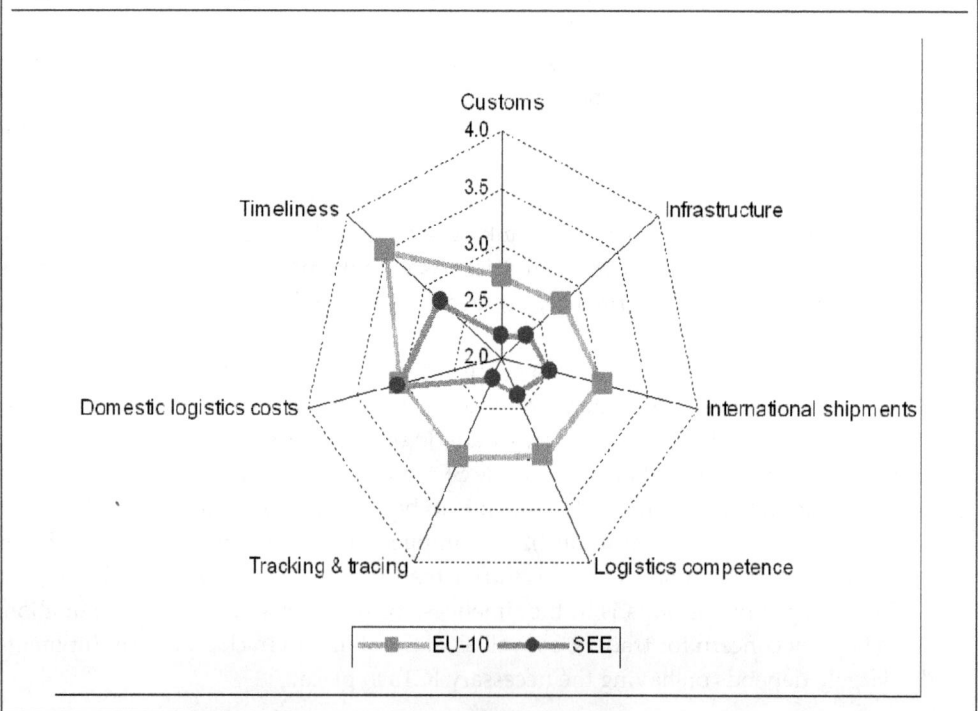

Source: www.worldbank.org/lpi.

Figure 3.4.Association of Trade Logistics Performance and Diversification of Exports

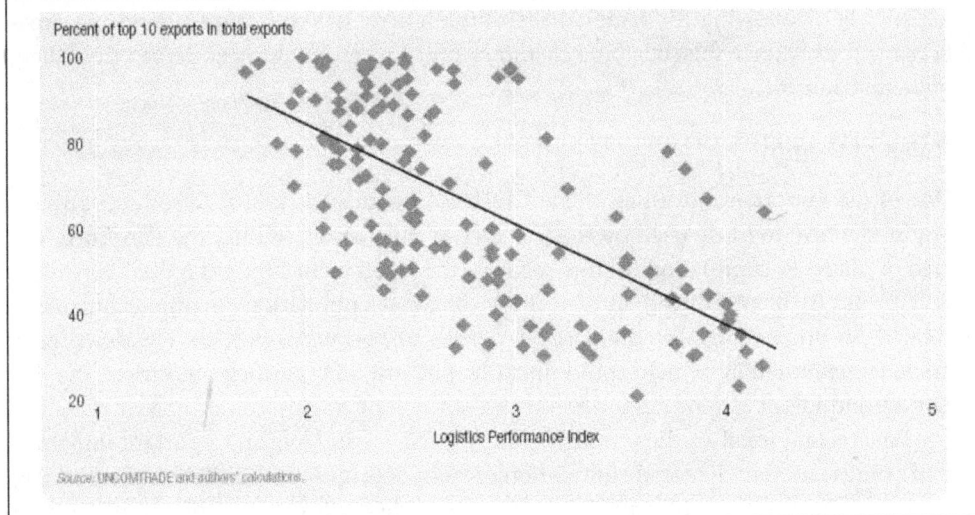

Percent of top 10 exports in total exports

Logistics Performance Index

Source: UNCOMTRADE and authors' calculations.

Efficient logistics are relevant not only for trade expansion but also for trade diversification and integration. The global production networks of the modern economy go beyond having access to markets and put a premium on moving goods in a predictable, timely, and cost-effective way. Logistics performance is positively correlated with the diversification of exports (figure 3.4). To be able to increase and diversify its export structure and move up the value-added ladder, the region ought to become 'well connected'. By becoming logistically friendly, SEE countries could gain a significant competitive and cost advantage and this in turn would lead to better value chain integration and would attract export-oriented FDI. This holds in particular if the region strives to attract foreign investment in sectors which look at the region as a single market, such as the automotive industry or ICT sector (see the OECD (2008) study "Defining and Strengthening Sector Specific Sources of Competitiveness in the

Box 3.5. Logistics Costs in Albania

According to the World Bank's Albania Country Economic Memorandum (forthcoming), Albania has among the highest logistics costs in Europe, which is also confirmed by its low ranking on the LPI regarding this component. In 2007, these costs were estimated around 22 percent of imports and 19 percent of exports; and these figures exclude unofficial payments to, for example, customs officers, road police, inspection services, and so forth.

Total logistics costs, including costs for domestic non-trade related logistics operations, in Albania were estimated at around $2 billion in 2007, or about a fifth of its GDP, a high figure both in a European and a worldwide comparison. For example, the equivalent costs in the EU-15 range between 10 and 16 percent of GDP, and in the EU-10 from 12 to 17 percent of GDP.

It should be noted though that the Albanian authorities have undertaken notable improvements related to the logistics environment in past three years, including major infrastructure investment, which has likely had a significant impact on logistics costs. The upcoming LPI 2009 index should shed more light on the impact of these reforms on logistics costs.

Source: Albania Country Economic Memorandum, World Bank (forthcoming).

Western Balkans," which identifies these sectors as most attractive for regional investment approach). One way, for example, to improve the quality and cost of logistics is by allowing for regional distribution activities to serve neighboring areas. However, to achieve this, customs clearance procedures would need to be streamlined to the maximum.

Rules of Origin

One of the important novelties of the CEFTA Agreement is that it introduces rules of origin identical to those used by the EU, EFTA, and Turkey (within the Pan-Euro-Med area of diagonal cumulation. In this regards, the Agreement brought a dual benefit for SEE firms: (i) it introduced intra-CEFTA diagonal cumulation of origin, and (ii) it created an opportunity for the CEFTA parties to become a part of a wider area of diagonal cumulation which could include key trading partner countries: the EU, Turkey and EFTA.

Several empirical studies confirm that rules of origin have an important impact on trade flows and that diagonal cumulation of rules of origin can facilitate trade (box 3.6). Gasiorek (2008) shows that in the European trade context, rules of origin serve to restrict trade flows with non-cumulating countries, and trade with those countries could be lower by up to 50 percent (or even 70 percent for some sectors). Woolcock (2007) finds that "rules of origin can be equivalent to a 4 percent tariff and incompatible rules of origin [that prevent diagonal cumulation] in different FTAs are the antithesis of trade facilitation". To eliminate these trade distortive effects of rules of origin, the EU in 1997 established a unified system of diagonal cumulation comprising EFTA, the then CEFTA countries and the Baltics. The creation of this Pan-European system of cumulation had a strong impact on trade flows within the EU-10 countries and between the EU-10 and the EU blocs (see Augier et al., 2005). Trade growth within the area was up to 43 percent higher than rise in trade with non-cumulating countries in 1997–99.

Box 3.6. The Benefits of Diagonal Cumulation

The largest benefit of using identical rules of origin among three or more trading partners is the possibility to apply diagonal cumulation of origin. Bilateral cumulation of origin is allowed in any FTA, it allows one partner country to import intermediary products from the other partner, and export a final product to the other partner duty-free. For example, Montenegro would import raw materials from the EU, process them, and export them back to the EU duty-free. However, in the absence of diagonal cumulation, a Montenegrin product would not be allowed duty-free access to the EU if it uses significant amount of inputs from another country (for example, Albania) even if Albania also has duty-free access to the EU for that product. Allowing for diagonal cumulation overcomes this anomaly as it enables the use of inputs from all trading partners participating in the diagonal cumulation area, as long as they are linked by free trade agreements providing for diagonal cumulation.

Hence, diagonal cumulation promotes trade within the area of diagonal cumulation by encouraging sourcing and processing within that area. In case of a trade area which involves one major trading partner (in this case the EU) and several other smaller countries, diagonal cumulation could encourage trade within the smaller countries as firms could now get inputs from any of these countries instead of from the EU or domestic production as was previously.

Source: Author.

Diagonal cumulation of origin within CEFTA became automatically possible with the entry into force CEFTA. So, a Serbian company can import raw materials from Albania, process them, and export a final product to Croatia at a zero tariff (assuming trade for that product is duty-free). In this and all other cases of within-CEFTA diagonal cumulation, the rules of origin (and the accompanying movement certificate) are the same, which greatly reduces the administrative burden for firms to prove compliance with the rules of origin. The actual impact of the intra-regional diagonal cumulation, unfortunately, cannot be assessed as data on the use of diagonal cumulation is not available. It would be of great importance for CEFTA parties to gather such data in order to analyze the trade creation impact of this policy.

The second, and more important, benefit of the CEFTA rules of origin is the possibility to engage in a diagonal cumulation with the EU, Turkey, and EFTA. So, for example, a Montenegrin product with Albanian inputs could also be exported to the EU. Moreover, the CEFTA countries which have an FTA with both the EU and Turkey could engage in a diagonal cumulation of origin among each other. For example, since July 1 2009, a firm in FYR Macedonia can import fabric and other raw materials from Turkey, process them and then export final textile products to the EU market at a zero tariff (assuming trade for that product is duty-free). For this arrangement to become operational, FYR Macedonia and its trading partners (the EU and Turkey) had to modify the rules of origin protocols of their bilateral FTAs. The same needs to be done for all other SEE countries, and once these legal requirements are fulfilled (and this is likely to happen in the course of 2009 for most SEE countries), the diagonal cumulation possibility would become reality.

The entry into the Pan-Euro-Med area of cumulation, once the conditions are in place, should be expected to have significant trade creation effects. Kejzar (2009) presents the possible effects of allowing diagonal cumulation with the EU, EFTA, and Turkey, and finds a positive effect in all cases on trade creation and trade expansion. The same study also shows that the Mediterranean countries which entered the Pan-Euro-Med area of diagonal cumulation also benefited from diagonal cumulation, and non-participating countries have lower trade with the EU and EFTA by up to 45 percent.

The full use of diagonal cumulation for achieving free trade among the EU, EFTA, SEE, and Turkey is, however, hampered by several issues. Firstly, Turkey does not have free trade agreements with Serbia, Montenegro, and Kosovo. In addition, the protocols providing for diagonal cumulation have yet to be fully concluded in the case of the existing free trade agreements with some of the other countries in the region. So, Croatian imports of raw materials from Turkey, used for products exported to the EU, would still be subject to customs duties. Second, the inclusion of the EFTA countries in the area of diagonal cumulation (EU-EFTA-Turkey-CEFTA) remains to be resolved (as it might require modifications of protocols with the Mediterranean countries as well). To resolve the latter issue, it is planned to include SEE countries in the Pan-Euro-Med system through the Regional Convention on Pan-Euro-Med preferential rules of origin. Lastly, Kosovo is in a unique, unenviable, position that it does not have an FTA with the EU, nor with Turkey or EFTA. Until this is remedied, Kosovo will not be able to benefit from the diagonal cumulation, apart from the intra-CEFTA cumulation.

Notes

[1] According to the OECD, technical barriers to trade (TBT) refer to technical regulations and voluntary standards that set out specific characteristics of a product, such as its size, shape, design, functions and performance, or the way a product is labeled or packaged before it enters the marketplace. Included in this set of measures are also the technical procedures which confirm that products fulfill the requirements laid down in regulations and standards

[2] Sanitary and phytosanitary (SPS) measures refer to any of the laws, rules, standards, and procedures that governments employ to protect humans, other animals, and plants from diseases, pests, toxins, and other contaminants.

[3] Albania, Croatia, FYR Macedonia, and Moldova are WTO members, and Montenegro is expected to join in 2009.

[4] The national quality infrastructure comprises a set of public and private institutions that enable firms to demonstrate that they are complying with the defined standards. This includes: testing laboratories and inspection bodies, certification bodies, calibration laboratories, a national standards body, a national accreditation body, and a national metrology institute.

[5] APEC's Telecommunications MRA was concluded at a gathering of Ministers for Telecommunications and Information in Singapore on May 8, 1998. It entered into effect on July 1, 1999.

[6] www.enterprisesurveys.org

[7] "Identifying and Eliminating NTBs: Annual Reports by SEE countries—An Assessment," prepared by WTI Advisors, May 2007.

[8] "Harmonization of Technical Regulations and Standards and Mutual Recognition of Conformity Assessment Procedures under CEFTA."

[9] "Identification of Potential of Harmonization or Mutual Recognition of Sanitary and Phytosanitary Measures under CEFTA."

[10] Trade costs encompass all costs related to the transfer of goods to a final user (in a different country), other than the costs of producing the goods. Trade costs also include the costs of compliance with standards and technical regulations in foreign markets if those are different from the ones in the domestic market.

[11] The ASEAN FTA was signed in 1992 and envisaged setting up a free trade area within 15 years.

[12] The "Trading Across Borders" component of Doing Business captures the total official cost for importing or exporting a standardized cargo of goods, excluding ocean transit and trade policy measures such as tariffs.

[13] See B92 article for more information: http://www.b92.net/info/vesti/index.php?yyyy=2009&mm=07&dd=23&nav_id=372878.

[14] The index composes 10 pillars grouped in four sub-indexes: (1) Tariffs and nontariff barriers, (2) Proclivity to trade, (3) Efficiency of customs administration, (4) Efficiency of import-export procedures, (5) Transparency of border administration, (6) Availability and quality of transport, infrastructure, (7) Availability and quality of transport services, (8) Availability and use of ICTs, (9) Regulatory environment, (10) Physical security.

CHAPTER 4

How Are Firms Reacting to Regional Trade Integration?

The Case of Agrokor

Agrokor is the largest private Croatian company, with revenue of some €3.8 billion in 2008. Most of it revenues come from sales in Croatia, SEE and some of its EU neighbors (Slovenia, Hungary, and so forth). It is also one of the biggest companies in the region. At the same time, Agrokor is an important trader in the region with around €200 million of intra-regional trade. It has trade relationships with each country in the region, while most of its assets (and production) are located in Croatia, Bosnia and Herzegovina, and Serbia. The company employs up to 38,000 employees, most in Croatia, but also some 2,400 in Bosnia and Herzegovina and more than 5,400 in Serbia.

As a truly regional company with production sites, suppliers and buyers throughout SEE, Agrokor sees great advantages from trade integration in the region and sees CEFTA as a major step forward to unleashing the potential of such integration. One of the most important benefits from CEFTA is the reduction/elimination of tariffs (and quotas) within the region, though the company would wish to see trade in the region fully liberalized as soon as possible. Being focused mostly on food products, tariffs and import bans on certain products (for example, pork, beef, and so forth.) in some of the CEFTA countries continue to hamper trade. Recent import-restricting measures in some of the countries have clearly demonstrated the negative effects of trade protectionism.

Another important benefit for Agrokor is the introduction of unified rules of origin in CEFTA and the possibility for using diagonal cumulation of origin. The firm sees numerous opportunities from implementing diagonal cumulation in the region and the EU. It would enable the company to better access EU markets and to make better investment decisions (based on economic/cost factors rather than on factors such as borders). Fully implemented DCO is very much needed in the region, and would have great impact on trade creation.

Nontariff barriers continue to be a constraint to trade in the region and the company finds that technical regulations and standards are used as trade protectionism measures. For example, sometimes trucks with food products (for example, meat) spend several days at a border before sanitary inspection clears the goods. In such cases, these measures prohibit trade of perishable goods. Although Agrokor does not face great difficulties in meeting technical requirements (for example, obtaining certification, and so forth) for the products its trades, the variety of regulations poses challenges for the company. For example, even a simple product such as bottled water (Jana water is one of Agrokor's most well-known brands) have different regulations among the countries. Harmonization of standards would facilitate trade and reduce costs of exporting to several markets in the region.

Removing the remaining nontariff barriers would enhance not only trade but also investment flows to the region. The costly and timely border-crossing procedures have great impact on investment decisions for regional and foreign companies. Agrokor, as well as many European and other foreign investors, would like to see the region as a more integrated economic space where investment decisions could be based solely on economic basis. However, this is not the case yet and decisions on locating production and distribution sites are strongly affected by these border-crossing issues.

Concerning other aspects of the trade environment, Agrokor would benefit from improvements in the transport infrastructure, in particular rail. Rail transport is important for many products, especially seasonal products such as wheat. Yet, rail transport is for many reasons limited and the firm relies mostly on road transport which at this stage is much more efficient. In terms of logistics, due to its size Agrokor manages its logistics internally (for example, has its own distribution channel) and does not find them to be a constraint to doing business. Trade finance is also not an issue; being a large company, it has access to banking services across the region, and it helps that European banks are present in practically all countries in the region. And to ensure access to inputs, Agrokor sometimes helps its own suppliers with getting access to finance.

The Case of ArcelorMittal

ArcelorMittal, previously Mittal Steel, is one of the largest steel product manufacturers in SEE offering various steel products (for example, flat products, long products, automotive grades, and so forth). It operates two production facilities in the region, one in Skopje (FYR Macedonia) and one in Zenica (Bosnia and Herzegovina) both of which it acquired in 2004. The two plants sell their products to the region and to the EU. In the case of the steel plant in Skopje, between a quarter and half of total revenue comes from the CEFTA region.

In terms of tariffs and quotas, steel trade was largely liberalized prior to CEFTA, so in this regard the Agreement did not bring any additional benefits for the company. However, trade flows remain to be hampered by some nontariff barriers. The company faces situations when technical regulations are used as a barrier to trade. For example, when exporting to Serbia, goods cannot cross the border before the company provides a quality certificate (MTC) to the Serbian Customs Administration. This often delays the transport and the Serbian Customs Administration is the only one in the region that requests the quality certificates to be shown prior to entry.

One of the most important challenges that the company is facing in the region is dealing with unfair competition offering products at "dumping prices." However, these low-priced products come from non-CEFTA countries, mostly from companies in the CIS region and from Bulgaria (mainly hot rolled material). In this regard, the provisions in CEFTA on state aid and anti-dumping are perceived as important for ensuring fair competition in the region.

More efficient border crossings should be one of the top priorities for trade enhancement as seen my ArcelorMittal. Unnecessary delays at border crossings and at customs terminals, has important implications on the total transport costs. Opening times at border crossings and customs terminals are short, and if a truck is not cleared, for example, by Friday afternoon, it has to wait until Monday to clear customs. This results in unnecessary increase in transport costs.

Infrastructure availability and efficiency is also one of the most important determinants of transport costs, and the company sees a lot of room for improving infrastructure throughout the region. The Skopje plant transports some 40 percent of its exports by rail, however, the rail infrastructure is quite underdeveloped. For example, the Nis-Solun track is one rail which presents a major bottleneck for larger loads. Moreover, since there is no rail connection between FYR Macedonia and Bulgaria, rail cargo to Bulgaria also goes via Nis. The quality of the transport services is also a constraint as the company sometime faces insufficient wagons (in particular closed wagons). ArcelorMittal also sees room for improvement of road transport. For example, exports to Albania can only be cleared by customs in Struga (at the very south of FYR Macedonia) which extends the distance for trade with Albania.

CHAPTER 5

Conclusions and Recommendations

Intra-regional trade performance in SEE has improved considerably in recent years. Formal trade liberalization policies, first through bilateral FTAs and later through CEFTA, have contributed to this increase. Nonetheless, intra-regional trade integration could be further enhanced. Despite the increase in trade flows, the structure of does not signal a high level of integration. Commodities continue to dominate, and intra-industry trade remains low compared to intra-industry trade performance in the EU-10 countries. Greater trade integration could be an important driver of economic growth in the region, and a number of policy options are available to achieve this. Many of these policy options are specifically addressed in the CEFTA Agreement, hence, include a clear commitment for action.

Achieving complete trade liberalization should be one of the first priorities. The visible benefits of zero tariffs and quotas for manufactured goods and many agriculture products, should urge the authorities to complete the formal trade liberalization agenda. The CEFTA Agreement itself requires countries to move forward on this, and substantial progress has been made within the CEFTA framework already. Negotiations on agriculture liberalization have been initiated and it is likely that a decision could be taken by the end of 2009. At the same time, the countries should refrain from introducing protectionism measures, such as tariffs, quotas and other import-restrictions, as these are not only a breach of the Agreement, but also have negative economic consequences in the long-term.

With tariffs and quotas being largely eliminated within CEFTA, the impact of NTBs on trade flows becomes more prominent. In this regard, TBTs and SPS measures could become important barriers to trade. The possibility of some of these measures to act as a barrier to trade has been well elaborated in the trade literature, and is also confirmed by the reactions from the SEE business community. As all SEE countries aim to join the EU, the best and easiest way to harmonize technical, sanitary and phytosanitary standards is by converging to EU rules (*acquis*) in these areas. At present, there is great discrepancy among the countries in the level of transposition of the EU *acquis*. Moreover, enhanced collaboration on these matters is of almost equal importance. As committed, the countries should co-operate closely in the fields of SPS and TBTs, apply regulations in non-discriminatory manner, and refrain from introducing new barriers to trade.

In addition to the trade measures that are part of CEFTA, other more general trade-facilitation policies could also enhance intra-regional, and overall, trade. The time and costs to export and import in some of the SEE countries are high compared to well-performing EU-10 countries. At the same time, logistics performance is weak. The transport infrastructure also could benefit from improvements. These findings are confirmed by the two case-study firms, which would like to see more efficient customs procedures and better transport infrastructure. More detailed analysis would be needed to determine where exactly should improvements be targeted and how much of these impediments are related to intra-regional trade. The recent World Bank's Country Economic Memoranda for some of the SEE countries contain a more specific diagnosis on these issues.

The rules of origin, and the possibility to apply wider diagonal cumulation of origin, are another potential benefit of the CEFTA Agreement. The rules allow not only for intra-CEFTA cumulation of origin, but also for future inclusion in the Pan-Euro-Med system of cumulation. Allowing for diagonal cumulation, for example, with the EU and Turkey, requires changes in bilateral trade protocols, and not all countries have completed this process. At the same time, the authorities would need to engage with the private sector and to promote the opportunities offered in this area.

While this study does not address many of the other areas that are included in the Agreement, some of them are of great importance and should deserve greater attention of policy makers. For example, trade in services could be greatly enhanced by moving forward on some of the areas in the Agreement, such as public procurement, intellectual property rights, competition and state aid rules, and so forth. The countries have committed to collaborate on all these areas, and a more prompt action is needed, in particular on those for which the Agreement does not contain any deadlines for action.

Last but not least, trade statistics deserve greater attention. The reasons for the discrepancies in mirror trade statistics, beyond those that are to be expected due to recording differences, should be investigated in greater detail. Unrecorded trade has fiscal implications and distortive effects on markets. Moreover, greater transparency and availability of trade statistics would be valuable for policy and market analysis.

The implementation of the commitments of the CEFTA agreement will help the SEE countries' EU accession prospects. External trade is one of the core, and sole, Community competencies and many of the areas of co-operation are part of the EU *acquis*, so making progress on these will require harmonization with EU standards. Upon joining the Union SEE economies will be fully integrated into the EU's Single Market. Hence, greater trade and economic integration prior to becoming part of the EU will have multiple benefits: (i) firms will be better able to cope with the competitive pressures within the Union; and (ii) national administrations will have gained experience in regional cooperation, which is essential for well-functioning within the EU.

Annexes

Annex I.A. Trade Structure by HS-2 Product Category in 2007

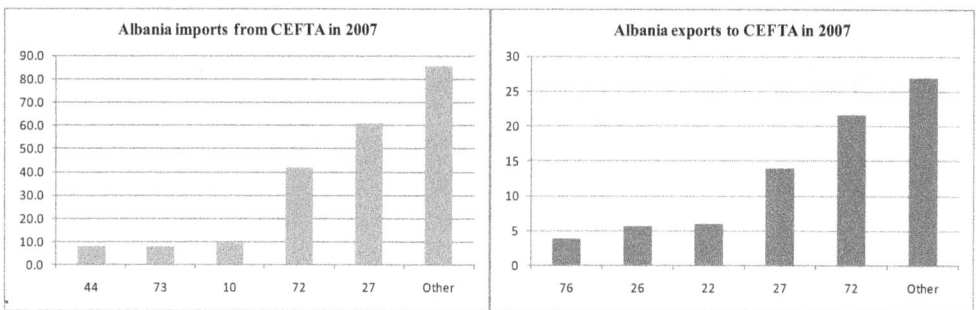

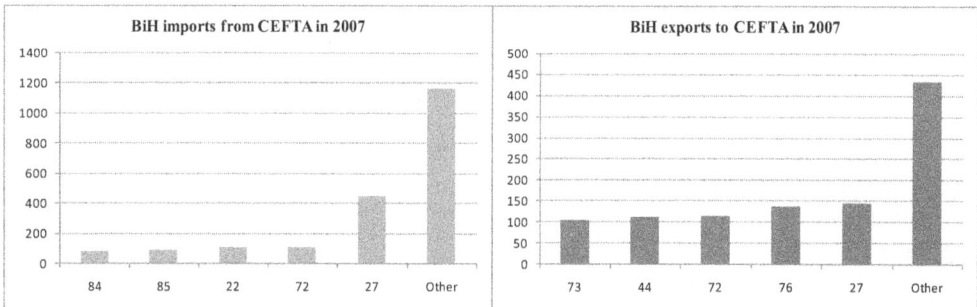

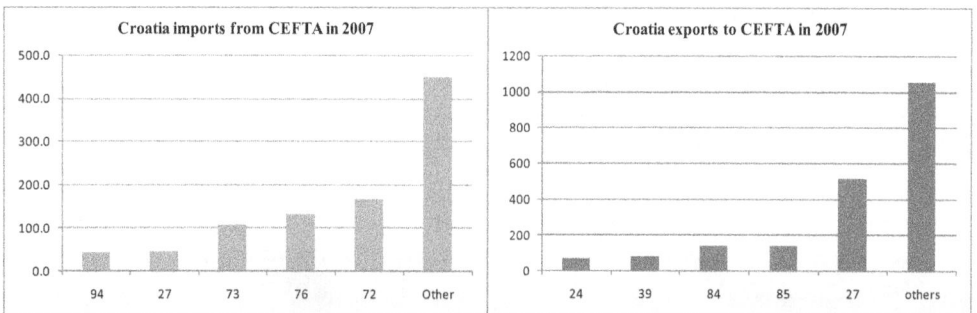

Albania imports from CEFTA in 2007

Categories: 44, 73, 10, 72, 27, Other (y-axis 0.0 to 90.0)

Albania exports to CEFTA in 2007

Categories: 76, 26, 22, 27, 72, Other (y-axis 0 to 30)

BiH imports from CEFTA in 2007

Categories: 84, 85, 22, 72, 27, Other (y-axis 0 to 1400)

BiH exports to CEFTA in 2007

Categories: 73, 44, 72, 76, 27, Other (y-axis 0 to 500)

Croatia imports from CEFTA in 2007

Categories: 94, 27, 73, 76, 72, Other (y-axis 0.0 to 500.0)

Croatia exports to CEFTA in 2007

Categories: 24, 39, 84, 85, 27, others (y-axis 0 to 1200)

Kosovo imports from CEFTA in 2007

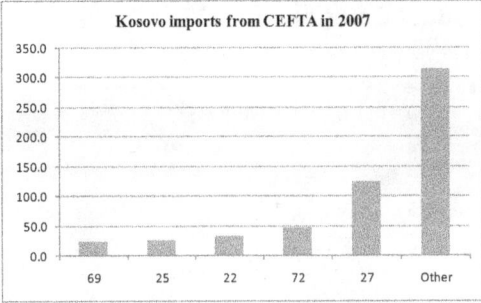

Kosovo exports to CEFTA in 2007

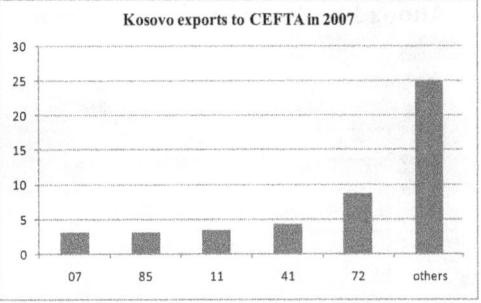

FYR Macedonia imports from CEFTA in 2007

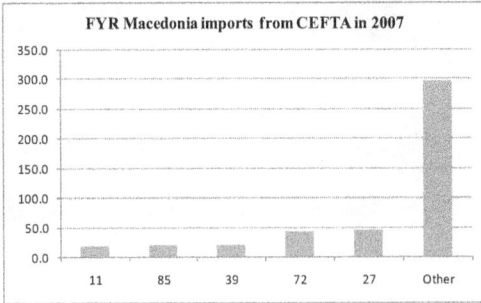

FYR Macedonia exports to CEFTA in 2007

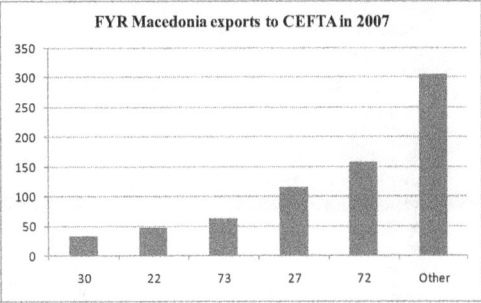

Montenegro imports from CEFTA in 2007

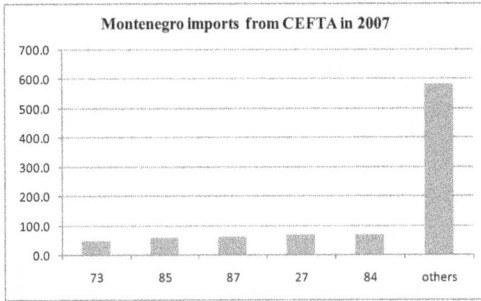

Montenegro exports to CEFTA in 2007

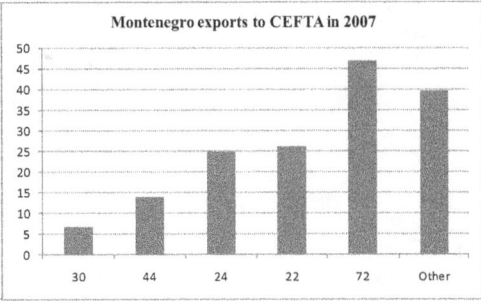

Serbia imports from CEFTA in 2007

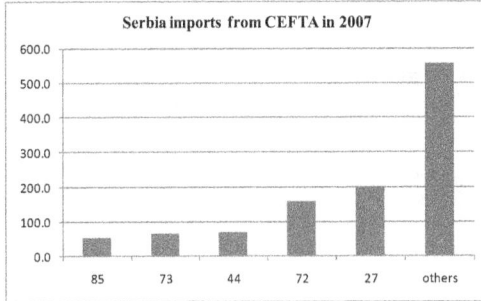

Serbia exports to CEFTA in 2007

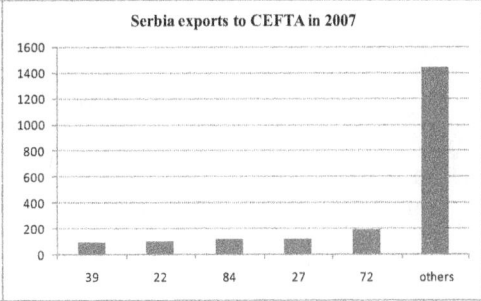

Annex I.B. Trade Structure by HS-2 Product Category in 2008

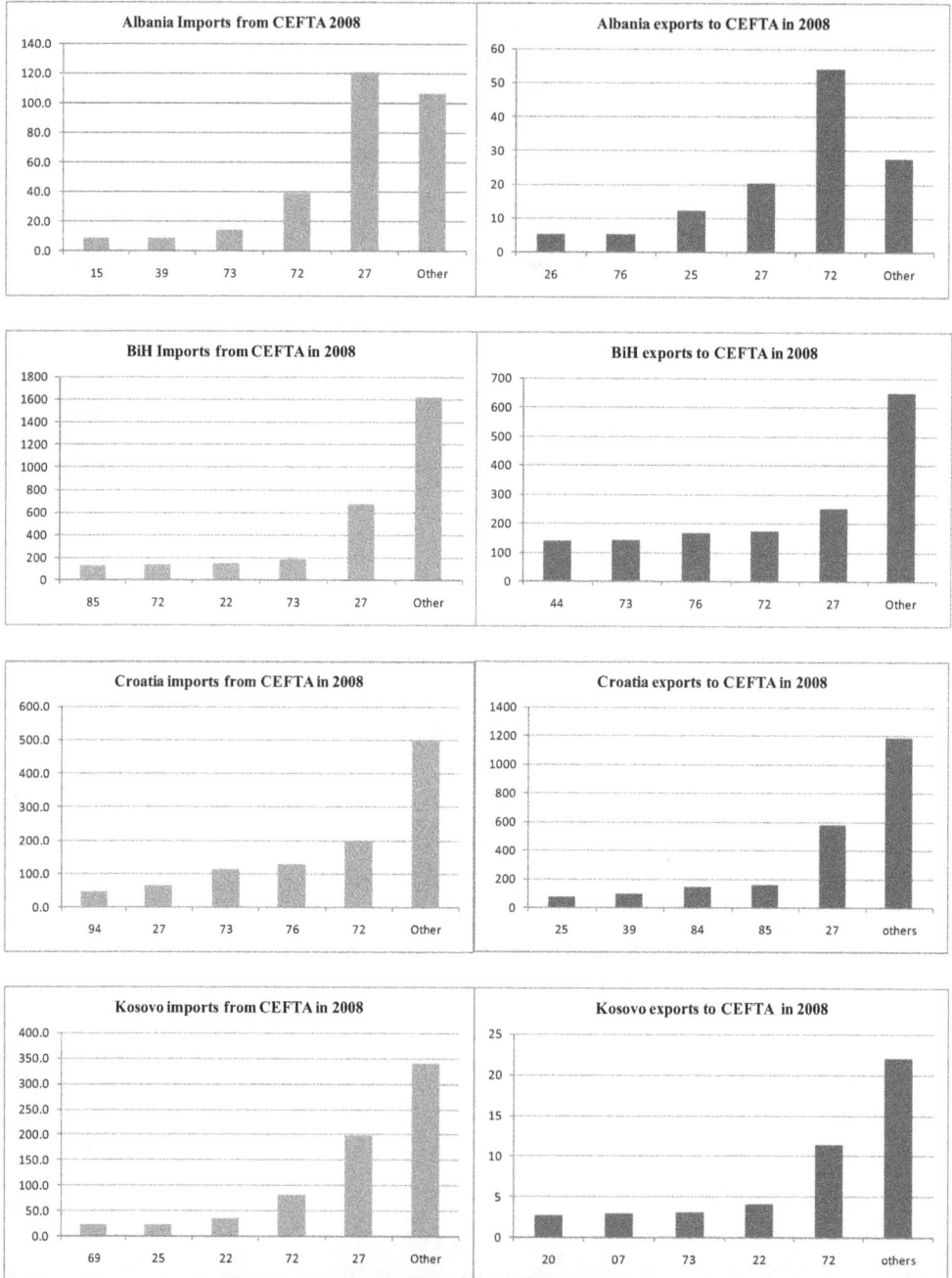

Albania Imports from CEFTA 2008

Albania exports to CEFTA in 2008

BiH Imports from CEFTA in 2008

BiH exports to CEFTA in 2008

Croatia imports from CEFTA in 2008

Croatia exports to CEFTA in 2008

Kosovo imports from CEFTA in 2008

Kosovo exports to CEFTA in 2008

FYR Macedonia imports from CEFTA in 2008

FYR Macedonia exports to CEFTA in 2008

Montenegro imports from CEFTA in 2008*

Montenegro exports to CEFTA in 2008*

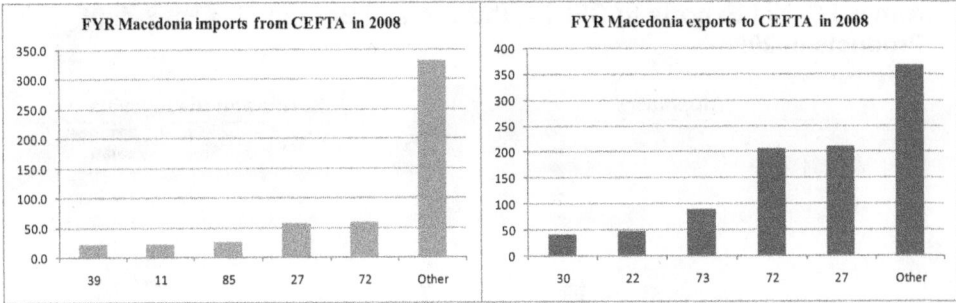

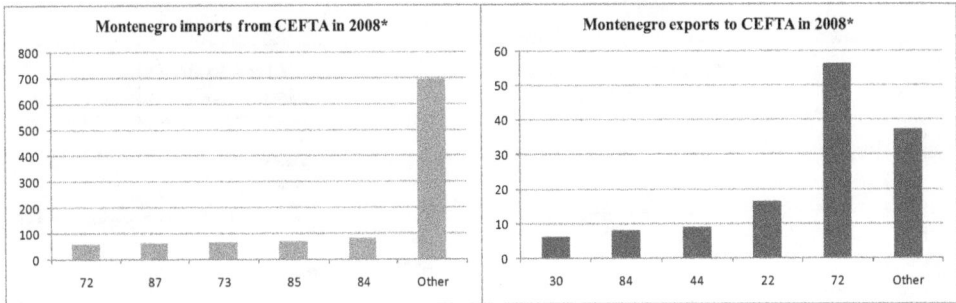

* Data for January-October only.

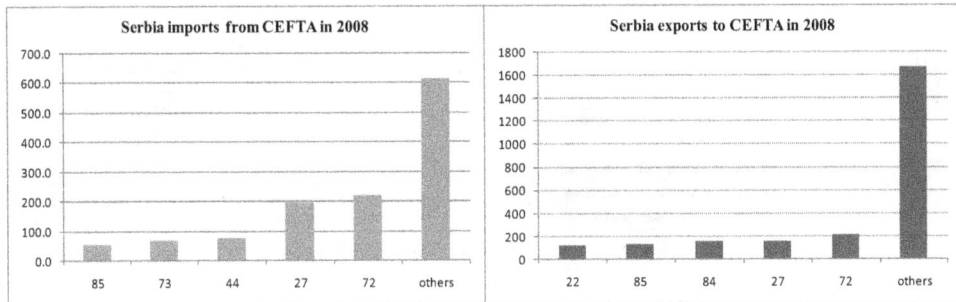

Serbia imports from CEFTA in 2008

Serbia exports to CEFTA in 2008

Annex I.C. Net Exports to CEFTA, the Top and Bottom Five HS 2-digit Products in 2008

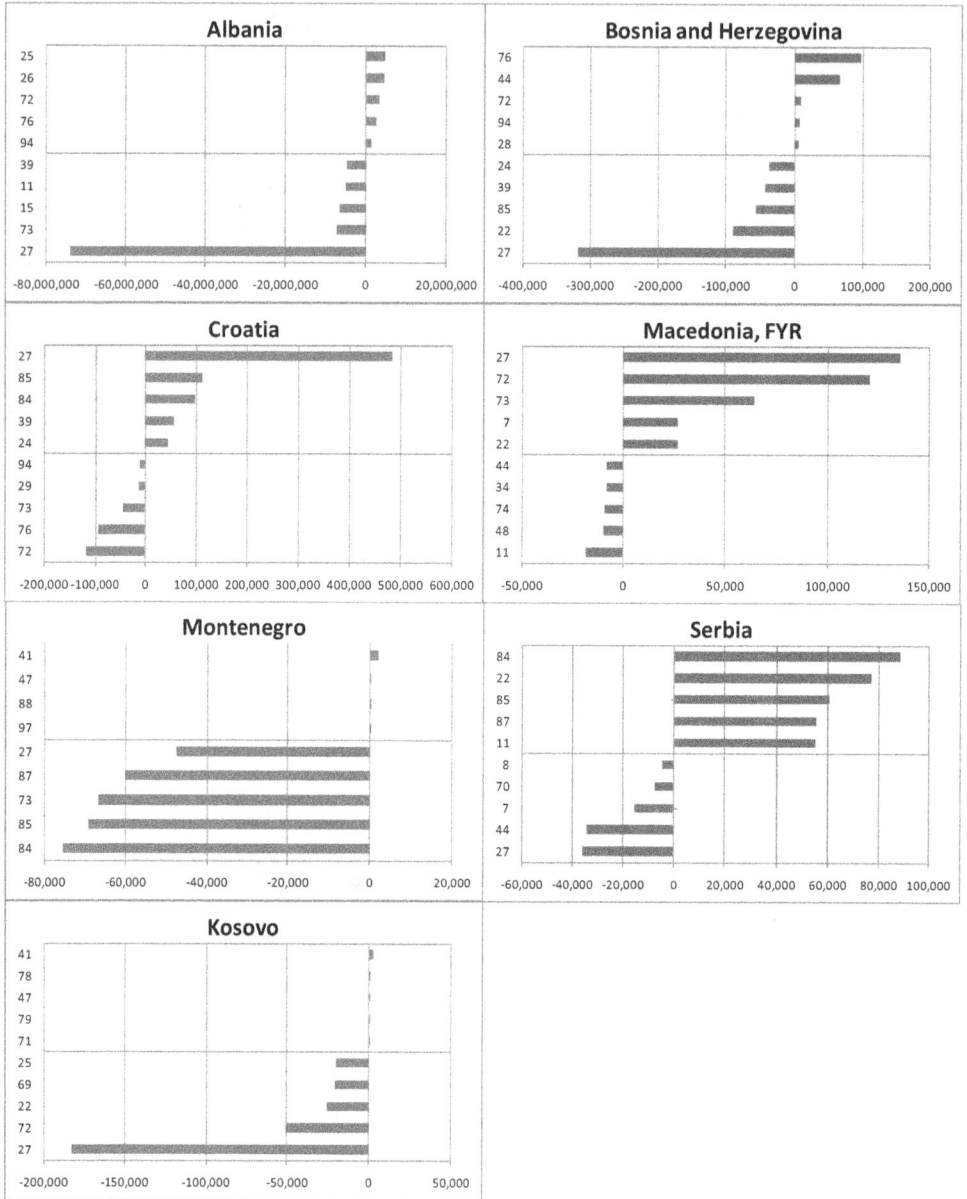

Source: National authorities.

* Data are for first three quarters, except Croatia (includes October data).

Annex I.D. Description of 2-digit HS Categories

Code	Description	Code	Description
1	Live animals	49	Printed books,newspapers,pictures;typescripts and plans
2	Meat and edible meat offal	50	Silk
3	Fish and crustaceans,molluscs & other aquatic invertebrates	51	Wool,fine or coarse animal hair;horsehair yarn and woven f
4	Milk and products of milk;birds' eggs; natural honey	52	Cotton
5	Products of animal origin not elsewhere included	53	Other vegetable textile fibres;paper yarn
6	Live trees and other plants;roots and the like;cut flowers	54	Man-made filaments
7	Edible vegetables and certain roots and tubers	55	Man-made staple fibres
8	Edible fruit and nuts;peel of citrus fruits or melons	56	Wadding,felt and non-wovens;special yarns;twine,cordage
9	Coffee,tea,mate and spices	57	Carpets and other textile floor coverings
10	Cereals	58	Special woven fabrics;tufted textile fabrics;lace
11	Products of the milling industry;malt;starches;inulin	59	Impregnated,coated,covered or laminated fabrics
12	Oil,seeds and oleaginous fruits;miscellaneous grains,	60	Knitted or crocheted fabrics
13	Lacs;gums,resins and other vegetable saps and extracts	61	Articles of apparel and clothing accessories,knitted
14	Vegetable plaiting materials	62	Articles of apparel and clothing accessories,not knitted
15	Animal or vegetable fats and oils;their cleavage products	63	Other made up textile articles;other
16	Preparations of meat,of fish or of crustaceans,molluscus	64	Footwear,gaiters and the like;parts of such articles
17	Sugars and sugar confectionery	65	Headgear and parts thereof
18	Cocoa and cocoa preparations	66	Umbrellas,sun umbrellas,walking-sticks,seat-sticks,whips
19	Preparations of cereals,flour,starch or milk;	67	Prepared feathers and down and articles made of feathers
20	Preparations of vegetables,fruit,nuts	68	Articles of stone,plaster,cement,asbestos,mica or similar
21	Miscellaneous edible preparations	69	Ceramic products
22	Beverages, spirits and vinegar	70	Glass and glassware
23	Waste from the food industries;prepared animal fodder	71	Natural or cultured pearls,precious or semi-precious stones
24	Tobacco and manufactured tobacco substitutes	72	Iron and steel
25	Salt;sulphur;earths & stone;plastering material,lime,cement	73	Articles of iron or steel
26	Ores,slag and ash	74	Copper and articles thereof
27	Mineral fuels,mineral oils and waxes;bituminous substances	75	Nickel and articles thereof
28	Inorganic chemicals	76	Aluminium and articles thereof
29	Organic chemicals	78	Lead and articles thereof
30	Pharmaceutical products	79	Zinc and articles thereof
31	Fertilizers	80	Tin and articles thereof
32	Tanning or dyeing extracts;tannins and their derivates;dyes	81	Other base metals;cermets;articles thereof
33	Essential oils and resinoids;perfumery,cosmetic preparations	82	Tools,implements,cutlery,spoons and forks,of base metal
34	Soap,organic surface-active agents,washing preparations	83	Miscellaneous articles of base metal
35	Albuminoidal substances;modified starches;glues;enzymes	84	Nuclear reactors,boilers,machinery and mechanical appliances
36	Explosives;pyrotechnic products;matches;pyrophoric alloys	85	Electrical machinery and equipment and parts thereof
37	Photographic or cinematographic goods	86	Railway or tramway locomotives,rolling-stock & parts thereof
38	Miscellaneous chemical products	87	Vehicles other than railway or tramway rolling-stock,parts
39	Plastics and articles thereof	88	Aircraft,spacecraft and parts thereof
40	Rubber and articles thereof	89	Ships,boats and floating structures
41	Raw hides and skins(other than furskins) and leather	90	Optical,photographic,cinematographic,measuring;parts thereof
42	Articles of leather;saddlery and harness	91	Clocks and watches and parts thereof
43	Furskins and artificial fur;manufactures thereof	92	Musical instruments;parts and accessories of such articles
44	Wood and articles of wood;wood charcoal	93	Revolvers,pistols,shotguns&the like;cartridges&parts thereof
45	Cork and articles of cork	94	Furniture;bedding,mattresses,mattress supports,cushions
46	Manufactures of straw,of esparto,of other plaiting materials	95	Toys,games and sports requisites;parts thereof
47	Pulp of wood or of other fibrous cellulosic material	96	Miscellaneous manufactured articles
48	Paper and paperboard;articles of paper pulp	97	Works of art,collectors' pieces and antiques

Part II

Labor Mobility in Southeast Europe

Robert Lucas
Philip Martin

Abstract

The eight CEFTA member states aim to join the European Union,[1] which is based on the free movement of goods, capital, services, and workers over national borders. There is labor migration between CEFTA member states, but few formal mechanisms allow and encourage the freer mobility of workers that could allow economies of scale and FDI to speed up economic growth and job creation.

This report examines the mobility provisions of free trade agreements (FTAs); its purpose is to show how to implement freer migration of especially professional and skilled workers between CEFTA member states. The EU experience highlights the need for strong leadership, firm time lines, and institutions that can provide redress to individuals whose mobility rights were impeded and set precedents that encourage freedom of movement. The examples of other FTAs, such as NAFTA or CARICOM, may provide some useful lessons as to how to approach labor mobility.

The benefits of more skilled worker mobility within CEFTA range from filling skill gaps to attracting FDI, promoting cross-border bids for infrastructure projects in third countries, and encouraging investment in education. CEFTA member states could begin liberalizing with intra-company transfers, student migration that includes part-time work and the opportunity to seek employment after graduation, and freedom of movement for those with university degrees.

Note

[1] The countries of the Western Balkans, unlike Moldova, have been offered EU membership once they fully meet the criteria for joining the EU.

CHAPTER 6

Introduction

Labor mobility clauses are commonly included in free trade agreements (FTA). The purpose of this report is to review the labor mobility agreements in selected FTAs and their applicability to members of the Central European Free Trade Agreement (CEFTA). The report is organized in five main sections:

- The first section provides some background information on CEFTA, including a brief history, population, and labor force profiles of the various member countries, economic growth, and status of labor markets in the region, and prevailing patterns of migration and remittances.
- The second section outlines the labor mobility provisions of other free trade agreements and draws lessons for CEFTA.
- The third section lays out some of the potential benefits and costs of enhanced labor mobility, with particular reference to the CEFTA countries.
- The fourth section turns to the existing barriers to labor mobility among the CEFTA member countries, including visa regulations, work permit requirements, social barriers, and the role of EU member states as a destination for migrants.
- The fifth section draws some broad conclusions.

CHAPTER 7

CEFTA: The Setting

The new CEFTA Agreement (also called CEFTA 2006) was signed by all CEFTA parties in late 2007 and entered into force in the second half of 2008.

CEFTA is thus a very young association, and its membership may again change, as Croatia and FYR Macedonia are candidates for accession to the EU and all of the remaining Western Balkan states[1] are considered potential candidates.[2] The fact that all CEFTA members aim to join the EU is an important background fact in considering potential labor mobility among current CEFTA members, since freedom of movement is a core component of the four freedoms on which the EU is built, freedom to move goods, capital, services, and labor among EU member states.

The eight members of CEFTA differ substantially in size and level of economic development. After laying out basic facts on the population and the labor force of each member state, we review economic and employment growth since 1990. There are limited migration data, but those available are reviewed and assessed in the closing section.

Population and Labor Force

The CEFTA member states have relatively small populations and geographic areas, making foreign direct investment (FDI), trade, and migration key drivers of the increased competition, larger markets, and economies of scale that can sustain economic growth in member states (table 7.1). The combined population of the CEFTA member states is about 28 million, and most members have stable or declining populations, except for Kosovo, which continues to have a high rate of natural increase (of 1.4 percent a year).

Table 7.1. CEFTA Population Indicators: 2008, 2025

	2008			2025	Population Change 2008-2025 (%)
	Population (millions)	Natural Increase (%)	Total Fertility Rate (%)	Population (millions)	
Albania	3.2	0.7	1.6	3.5	9
Bosnia and Herzegovina	3.8	0	1.2	3.7	−3
Croatia	4.4	−0.3	1.4	4.3	−2
Kosovo	2.2	1.4	2.5	2.7	19
FYR Macedonia	2	0.2	1.5	2	0
Montenegro	0.6	0.3	1.6	0.6	0
Serbia	7.4	−0.4	1.4	6.7	−10
Sum/Average	27.7	0.2	1.6	27.3	−1

Source: Population Reference Bureau (www.prb.org).
Note: Data for 2025 are projections.

The population of the CEFTA member states is expected to shrink slightly by 2025, with the sharpest population decline expected in Serbia. Despite a projected 10 percent drop in population, Serbia is still expected to include a quarter of CEFTA residents. The most significant population increase is anticipated for Kosovo, which is projected to have four times more residents than Montenegro in 2025. All CEFTA member states except Albania were affected directly by the break-up of larger entities. As a result there was migration both as people moved over borders and as borders moved over people (with the dissolution of former Yugoslavia). In the latter case, people became "migrants" without moving (Martin and Zuercher, 2008).

ILO's most recent labor force projections cover all CEFTA members except Kosovo, but do not show Montenegro and Serbia separately (table 7.2). The economically active population of the CEFTA member states (without Kosovo) is projected to shrink by over 10 percent between 2010 and 2020, and the labor force aged 25–29, the age group that includes the most mobile professional workers, is projected to shrink by a similar 10 percent. The labor force in Croatia is projected to shrink faster than the labor force in Serbia and Montenegro.

Table 7.2. CEFTA: Economically Active Population, 2005–2020 (thousands)

	2005	2010	2015	2020	2010–2020 change
Albania	1,405	1,486	1,556	1,597	110
Age 25–29	166	186	220	211	25
Bosnia–Herzegovina	1,930	1,969	1,959	1,922	–47
Age 25–29	249	225	231	201	–24
Croatia	2,022	1,992	1,924	1,846	–146
Age 25–29	268	265	236	216	–49
FYR Macedonia	863	905	918	909	4
Age 25–29	117	122	117	112	–10
Serbia	4,760	4,840	4,830	4,786	–55
Age 25–29	591	604	583	528	–75
Subtotal	12,484	12,585	12,564	12,447	–137
Age 25–29	1,501	1,514	1,499	1,352	–162

Source: ILO Labor Statistics, Economically Active Population Projections.
Note: No data available for Kosovo; Serbia includes Montenegro.

Among the 1.3 million CEFTA nationals in Southeast Europe SEE)[3] in the 25–29 age group (removing an assumed 200,000 in this age group in Kosovo and Moldova), how many would qualify for freedom of movement if the requirement was to have at least a first university degree?

The ILO database includes limited information on educational levels of economically active people, and some of the data may be suspect, such as no university educated workers in Bosnia and Herzegovina. If we assume that 15 percent of those in the more advanced CEFTA nations of Croatia and Serbia have at least a first university degree, and 10 percent of those in Albania, Bosnia and Herzegovina, and FYR Macedonia have at least a first university degree, the number of first-degree persons who would enjoy free-movement rights in the most mobile age group is relatively small (table 7.3). For example, even assuming that the share of university-educated persons age 25–29 is 30 percent means that only 80,000 Croatians in this age group would qualify for freedom of movement in 2010.[4]

Table 7.3. CEFTA Labor Force by Education, 2001-07

	Year	Labor Force (millions)	University degree or more	% share with university degree
Albania	2001	1.4	107,339	8
Bosnia and Herzegovina	2007	1.2	100	0
Croatia	2007	1.8	324,000	18
Montenegro	2005	0.3	30,433	12

Source: ILO Labor Statistics, Total and Economically Active Population, Table 1B.
Notes: Year is year of most recent census. University degree or higher corresponds to ISCED levels 5–7. No data are available for Kosovo, FYR Macedonia, and Serbia.

Economic Growth and Employment

GDP per capita in CEFTA member states fell sharply in the early 1990s in the transition from centrally planned to market systems. Thereafter, economic recovery has been sustained, although accelerated growth came to FYR Macedonia only after 2000 and Albania's economy shrank after the collapse of pyramid investment schemes in 1997. By 2000 most of the current CEFTA countries had re-achieved or surpassed their real 1990 income levels.

Most of the SEE countries have similar GDP per capita levels, with Croatia being outlier together with Kosovo though in the latter case PPP data are not available (see figure 7.1). The sectoral pattern of production shifted quite dramatically in some of the CEFTA countries, as the services sector expanded with rising income levels and a transition from a socialist model, while both agriculture and industry shrank as a share of GDP. These transformations have been most dramatic in Albania, although the

Figure 7.1: GDP Per Capita 2007 (PPP International Dollars)

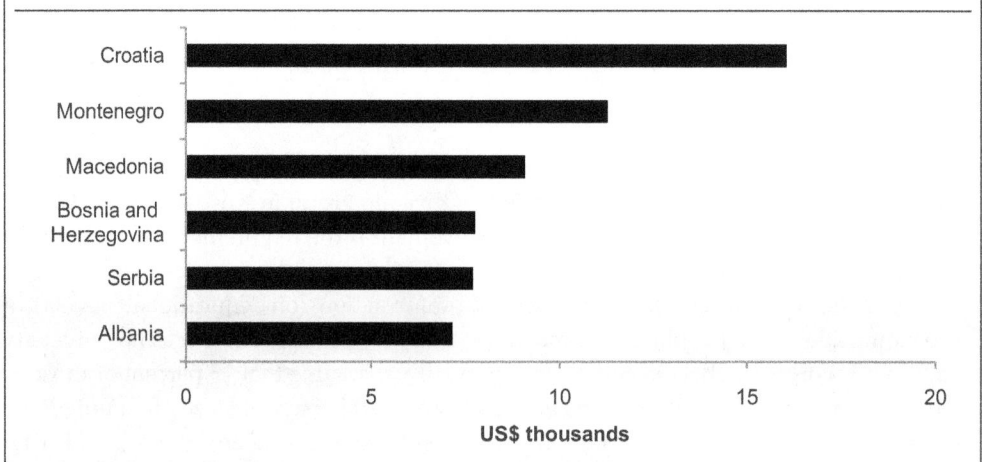

Source: World Bank data.

declining shares of agriculture in Bosnia and Herzegovina and of industry in FYR Macedonia are also apparent.

Despite rising GDP, employment has not recovered in some of the CEFTA members, especially FYR Macedonia and Kosovo, where employment stood at about two thirds the 1990 levels as late as 2007–08 (figure 7.2). In Albania, employment stabilized after 2000. No data are available on Bosnia and Herzegovina, and the data on Serbia and Montenegro are very incomplete, but the substantial loss of jobs from 1995 through 2003 is apparent. By 2008 Croatia had regained the 1990 aggregate employment level, and the dip in the interim was generally less dramatic than in some of the other member states.

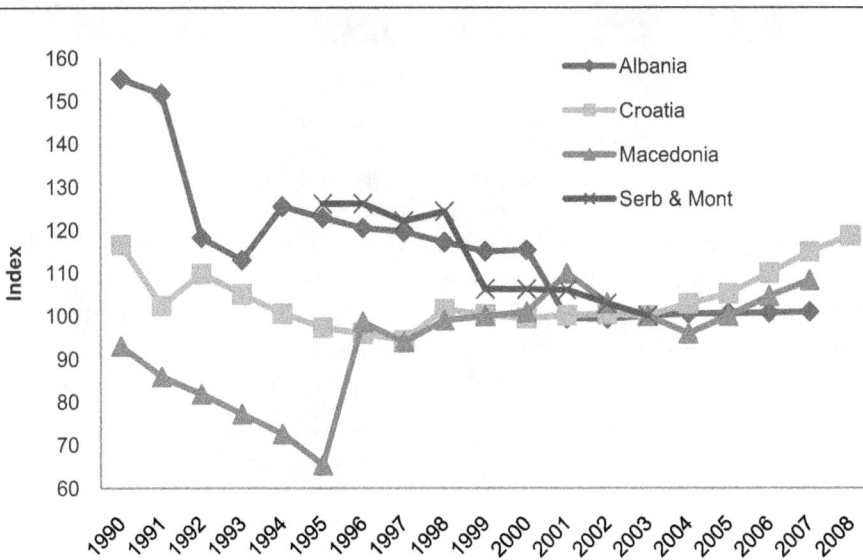

Figure 7.2. Indices of Total Employment (2003=100)

Sources: International Financial Statistics.
Except Serbia & Montenegro from ILO at http://laborsta.ilo.org/.

The restructuring after 1990 was accompanied by unemployment (figure 7.3),[5] but the persistence of the very high rates of unemployment points to inflexibility in the labor markets of CEFTA member states. Micevska (2004) examined the labor market institutions of Southeastern European countries, concluding that their unemployment insurance schemes were less generous than those of EU member states, but their employment protection legislation (EPL) was comparatively strict, especially in the former Yugoslav states, with some relaxation of EPL after 2000. Micevska concluded that EPL was not a major contributor to overall unemployment but its strictness, especially with respect to temporary employment and collective dismissals, contributed to higher unemployment among women and young people and encouraging an underground economy that generates lower official labor force participation rates.

Figure 7.3. Unemployment Rates 2006

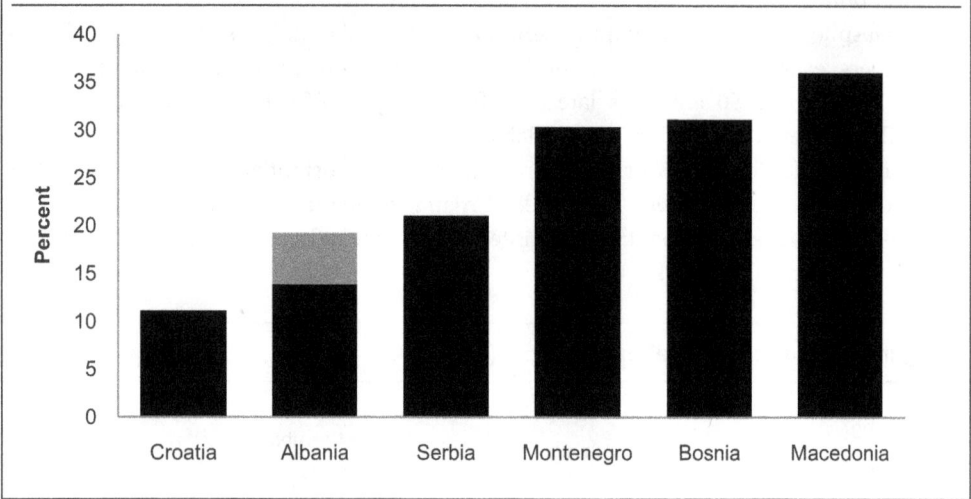

Source: Eurostat Pocketbook on Candidate and Potential Candidate Countries, 2008 edition.
Except Albania = Authors' calculations from ILO at http://laborsta.ilo.org/

The unemployment rates of females are generally higher than among males in CEFTA member states, except in Serbia (figure 7.4).[6] As in most countries, unemployment rates for youth are higher than overall rates, but the absolute levels of these rates in CEFTA member states, nearly 60 percent in FYR Macedonia and Bosnia and Herzegovina and 50 percent in Serbia, are a major concern.

Figure 7.4. Unemployment Rates among Males, Females, and Youths

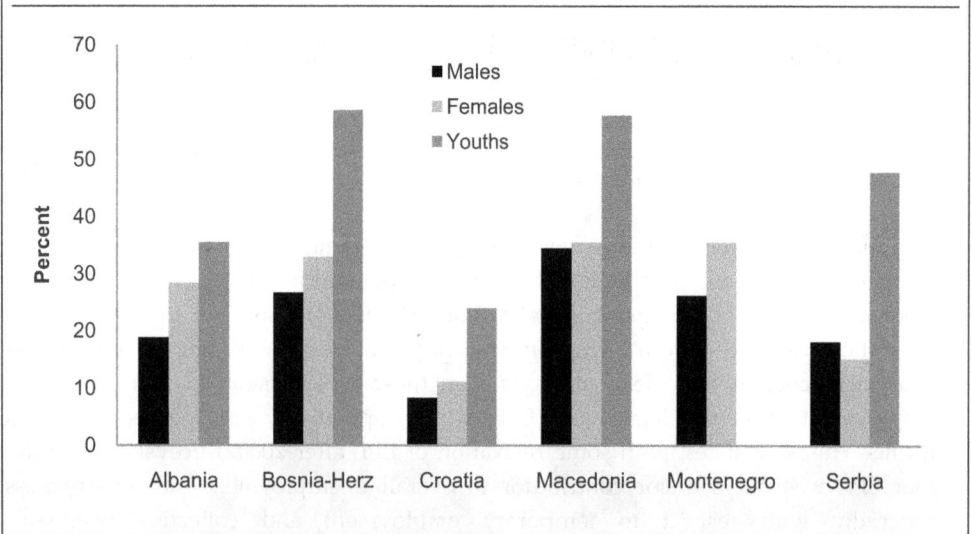

Source: Authors' calculations.

Migration Patterns

Migration patterns especially in the ex-Yugoslav CEFTA member states were influenced by the dissolution of the former Soviet Union and Yugoslavia, subsequent conflicts, and their economic aftermath. To place these changes in longer run perspective, Figure 7.5 shows the UN estimates of net migration rates (in-migration minus out-migration per thousand population) over half a century, from 1950–55 through 2000–2005, for each CEFTA member.[7] Although each of the states exhibits a shift in migration patterns after 1990, the nature of these changes differs significantly.

Figure 7.5. Net Migration Rates 1950–2005

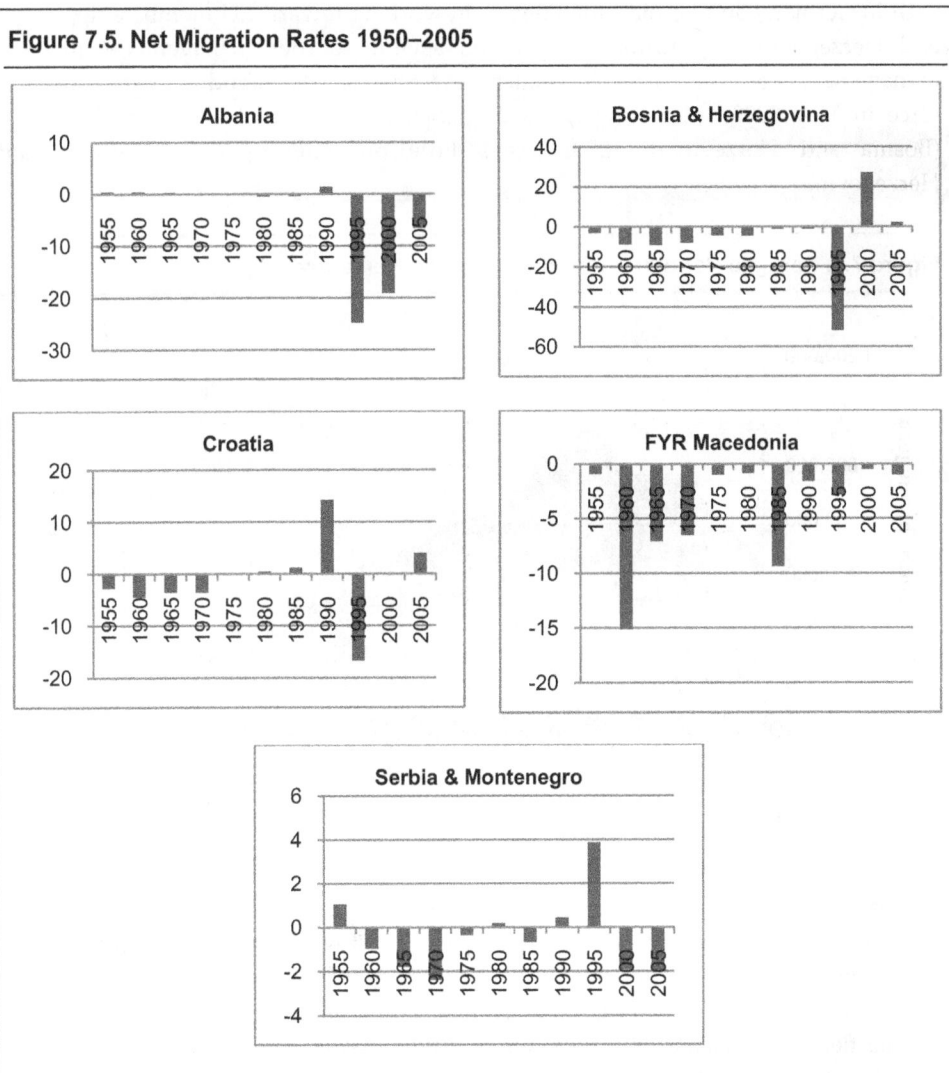

Source: UN Population Division.

Bosnia and Herzegovina

Bosnia and Herzegovina experienced significant net out-migration during the late 1950s and 1960s, after which there was less until after 1990. By 1992, armed conflict resulted in a massive exodus from Bosnia and Herzegovina, a net departure of 50 persons per 1,000 residents between 1990 and 1995, according to the UN estimates. At the peak of the exodus in 1996, the UNHCR recognized almost a million refugees from Bosnia and Herzegovina, including 25 percent in Serbia-Montenegro and 16 percent in Croatia (figure 7.6). Substantial return migration in the second half of the 1990s resulted in high levels of net in-migration, reflected in Figure 6. By 2007, the UNHCR reported that there were 60,000 refugees from Bosnia and Herzegovina, with about half each in Germany and Serbia-Montenegro. In working toward EU membership, Bosnia and Herzegovina has focused largely on asylum, border management, and visa management; the Law on the Movement and Stay of Aliens and Asylum came into force in May 2008. Interestingly, the *Migration and Asylum Action Plan: 2008–2011*, (Bosnia and Herzegovina, 2008), says little on emigration from Bosnia and Herzegovina.

Figure 7.6. Refugee Population from Bosnia and Herzegovina

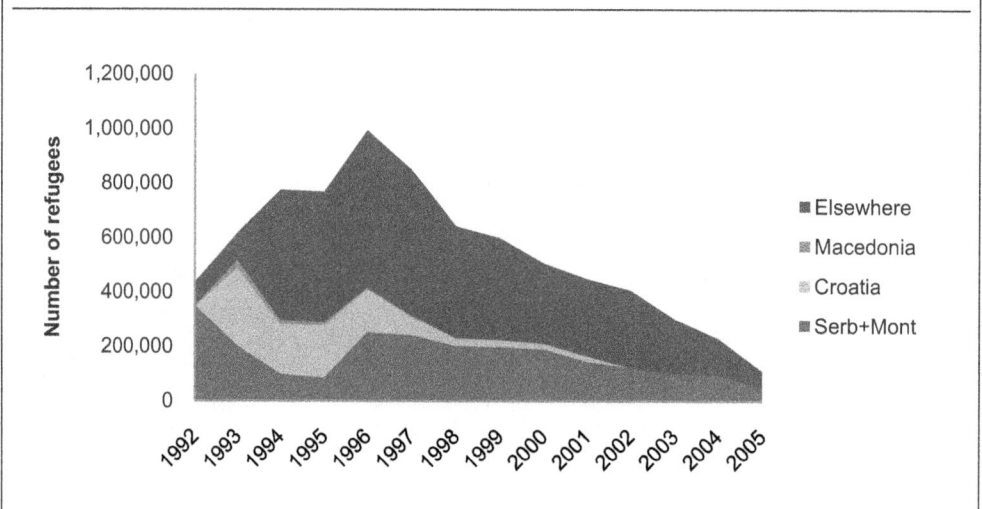

Source: UNHCR Statistical Yearbook.

Croatia

Many Croatians migrated to Western Europe as guest workers in the 1950s and 1960s, and labor migration was replaced by a lower level of family unification in the late 1970s and 1980s. After 1985 Croatia became a net immigration area, especially as people fled from Bosnia and Herzegovina into Croatia. After 1995, many Serbs in Croatia left, and 350,000 were recognized as refugees by UNHCR; most moved to Serbia and Montenegro. Since then, there has been little net movement either in or out of Croatia, although some reports suggest a substantial return of ethnic Serbs to Croatia.

Croatia has low fertility and the highest per capita income in the CEFTA area, prompting the prediction that: "In view of demographic decline and aging population, more sustained immigration flows will increasingly be required to meet the needs of the Croatian labor market."[8] The Croatian government introduced a quota system for the recruitment of foreign workers to meet specific perceived shortages. As of December 2006, the *Migration Policy Strategy of the Republic of Croatia, 2007* reported almost 10,000 foreign workers in Croatia, 85 percent male, and mostly less skilled.[9]

Serbia and Montenegro.

Migration from Serbia and Montenegro also fluctuated considerably over time, though the UN estimates suggest low rates of net migration. Between 1955 and 1975, there was slight net out-migration, followed by 15 years of little net movement until the early 1990s, when Serbia and Montenegro became net immigration areas. The UN estimated this net inflow at less than four per thousand per year, which seems low in light of the refugee inflows reported by UNHCR. Since 1995, the UN reports modest net emigration, while the International Organization for Migration (IOM, 2008a, 12) reported that "Serbia (and Montenegro) is among the countries in the region that has evolved from a net emigration country to a net immigration one. Moderately increasing immigration flows also call for renewed immigration policies and enhanced cooperation with third countries of origin."

Serbia seeks to maintain active contact with its diaspora, as reflected in the establishment of a Ministry of Diaspora and the Diaspora Action Plan 2005.[10] Serbia is bringing its migration policies into conformity with those of the EU via the Law on Identification of Documents, the Law on Travel Documents, and the Law on Conditions for Employment of Foreign Nationals.

Kosovo

There was a mass exodus of Kosovars in 1998–99 amidst conflict between ethnic Serbs and Albanians, and significant return migration since the conflict ended. However, there are almost no data on migration flows, and the dominant migration policy issue is the reintegration of returning Kosovars.

FYR Macedonia.

FYR Macedonia has had net emigration for the past half century. Net departures were particularly high between 1955 and 1970 and again in the early 1980s but, unlike most other CEFTA countries, FYR Macedonia has not had especially high rates of net emigration since 1990 despite the uprising and events of 2001, according to UN estimates. The Government of FYR Macedonia (2009) apparently disagrees with the UN data noting that immigration remains low and that emigration has been high in recent years (reportedly 20 percent of those born in FYR Macedonia are abroad).

Given high unemployment rates, high emigration rates are to be expected. The government of FYR Macedonia is concerned about depopulation and the brain drain, and is making efforts to reach out to the diaspora with a Coordinative Emigration Body. In 2009, the government announced that "Temporary stay and permanent residence of foreigners in the Republic of Macedonia is regulated with legislation and transparent procedures that have been entirely harmonized with those of the European Union."[11]

Albania

Albania was almost closed to emigration or immigration until 1990, and has since then experienced one of the world's highest rates of net out-migration. There were two major waves of emigrants: in 1990-91 and again in 1997. Since then, the net emigration has decreased.

Much of the emigration from Albania is temporary, as Albanians leave (often in irregular status) for Greece and Italy to fill jobs in agriculture, construction, and domestic services: "Albania has been particularly targeted on different occasions by the European Union as one of the top priority third countries for the fight against irregular migration. The management of migration flows has therefore become an integral part of the Stabilization and Association Process" (Albania, 2004, 3). The Albanian government deals with emigration management by increasing "the protection of the rights of Albanian emigrants abroad, building up and linking Albanian communities abroad, driving remittances of emigrants into business investments, organizing an adequate policy for labor migration, facilitating the travel of Albanian citizens confronted with short term visa requirements and finally, the development of the adequate legal and institutional framework" (Albania, 2004, 4).

The Diaspora

By 2000, the CEFTA diaspora, (people born in the CEFTA countries living in another country), were about 19 percent of those still in CEFTA countries. The size of the diaspora varied from nearly a third of those born in Bosnia and Herzegovina, a quarter of Albanians, and 13 percent of those born in Croatia and FYR Macedonia[12] (table 2.4).

Nearly half of Albanians abroad are in Greece and another fifth in Italy. More than a third of the diaspora of Bosnia and Herzegovina is in other CEFTA states, and another quarter is in Germany and Austria. Similarly 40 percent of Croatia's diaspora is in Germany and a significant share is in North America, and a similar pattern holds for the diaspora of Serbia and Montenegro. Emigrants from FYR Macedonia are in Australia, Switzerland, Turkey, North America, and Italy.

An important feature of the diaspora data in table 7.4 is that, apart from Bosnia and Herzegovina, the other CEFTA countries have less than 10 percent of their overseas populations in other CEFTA countries. Moldova, in particular, has been essentially isolated from migration to the SEE states.

Migrants' Education Levels

The educational profile of CEFTA nationals in the OECD countries was roughly comparable in 2000 (table 7.5). About half had less than a secondary education, while close to a fifth had some form of tertiary level education. The data for Moldova no doubt look quite different in large part because, as we have seen, most of the diaspora is not in the OECD countries but in the Commonwealth of Independent States (CIS).

Table 7.4. Diaspora of the CEFTA Countries in 2000

	Albania	Bosnia and Herzegovina	Croatia	Serbia and Montenegro	FYR Macedonia
Percent of Home Population	26.2	32.4	13.4	16.0	12.7
Percent of diaspora in:	4.75	37.03	6.87	8.97	4.92
CEFTA	0.39	2.77	0.94	3.43	1.24
Other Eastern Europe	11.27	17.06	40.05	25.30	6.29
Germany	49.27	0.03	0.06	0.30	0.36
Greece	0.26	10.63	6.41	8.54	5.41
Austria	0.42	3.78	4.15	9.58	16.16
Switzerland	20.43	1.10	3.28	2.81	10.01
Italy	0.40	0.19	0.04	6.69	12.17
Turkey	0.07	4.26	0.94	4.47	1.15
Sweden	0.35	1.90	5.03	0.52	3.81
France	0.05	0.04	0.02	3.16	0.01
Netherlands	0.38	0.58	1.23	1.93	0.55
United Kingdom	0.10	2.94	2.74	2.84	2.37
Other Western Europe	0.81	0.87	0.84	0.84	0.85
CIS	1.43	1.46	1.41	2.79	3.94
MENA	5.63	9.98	13.44	10.84	10.19
North America	0.22	1.96	8.96	3.49	17.11
Australasia	3.76	3.43	3.59	3.51	3.47
Other	100.00	100.00	100.00	100.00	100.00
TOTAL					

Source: Winters, Alan L., Terrie L. Walmsley, Ronald Skeldon, and Christopher R. Parsons, *Global Migrant Origin Database*, Updated March 2007, at http://www.migrationdrc.org/research/typesofmigration/global_migrant_origin_database.html.

Table 7.5. Expatriate Adults in the OECD Countries by Education: 2000

Education Level	Albania	Bosnia and Herzegovina	Croatia	Serbia and Montenegro	FYR Macedonia
	Education Levels of Expatriate Adults in OECD (%)				
Primary	46.2	44.4	54.2	44.9	52.2
Secondary	35.3	38.6	25.3	34.3	28.1
Tertiary	18.4	17.0	20.5	20.7	19.6
Total	100.0	100.0	100.0	100.0	100.0
	Percent of Working Age Population in OECD				
Primary	9.3	14.4	14.6	7.9	18.2
Secondary	7.2	15.2	8.9	10.3	12.8
Tertiary	9.0	23.9	24.1	13.6	29.1
	Tertiary Educated Adults in OECD by Region (%)				
Europe	53.6	51.2	39.6	60.4	57.4
North America	44.8	39.5	48.4	28.3	19.3
Asia and Oceania	1.7	9.3	12.0	11.2	23.3
Total	100.0	100.0	100.0	100.0	100.0

Source: Docquier, Frédéric and Abdeslam Marfouk. 2006. "International Migration by Educational Attainment," in Schiff, Maurice and Çaglar Özden (eds.), *International Migration, Remittances, and the Brain Drain*, Washington DC: World Bank.

One brain-drain indicator is the fraction of college-educated adults abroad. There are no overall measures but much of the migration from the CEFTA countries is to the OECD member countries. The middle panel of table 7.5 shows the selection rate of expatriates in the OECD from each education level, relative to the working age population, at home and abroad, with that level of education. Tertiary educated migrants from Bosnia and Herzegovina, Croatia, and FYR Macedonia in OECD countries are over a fifth of the total population with a college-level education. The rates at which the college-educated leave Serbia, Montenegro, and Albania were lower in 2000.

Anecdotes suggest that large numbers of college-educated nationals leave. For example, half of the lecturers and research staff of Albanian universities reportedly left the country between 1991 and 2001, prompting a new policy to allow Albanian universities to hire foreigners to replace them.[13] Apparently few Albanian students return from study abroad, prompting a 2005 Brain Gain initiative to tap the expertise of the diaspora to stimulate Albanian development.[14] It appears that many highly qualified Albanians work in quite low-skill occupations abroad.

The Government of FYR Macedonia (2009, 31) asserted that "the scale of the brain-drain problem has reached alarming proportions" and that "The solution ought to be found in a well conceived policy in the medium and long term, which in essence should be aimed at … creating conditions conducive to a decrease in the volume of highly educated emigrants and gradual return of part of the Macedonian population living abroad."

The European OECD member countries are the major destination for highly skilled CEFTA migrants, as may be seen from the lower panel of Table 6. However, the brain drain to North America has been very significant (as well as to Australasia from FYR Macedonia).

Migrant Stocks in the CEFTA Countries

Prior to 1990, none of the CEFTA countries had a significant stock of migrants, defined by the UN as foreign born persons present in the country for at least one year (figure 7.7). Since 1990, immigration has increased, especially in Croatia, where the migrant stock is estimated to have reached nearly 15 percent of the population in 2005. For the other CEFTA countries the proportion of migrants is much lower, especially in Albania and Bosnia and Herzegovina.

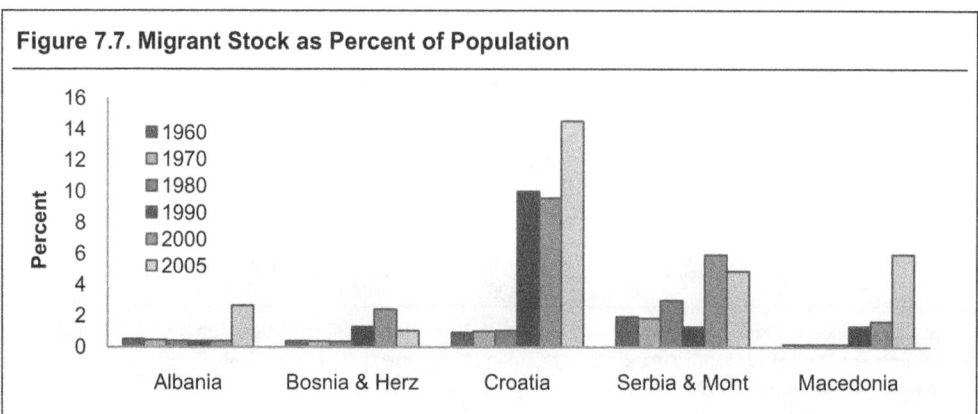

Figure 7.7. Migrant Stock as Percent of Population

Source: UN Population Division.

Most migrants in Bosnia and Herzegovina, Croatia, and FYR Macedonia are from the other ex-Yugoslavia states, as might be expected. However, a third of migrants in Serbia-Montenegro are from the EU, and there are significant groups from the Middle East (Turkey and the Maghreb), Asia (notably South Asia) and the Americas (including a significant U.S. presence). Albania's migrants in 2000 were mostly from CIS states (Winters et al., 2007).

Table 7.6 examines movements from one CEFTA country to another in greater detail. As Winters et al emphasize, their migrant stock estimates are based on the country of birth and are approximate. There are discrepancies between the Winters et al. database and other data, in part reflecting the prevalence of dual citizenship status and ethnic identity. For example, the larger Serbian diaspora estimate made by MARRI probably reflects ethnic identity, but the 45,000 Serbs reported by MARRI in FYR Macedonia are about the same as were reported in the Macedonian Census for 2002.

Table 7.6. Migrant Stock in CEFTA Countries: 2000 (Percent)

	Albania	Bosnia and Herzegovina	Croatia	Serbia and Montenegro	FYR Macedonia
CEFTA	19.1	98.7	92.3	5.5	84.6
CIS	43.6	0.3	0.6	3.6	0.2
EU	26.8	0.4	6.2	34.9	0.6
Other Europe	6.2	0.0	0.2	8.7	13.4
MENA	0.8	0.1	0.0	15.6	0.6
Asia	1.7	0.2	0.1	12.1	0.3
Americas	1.3	0.2	0.3	10.1	0.2
Other	0.5	0.1	0.2	9.4	0.1
TOTAL	100.0	100.0	100.0	100.0	100.0
Number	12,188	95,998	600,115	625,996	32,995

Source: Winters, Alan L., Terrie L. Walmsley, Ronald Skeldon and Christopher R. Parsons, *Global Migrant Origin Database*, Updated March 2007, at http://www.migrationdrc.org/research/typesofmigration/global_migrant_origin_database.html.

Table 7.7 shows that the largest intra-CEFTA movements have been from Bosnia and Herzegovina to Croatia (including refugees recognized by the UNHCR) and from Serbia-Montenegro to Bosnia and Herzegovina and to Croatia. FYR Macedonia appears not to have played host to large numbers of CEFTA migrants there are few CEFTA nationals in Albania, although there are estimated to be large numbers of Albanian nationals in FYR Macedonia.

Thus migration among the CEFTA states has been dominated by the consequences of the break up Yugoslavia, with mass movements in and out of Bosnia and Herzegovina, Serbia and Montenegro, and Croatia. To the extent that networks are important in shaping migration, we could expect these patterns to persist.

Table 7.7. CEFTA Diaspora in CEFTA Countries: (2000–05)

Country of Origin	Country of Residence				
	Albania	Bosnia and Herzegovina	Croatia	Serbia and Montenegro	FYR Macedonia
Albania		218	129	13,451	25,001 (91,891)
Bosnia and Herzegovina	1,645		456,580	10,201	387
Croatia	56	33,637		7,858	127
Serbia and Montenegro	453 (128) [10-20,000]	60,840 [1.000,000]	86,830 (95,699) [200,000]		2,411 [45,000]
FYR Macedonia	55 (5991)	71 (2278)	10,329 (4270)	2,224 (25,847)	

Sources: Main entries: Winters, Alan L., Terrie L. Walmsley, Ronald Skeldon, and Christopher R. Parsons, *Global Migrant Origin Database*, Updated March 2007, at http://www.migrationdrc.org/research/typesofmigration/global_migrant_origin_database.html.
Entries in ( ): Country migration profiles for Albania, Croatia, Serbia, and FYR Macedonia.
Entries in [ ]: Country migration profile for Serbia, derived from MARRI survey.

Irregular Migration

Irregular migration is common in CEFTA states. These new states had to develop migration mechanisms, including passports, visas, and border controls. While some CEFTA member countries have made significant strides to control entries over borders and the activities of foreigners inside them, border and interior control systems vary in effectiveness. For example, Bosnia and Herzegovina is still struggling to establish effective border controls and, since it allows visa-free entry of Serbians, Montenegrins and Macedonians, there is significant transit migration via Bosnia and Herzegovina to the EU.

Many Albanians pass through other SEE states *en route* to the EU, though certainly some stay within the region. IOM (2008b) reports that Albania is improving its border management, particularly since 2005, and Albania signed a border police cooperation agreement with FYR Macedonia, Montenegro, and Kosovo in 2007. FYR Macedonia (2009) reports Albanians were 80 percent of persons detected attempting to enter the country without appropriate documents between 2002 and 2008, but "As a result of the strengthened measures by the border police and the regular cooperation with the neighboring countries' border authorities in 2007 and 2008, the number of illegal crossings recorded was three times lower in comparison with 2006."[15]

The relative prosperity and EU-candidate status of Croatia make it attractive for irregular migrants: "According to the Croatian Ministry of Interior (MOI) statistics, irregular migration is on rise since 2004. The vast majority (over 90%) of apprehended migrants in irregular status originate from South-eastern Europe, with main source countries being Kosovo, Albania and Bosnia and Herzegovina."[16]

Remittances

Rising remittances are extremely important to several CEFTA economies. Table 7.8 and figure 7.8 show gross reported remittance receipts per capita since 1992.[17] FYR Macedonia reported the lowest remittance receipts per capita, US$131 in 2007, versus US$665 in Bosnia and Herzegovina, however, this is partly a recording issue (remittances are considered to be much higher than that). The other CEFTA countries received US$400 to US$470 in remittances per capita.

Table 7.8. Remittances' Share of GDP: 2006 (percent)

Albania	14.9
Bosnia and Herzegovina	17.6
Croatia	2.9
Serbia and Montenegro	13.6
FYR Macedonia	4.3

Source: World Bank and IMF Data

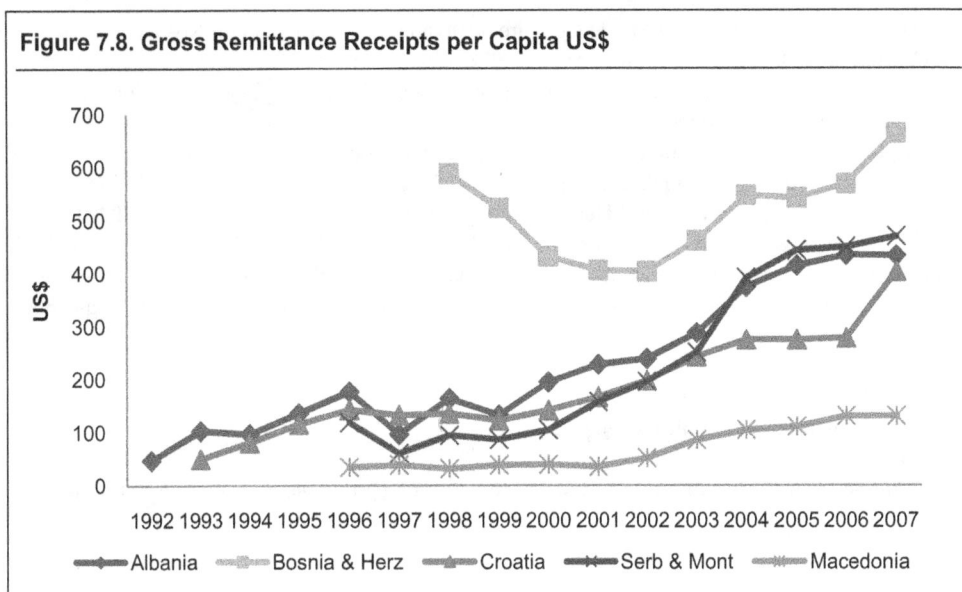

Figure 7.8. Gross Remittance Receipts per Capita US$

Source: World Bank and IMF data.

The World Bank reports remittance-to-GDP ratios of 174 countries. With the exceptions of Croatia and Macedonia, the remaining CEFTA countries are among the top 20 recipients on this list.[18] Remittances are critical both to the families that receive them and to the macro-economic performance of the CEFTA countries. It must be remembered, however, that in thinking about intra-regional migration, remittance inflows to one country also imply remittance outflows from the host.

Notes

[1] The terms "Western Balkans" and "Southeast Europe" are used interchangeably throughout the text.

[2] All CEFTA member states except Moldova are official candidates for EU accession or have signed Stabilization and Association Agreements (SAAs). Kosovo is part of the Stabilization and Association Process but has not signed an SAA or a trade agreement with the EU.

[3] The terms Southeast Europe and Western Balkans are used interchangeably and include all CEFTA parties except Moldova.

[4] There are projected to be 265,000 economically active Croatians 25–29 in 2010; 30 percent of this number is 79,500.

[5] With the exception of Albania, the unemployment measures shown in figure 7.4 for 2006 are drawn from Labor Force Surveys. For Albania, the implied rate of unemployment based on the number of registered unemployed is the lower figure shown. Albania's upper unemployment estimate is based on the difference between the official rate and the rate according to the Population Census in 2001. The rate shown for Montenegro is for 2005.

[6] Data are for 2007 except for Albania (2001), Montenegro (2005) and the youth unemployment rate for Serbia (2006). All measures are calculated from ILO data drawn from http://laborsta.ilo.org/ except the youth unemployment rate for Serbia which is reported in Eurostat Pocketbook on Candidate and Potential Candidate Countries, 2008 edition. "Youth" here refers to persons ages 15–24.

[7] Separate data for Serbia and Montenegro are not available, nor are data for Kosovo.

[8] International Organization for Migration (2007), p.24.

[9] About 15 percent of the 10,000 had a university degree, half had a high-school diploma and over a quarter apparently had less than high-school.

[10] http://www.mzd.sr.gov.yu/_eng/docs/action_plan_mfd.doc.

[11] Government of Macedonia (2009) p.29.

[12] Figures released by Bosnia and Herzegovina's Ministry of Foreign Affairs, in April 2007, show 1,343,805 citizens currently living abroad. More broadly defined concepts of a Diaspora typically depict far larger numbers. For instance, the national statistics for Croatia indicate that there are at least 3.5 million Croats living outside of Croatia, which is around 80 percent of the home population.

[13] Centre for Economic and Social Studies (2006).

[14] http://www.braingain.gov.al.

[15] Government of Macedonia (2009), p.22.

[16] IOM (2008a), p.20.

[17] Remittances include workers' remittances, compensation of employees and migrant transfers.

[18] The Macedonian national statistics indicate a much larger role for remittances at more than ten percent of GDP.

CHAPTER 8

Labor Mobility Provisions
in Free Trade Agreements

This section summarizes the labor mobility provisions of major Free Trade Agreements (FTAs). The purpose of FTAs is to allow the free flow of goods between member nations by reducing tariff and nontariff barriers to trade. Many FTAs also include provisions to foster cross-border investment, and some include provisions that facilitate the cross-border movement of at least some types of workers, including investors, business visitors, and workers.

The EU, which CEFTA members want to join, has some of the most comprehensive freedom of movement provisions, allowing and sometimes encouraging EU nationals to move from one EU member state to another. Individuals who believe that their freedom of movement rights were abridged can appeal to institutions for remedies, including the European Court of Justice (ECJ), whose decisions have generally struck down national attempts to limit the right of workers to move freely from one EU member state to another.[1]

Mobility provisions in the other FTAs reviewed below provide more limited freedom of movement rights and often lack institutions to which aggrieved individuals can appeal. In some cases there appears to be a trade-off between migrant numbers and migrant rights, meaning that states accepting more (especially low-skilled) migrants tend to accord them fewer rights to social services and settlement (Martin, 2008; Ruhs and Martin, 2008).

Asia-Pacific Economic Cooperation (APEC)

The Asia-Pacific Economic Cooperation (www.apec.org) is a 21-member forum established in 1989 to promote economic growth among member nations.[2] APEC bills itself as the only international intergovernmental forum that aims to reduce barriers to trade and investment by consensus, that is, without requiring its members to enter into legally binding obligations. APEC's three pillars are trade and investment liberalization, business facilitation, and economic and technical cooperation.

A major accomplishment of the business facilitation pillar is the APEC Business Travel Card (ABTC) program, which has facilitated the cross-border movement of business visitors since 1997 and included 17 participating countries in 2009 (www.businessmobility.org). Nationals of participating APEC member states apply to their home governments for ABTC cards, which transmit information on approved business visitors to other APEC member countries to obtain their approval before the

ABTC is issued.[3] ABTC-holders receive expedited admission via special lanes at participating-country airports, and can generally stay in another member country for 60 to 90 days. ABTC cards do not allow employment for wages abroad.

The APEC members participating in the ABTC have varying visa and immigration requirements. Having an ABTC, for example, does not exempt an Indonesian from the need to obtain a visa to enter Canada or the United States, but ABTC holders do get expedited visa-application interviews.[4]

ASEAN Free Trade Area (AFTA)

The ASEAN FTA, established in 1992, aims to create a free-trade area encompassing over 550 million people in 10 Southeast Asian nations. Almost half of these people are in Indonesia (www.aseansec.org).[5] The goal is to eliminate all tariffs between the original six member states by 2010, and tariff barriers for states joining later by 2015.[6] ASEAN has signed free-trade agreements with Australia and New Zealand, China, Japan, the Republic of Korea, and India.

The original ASEAN Vision 2020, endorsed by heads of government in 1997, did not mention migration, although it did emphasize a "free flow of goods, services and investment and capital."[7] However, in 1998, the Ha Noi Plan of Action revised Vision 2020 to call for a "freer flow of skilled labor and professionals in the region" and ASEAN Lanes at ports of entry to facilitate the intra-regional travel of ASEAN nationals. In 2006, ASEAN leaders agreed to allow nationals of ASEAN member nations to enter other ASEAN states without visas for up to 14 days.[8]

There is significant intra-ASEAN migration, including from Myanmar, Lao PDR and Cambodia into Thailand, from Indonesia and Vietnam into Malaysia, and from Malaysia, the Philippines and other ASEAN nations into Singapore; Brunei Darussalam also attracts migrant workers. Manning and Bhatnagar (2004) examined patterns of labor migration within ASEAN and recommended that liberalizing freedom of movement begin with the occupations that already have the highest share of most migrants, including seafarers, business executives, construction workers and domestic helpers. They argued that ASEAN could aim to achieve freedom of movement for professional, business and skilled workers by 2020 (2004, p. v).

ASEAN leaders signed the ASEAN Declaration on the Protection and Promotion of the Rights of Migrant Workers on January 13, 2007. It commits receiving states to draw up charters that ensure decent working conditions, protection from all forms of abuse, and a minimum wage to protect ASEAN nationals employed in other ASEAN countries. The Declaration calls for tougher penalties on smugglers and traffickers, but is not legally binding and does not require governments to change their labor laws; advocates hope that it will be followed by a legally binding convention.[9]

Caribbean Community (CARICOM)

The Caribbean Community (www.caricom.org) is an organization of 15 Caribbean nations and dependencies created by the 1973 Treaty of Chaguaramas that aims to promote economic integration, including freedom of movement, between member states.[10] The population of CARICOM was about 6.5 million in 2000. Three countries included almost three-fourths of CARICOM's residents, with 40 percent in Jamaica,[11] 20 percent in Trinidad & Tobago and 12 percent in Guyana.

There are two components to freedom of movement: (1) facilitation of travel with common travel documents and national treatment at ports of entry (Article 46 of the CSME) and (2) the free movement of skills (Articles 32, 34d, 36, and 37 of the CSME). CARICOM members began issuing a common passport in 2005.

The free movement of skills initiative originated in the 1989 Grand Anse Declaration. Article 45 of the revised Treaty of Chaguaramas says: "Member States commit themselves to the goal of the free movement of their nationals within the Community." CARICOM began the freedom-of-movement process with five types of workers: graduates of approved universities,[12] media workers, musicians, artists, and sports persons certified by national professional bodies.

Freedom of movement rights for these occupations within CARICOM went into effect in January 1996; extending free mobility to three more occupations--teachers, nurses, domestic helpers—has been discussed since 2007 (Girvan, 2007, 39). During the 30th meeting of CARICOM leaders in July 2009, domestic helpers were added to the list of occupations that enjoy freedom of movement rights, effective January 1, 2010. However, Antigua, Barbuda, and Belize were allowed to study the socio-economic impacts of free mobility for domestic helpers for up to five years before adding them to the freedom of movement list.

Those wishing to move between CARICOM member states first obtain a Certificate of Recognition of CARICOM Skills Qualification, usually from their home country Ministry of Labor, and present it to immigration authorities upon arrival to receive six-month work-and-residence permits while the certificate is reviewed. After the credentials are verified, the CARICOM national is to receive an indefinite work-and-residence permit. CARICOM recognized the importance of skills certification and social security transferability for wage earners, and created a register of the self-employed, although progress in achieving full transferability has been slower than expected. CARICOM governments made commitments to establish mechanisms for certifying and establishing the equivalency of degrees and credentials earned in member states and to harmonize and make transferable the social security benefits earned in various CARICOM members.

The CARICOM Single Market and Economy (CSME) treaty went into effect January 1, 2006, with Barbados, Belize, Jamaica, Guyana, Suriname and Trinidad and Tobago as the first full members; they were joined by Antigua and Barbuda, Dominica, Grenada, St. Kitts and Nevis, St. Lucia, and St. Vincent and the Grenadines July 3, 2006. The Single Market component includes freedom of movement of goods, services, capital, business enterprise,[13] and skilled labor within a customs union.

Barbados, with about 300,000 residents and a per capita gross national income (GNI) of US$16,000 (at PPP), is much richer than Guyana, which has about 750,000 residents and a per capita GNI of US$2,900. About 120,000 Guyanese arrived in Barbados in 2008, and some overstayed and worked illegally. Barbados in June 2009 began a six-month legalization program for CARICOM nationals who arrived before December 31, 2005, have been in Barbados at least eight years, and who undergo a criminal background check.[14]

East Africa Community (EAC)

The East Africa Community (www.eac.int) is a Customs Union that includes Burundi, Kenya, Rwanda, Tanzania, and Uganda. The implementation of this Union in Burundi and Rwanda was officially launched July 6, 2009, though the initial Treaty for its establishment was signed by Kenya, Tanzania, and Uganda a decade earlier. Negotiations are continuing for a protocol on establishing a Common Market.[15] This protocol includes annexes "to remove restrictions on the free movement of workers ... (*and*) ... on harmonization and mutual recognition of academic and professional qualifications...."

Assurances have been issued that this freedom-of-movement protocol will be in place by 2010, but the EAC has missed other deadlines. Fallon (2008) distinguishes five major barriers to labor mobility, including restrictions among the original three Treaty signatories of Kenya, Tanzania and Uganda.

1. Distinct systems of work permits are maintained in each country, restricting the access of workers from other member countries and their ability to change jobs after entry. Specifically, to obtain a permit, migrant workers must first obtain a job offer, prove their qualifications, and show that their presence will contribute to economic growth. The wording of these requirements is sufficiently vague that it is relatively simple to justify rejection of a permit and rejection rates are high. Delays in processing the permits are reported to be long and the costs of preparing the paper work are quite substantial. Moreover some of the member countries require that a national understudy be employed alongside the migrant to learn and eventually take over the job.
2. The portability of social security entitlements, pensions, and health benefits is very limited. However, Fallon does point out that this is less of an issue for workers posted by home state employers to work elsewhere within the EAC.
3. Although significant progress has been made toward harmonizing standards for university degrees and honoring mutual recognition of university qualifications, there is less harmonization and mutual recognition of vocational and technical training.
4. Not surprisingly, obtaining information about job opportunities in the other member states limits mobility, though a few multinational firms do transfer employees between branches in the various member countries.
5. The cost of remitting funds is also cited as a barrier to mobility, though comparatively little is known about intra-African international remittances.

Four of the five EAC countries (not Tanzania) are also members of the Common Market for Eastern and Southern Africa (COMESA), comprising 19 countries with a combined population of over 400 million stretching from Libya to Swaziland and Mauritius. COMESA has a separate protocol with respect to labor mobility, though it remains un-ratified.

The 50+ African states have thus negotiated several agreements aimed at facilitating freedom of movement, including the EAC and COMESA as well as the Economic Community of Western African States (ECOWAS) and the Southern African

Development Community (SADC). However, the migration experience under these agreements reinforces the conclusion that "regional agreements among developing countries have made little progress in easing constraints on migration, compared with the major agreements among industrial countries (notably the European Union and the treaty between Australia and New Zealand)" (Ratha and Shaw, 2007, p. 16).

It is not clear how important formal freedom-of-movement agreements are in the African context. Given the arbitrary drawing of borders by the former colonial powers in Africa, migration patterns transcending those borders have been long established. Moreover, most African states do not have the resources or capacity to monitor border crossings except at major points such as international airports. Irregular migration is widespread and the norm within the region (Lucas, 2006), so that implementing freedom of movement may serve largely to formalize the migration that is already occurring.

Mercado Comun del Sur (Mercosur)

The Treaty of Asuncin, signed March 26, 1991, created the Mercado Comun del Sur between Argentina, Brazil, Paraguay and Uruguay (www.mercosur.int). The key to Mercosur's success is cooperation between traditional competitors Argentina and Brazil, much as the EU's success hinges on cooperation between historic rivals France and Germany. República Bolivariana de Venezuela applied in 2006, and is on the verge of full membership in 2009 after national parliaments in the four member states ratify its full membership status. Bolivia, Chile, Colombia, Ecuador, and Peru have associate member status in Mercosur.

The major goal of Mercosur is economic integration between member countries, including freedom of movement. The Andean Community of Nations (Comunidad Andina or CAN) is a smaller trade bloc that includes Bolivia, Colombia, Ecuador, and Peru; República Bolivariana de Venezuela resigned from CAN to join Mercosur. While a member of CAN, the Andean Instrument on Labor Migration, signed in October 1973, is credited with encouraging República Bolivariana de Venezuela to legalize 250,000 unauthorized foreigners, mostly from Colombia, in 1981 (IOM, 2003, p. 180).

Mercosur aims for eventual freedom of movement. In theory, Mercosur nationals may currently move among member states, although the right to work is regulated by host governments. Progress in liberalizing labor mobility has been slow. A Mercosur social security agreement was signed in 1997, but many of the steps aimed at facilitating migration within Mercosur take far longer to be implemented than planned.

Much of the migration that occurs in the Mercosur region is outside formal channels. In the 1990s, IOM estimated there were 1.3 million migrants in the region, including 62 percent who moved from Bolivia, Chile, Paraguay, and Uruguay to Argentina and another 16 percent in Brazil (IOM, 2003, p188). Some migrants left Argentina during the economic crisis of 2001.

In December 2002, Mercosur leaders signed an Agreement on Residency for Mercosur Nationals aimed at providing them "equal civil, social, cultural and economic rights and freedoms" to citizens of the Mercosur country in which they are living, "particularly the right to work and to carry out any legal activity." The related Agreement on Regulating the Migration of Mercosur Citizens encouraged Mercosur governments to legalize unauthorized nationals of Argentina, Brazil, Paraguay, and Uruguay as well as nationals of associate Mercosur members (Cerruti, 17–20).

North American Free Trade Agreement (NAFTA)

The North American Free Trade Agreement (NAFTA), which went into effect January 1, 1994, aims to free up trade and investment between Canada, Mexico, and the United States. A Canada-U.S. FTA went into effect January 1, 1989, and Mexican President Salinas requested an FTA with the United States in 1990, which eventually led to NAFTA (Villarreal and Cid, 2008).

NAFTA has 22 chapters, and Chapter 16, Temporary Entry for Business Purposes, covers four types of business travelers: business visitors, traders and investors, intra-company transferees, and specified professionals.[16]

The United States is the major destination for NAFTA-related migrants (Martin, 2005). Under U.S. immigration law, the first three groups of NAFTA migrants, business visitors, traders and investors, intra-company transferees, enter with visas that existed before NAFTA went into effect, for example, business visitors use B-1 visas to enter the United States, treaty traders and investors use E-1 and E-2 visas, and intra-company transferees use L-1 visas. NAFTA created a new TN visa for the fourth group (TD visas for their dependents), allowing U.S. employers to offer jobs that require college degrees to Canadians and Mexicans who have college degrees.

These written job offers, plus proof of the requisite education and $50, suffice for Canadians and Mexicans to have indefinitely renewable employment and residence visas issued at U.S. ports of entry.[17] There are no limits on the number of TN visas that can be issued, U.S. employers do not have to try to recruit U.S. workers before hiring Canadians or Mexicans, and there is no requirement that TN-visa holders receive prevailing wages while working in the United States.

The number of Canadian professionals entering the United States with NAFTA-TN visas almost quadrupled between 1995 and 2000, but fell after the IT-bubble burst in 2000 to less than 60,000 in 2003 and 2005. Canadian admissions have since risen to almost 70,000 a year, but are still well below the almost 90,000 of 2000. The number of Mexican entries rose even faster, but from a very low base, doubling between 2006 and 2008 to almost 20,000.

The NAFTA experience shows that a liberal free-mobility provision can be included in an FTA with safeguards, viz, limiting entries to those with at least college degrees in specified fields and for 10 years, requiring US employers to show that U.S. workers were not available before extending job offers to Mexicans, where wages were significantly lower. Mexican admissions, and the Mexican share of total admissions, have risen significantly in recent years.

European Union (EU)

Two main bodies of legislation affect migration among the members of the European Union: the provisions for the free movement of workers within the EU and the Schengen Agreement on borderless travel within Schengen member countries. Freedom of movement is included in Article 39 of the EU treaty and implemented via

Regulation 1612/68 on freedom of movement for workers and Directive 2004/38/EC on the right to reside.

Freedom of movement was one of the founding principles of the then European Communities in 1957: freedom to move goods, capital, and services were the other three fundamental freedoms. "Free movement of workers entitles EU citizens to look for a job in another country, to work there without needing a work permit, to live there for that purpose, to stay there even after the employment has finished and to enjoy equal treatment with nationals in access to employment, working conditions and all other social and tax advantages that may help integrate in the host country.... Certain rights are extended to family members of the worker. They have, in particular, the right to live with the worker in the host Member State and the right to equal treatment as regards for example education and social advantages. Some members of the family have also the right to work there."[18] EU nationals employed at least five years continuously in another state automatically acquire the right to permanent residence in the host state.

There are several important limitations on freedom of movement in the EU. First, EU member states may restrict, to their own nationals, those jobs in the public sector that involve the exercise of national sovereignty, though privatization and court decisions have whittled away the share of jobs not open to foreigners. Second, existing EU member states may choose to restrict freedom of movement for the nationals of new entrants. For example, Italians had to wait 10 years before they got freedom of movement rights (until 1967), and Greeks, Portuguese and Spaniards had to wait seven years, but there were no restrictions on freedom of movement for Britons, Austrians, Swedes and other late EU entrants.

For the ten Eastern European countries that joined in 2004 and 2007, there were special transition rules to freedom of movement. The original EU-15 member states were allowed to restrict the freedom of movement rights of Eastern European nationals for up to seven years, although they had to justify to the European Commission their reasons for restricting mobility, initially, after two years, and after three years. Only Britain, Ireland, and Sweden allowed immediate freedom of movement of so-called EU-8 nationals in 2004, and far more Poles and other Eastern Europeans moved to Britain and Ireland than projected. One result was that none of the EU-15 member states allowed Bulgarians and Romanians freedom of movement when these countries joined the EU in 2007. Yet several observers in the UK have indicated that the UK gained economically from this influx, that it had relatively little impact on employment or wages of prior UK residents while contributing positively to both output and to the UK's fiscal balance.[19]

Under the EU's freedom to provide services, employers based in one EU state may win a contract in another and send employees over borders to "service the contract," which often means constructing or refurbishing a building or working in a factory or service business. The European Commission in 2008 estimated a million workers were "posted" from one EU member state to another.[20] To avoid "social dumping," EU governments can require that these posted workers are paid at least the local minimum wage, if there is one. Since Austria enacted a national minimum wage effective January 2009, 21 of the EU's 27 members have national minimum wages. Most of the others, including Germany, extend negotiated minimum wages to an entire sector.

In several cases, the European Court of Justice has interpreted freedom to provide services in ways that encourage more migration within the EU, which is the aim of the European Commission. Wages vary within the EU, and especially in construction there is widespread use of subcontractors from lower-wage countries in higher-wage countries.

Germany has no national minimum wage, but the 1949 Collective Bargaining Act allows the federal government to "extend" the wages negotiated between unions and employers that cover at least 50 percent of workers in a sector to all employers and workers in a sector. After workers from Ireland, Portugal and other lower-wage EU member states flooded into Germany during the reunification boom of the mid-1990s, the 1996 Employee Posting Act (Arbeitnehmer-Entsendegesetz) was enacted to allow the German government to require employers of EU nationals "posted" to Germany to pay at least the minimum wage that was negotiated in the German construction sector. Germany's state of Lower Saxony, and most other German government entities, required employers bidding on public projects to pay all workers employed on the project at least this negotiated wage. However, a contractor building a prison in Goettingen used a Polish subcontractor and 53 "posted" Polish workers who were paid less than half of the local union wage. In April 2008, the ECJ ruled that EU member state governments could require posted workers to receive minimum wages, but only if they were universal, not just for public projects.[21]

There is perception within the European Commission that there is too little intra-EU labor migration. The Commission made 25 recommendations in February 2002 to increase intra-EU labor migration, and Social Affairs Commissioner Anna Diamantopoulou highlighted four priorities to increase labor market flexibility and mobility: find the correct link between the education system and labor markets; overcome the problem of mutual recognition of qualifications and work experience; transfer pension rights and health rights more easily; and speed up the implementation of the common policy on immigration. The European Commission (2007, 2) cites a number of reasons for the lack of greater realized mobility:

> Aside from an uncertainty over the advantages of being mobile, individuals face a number of hurdles to their movement. These can range from legal and administrative obstacles, housing costs and availability, employment of spouses and partners, portability of pensions, linguistic barriers, and issues on the acceptance of qualifications in other Member States.

In 2000, about 225,000 EU residents, less than 0.1 percent of the total EU population, changed their official residence by moving between two EU countries. By contrast, about 2.5 percent of U.S. residents move between states each year.[22]

The second major agreement affecting mobility within the EU is the Schengen Agreement, originally signed by five members of the then 10-member European Community in Luxembourg in 1985. Under this agreement, border controls between Schengen member states were eliminated as each Schengen state maintains and agrees to strengthen border controls with non-member states.

The scope of the initial Schengen Agreement was considerably widened with the signing of the Amsterdam Treaty, which came into force in 1999, and subsequent EU enlargement; new EU member states are required to join Schengen, which involves agreeing to common visa-issuance rules for Schengen visas and joining the Schengen Information System that provides a common lookout database and EURODAC, which, inter alia, fingerprints asylum applicants so they can apply in only one EU member state.

In 2009, the Schengen Area encompassed 25 European countries, including all EU members except Ireland and the UK, which opted out, and Romania, Cyprus, and Bulgaria, which hope to join. Iceland, Norway, and Switzerland are not EU members but part of the Schengen Area. Thus, the Schengen Area is not conterminous with the EU, though there is considerable overlap between Schengen and EU countries. Moreover, while the EU is effectively a Customs Union (maintaining common external trade policies), the member states of the Schengen Area retain separate control over entry from non-member states.

Lessons from Labor Mobility Provisions of FTAs

There are at least 20 major multilateral FTAs, and an even longer list of bilateral FTAs.[23] The major purpose of FTAs is to free up trade in goods and flows of investment, but many also include provisions aimed at expediting the movement of business investors, service providers, and sometimes workers employed for wages in an FTA partner country. Most FTAs include contiguous or neighboring countries, and some aim to be more than simply free-trade areas, as with the EU. FTAs are normally signed between neighboring countries because of political opportunity and because of geography— distance matters, and most trade and migration is between countries that are close to each other, in part because of improved information flows (Rauch, 1999).

If trade and migration are substitutes, FTAs may reduce labor mobility over time by narrowing wage and income gaps between member countries. However, it should be emphasized that most FTAs are between countries at a similar level of development, reducing incentives for migration. Trade agreements are almost always struck first, with the implementation of clauses promising to liberalize or coordinate labor movement often delayed so that there will be less migration (Martin, 1993).

Trade agreements are complex and difficult to negotiate, particularly if they involve common external trade barriers, and free labor movement agreements are even more difficult to achieve. Reasons for lack of progress toward freedom-of-movement under FTAs include:

1. Immigration, whether within a free trade area or otherwise, can have major distributional consequences, as some parties in the host country gain while others are hurt economically by new arrivals. Moving forward can require considerable political will and capacity.
2. Although the motives of individuals are diverse, the net effect of migration is movement from low to higher income countries. If FTAs encompass countries with different income levels, there is likely to be net migration to the higher- income member states.
3. It is easier to negotiate agreements to liberalize skilled labor migration because the numbers are relatively small, the economic and public finance gains to

receiving countries may be greater, and they may generate positive externalities where they live.

4. Countries include both nationals and foreigners, so that liberalizing freedom-of-movement between two countries requires consideration of so-called "third-country nationals." In most FTAs, only nationals of member states are covered.

5. A distinction is sometimes made between temporary workers and permanent immigrants. It is well known that temporary workers may settle and that permanent immigrants can and do return to their countries of origin. Most FTAs, as well as GATS Mode 4 negotiations, emphasize the movement of temporary workers over borders rather than immigrant settlers, helping them to avoid often controversial issues that range from access to the social safety net to voting rights.

The experiences of some of the FTAs reviewed here may offer particularly relevant insights in moving forward toward enhanced labor mobility in the case of CEFTA.

CARICOM offers some interesting comparisons with CEFTA, both being composed of states with very small populations. The 15 English-speaking CARICOM member states have an advantage in being united by a common language, which aided the establishment of pooled university facilities and enhanced the mobility of graduates. The benefits of a shared language extend to only some portions of CEFTA, though there is a substantial history of student training and mobility, at least across the sates of former Yugoslavia. The mobility of graduates in CARICOM has probably accelerated economic integration, though some tensions remain over guest-worker programs for less-skilled workers.

Both NAFTA and CARICOM encompass states at very different income levels. As a result, the pressures for labor mobility tend to be in one direction. Here CEFTA has an advantage in that income disparities are not so large (with the exceptions of Moldova at one end and Croatia at the other). Nonetheless, NAFTA has come to terms with this by restricting freedom of movement to those with at least a university degree in specified occupations who have a job offer from an employer in another member state. Moreover, NAFTA initially imposed extra restrictions on the lowest wage member, Mexico.

The APEC business card shows that having the home country government issue a freedom of movement document with the approval of other member governments can ensure that there are fewer difficulties at fast-track entry points. This may be particularly important for companies doing business in more than one CEFTA state. However, it should be noted that the APEC business card does not allow holders to earn wages abroad.

Perhaps the most important lesson that emerges, though, is the contrast between the case of the EU, which has made the most progress toward labor market integration, in contrast with some of the developing country FTAs that have made little real progress in this direction despite their rhetoric. A weak institutional framework underlying some of the latter regional agreements serves to restrict progress. In contrast, the experience of the supranational institutions in the EU context played an important role in general, and regarding labor freedom in particular. The CEFTA member states may be able to take advantage of the EU case by emulating this experience and specifically by aligning their migration systems with those of the EU.

Notes

[1] http://curia.europa.eu/jcms/jcms/Jo1_6308/.

[2] The 21 member nations are: Australia; Brunei Darussalam; Canada; Chile; China; Hong Kong, China; Indonesia; Japan; Republic of Korea; Malaysia; Mexico; New Zealand; Papua New Guinea; Peru; the Philippines; The Russian Federation; Singapore; Chinese Taipei; Thailand; US; and Viet Nam.

[3] This means that one country's refusal to approve an individual blocks him or her from receiving an ABTC.

[4] In March 2008, there were 34,000 active ABTC cards; 40 percent were held by Australians (www.apec.org/apec/business_resources/apec_business_travel0.html, accessed 6-2-09).

[5] ASEAN was created August 9, 1967, and the ASEAN Charter of December 15, 2008 calls for an ASEAN community by 2015 (ISEASa, 2009).

[6] Average tariffs were reported to be about two percent in 2008, down from 4.4 percent in 2000. Surin Pitsuwan, Secretary-General of ASEAN, Progress in ASEAN Economic Integration since the Adoption of the ASEAN Charter, June 29, 2009 (www.aseansec.org/93.htm).

[7] www.aseansec.org/16572.htm.

[8] www.aseansec.org/18570.htm.

[9] The Declaration extends protections to families formed by migrants after legal entry and employment.

[10] The treaty establishing the Caribbean Community and Common Market (signed at Chaguaramas, Trinidad and Tobago, July 4, 1973. CARICOM members are Antiuga & Barbuda, Barbados, Bermuda, Bahamas, Belize, Dominica, St. Lucia, St. Vincent & the Grenadines, Grenada, Trinidad & Tobago, Jamaica, and Guyana.

[11] Jamaica has a very high emigration rate—about 20,000 people a year, almost one percent of the 2.6 million residents, are accepted as immigrants each year; 80 percent by the US. Short-term, seasonal movements to the US are even more common (Lucas and Chappell 2009).

[12] The University of West Indies began as an external college of the University of London in 1948, and became fully independent in 1962. Today it has about 39,000 students on three campuses: Cave Hill, Barbados; Mona, Jamaica; and St. Augustine, Trinidad. There is also an open campus, and the University graduates about 5,800 students a year.

[13] CARICOM nationals have had since January 1, 2006 the right to establish a business in any member state and be treated as a national of that state; their families are allowed to join them.

[14] Heppilena Ferguson, "Barbados open to 'structured' readmission of overstays," *Stabroek News*, July 2, 2009.

[15] http://www.news.eac.int/index.php?option=com_content&view=article&id=85:progress-registered-in-negotiations-on-the-annexes-to-the-draft-eac-common-market-protocol-in-kigali&catid=48:eac-latest&Itemid=69.

[16] www.worldtradelaw.net/nafta/index.htm.

[17] http://travel.state.gov/visa/temp/types/types_1274.html.

[18] European Commission, Employment, Social Affairs and Equal Opportunities at http://ec.europa.eu/social/main.jsp?catId=458&langId=en.

[19] See, for example, Sriskandarajah *et al.* (2005), Coats (2008), Reed and Latorre (2009).

[20] EU: Blue Cards, Minimum Wages. 2008. *Migration News*. Volume 14 Number 2. April. http://migration.ucdavis.edu/mn/more.php?id=3347_0_4_0.

[21] EU: Blue Cards, Minimum Wages. 2008. *Migration News*. Volume 14 Number 2. April. http://migration.ucdavis.edu/mn/more.php?id=3347_0_4_0.

[22] EU: Mobility, Enlargement. 2002. *Migration News*. Volume 8 Number 4. March. http://migration.ucdavis.edu/mn/more.php?id=2578_0_4_0.

[23] A listing of operating and proposed multilateral FTAs is at: http://en.wikipedia.org/wiki/List_of_free_trade_agreements. A listing of bilateral FTAs is at: http://en.wikipedia.org/wiki/List_of_bilateral_free_trade_agreements.

CHAPTER 9

The Benefits (and Costs) of Labor Mobility Provisions

Overall Production and Productivity

There is considerable potential for improving overall labor productivity within the region by relocating workers from low to higher productivity settings. In the CEFTA context, this is particularly true since the combined population of the eight CEFTA member countries is less than 28 million. To exploit the advantages of any scale economies in production will require access to more labor than is available in any one of the member states.

Since 1990, production in each of the CEFTA states has come to be dominated by service activities. Scale economies are likely to be more important in the industrial sector than in most services. Indeed, the decline of industry in the region may partly reflect this inability to exploit scale economies, though many other factors have contributed also. In any case, if manufacturing is to be revived within the region, then access to sufficient appropriate labor will play a role.

Competitiveness in professional service provision does not typically require very large numbers of personnel concentrated in any one location. Nonetheless, a sufficient pool of personnel with overlapping professional skills is normally an essential ingredient. Given the limited number of highly educated adults remaining within the region, achieving such pooling again raises demands for the mobility of workers.

To attract more direct investment into the region will probably thus require the ability to hire workers from other countries within the region. Moreover, the ability to transfer workers and managerial staff among branches in other CEFTA member states may be important to attract some forms of business.

Enhancing labor mobility within the region can thus potentially increase productivity, enable exploitation of scale economies, and attract foreign investment. In turn, each of these will alter the region's competitiveness in international trade. But what ranges of skills are likely to prove most critical to these possibilities?

While some other free trade agreements have been extended to permit freer mobility of those with a university education or specific profession (such as CARICOM), other agreements have encompassed a much wider range of skills (such as the EU). For CEFTA, much will depend upon the proposed development strategy and the kind of activities that will become the focus of this.

The Serbian National Employment Action Plan for 2006–2008 foresees a focus on new technologies in agriculture and forestry, tourism and services, rather than industry. In this process a gap persists between the fields of emphasis in both university and vocational education on the one hand, versus perceived labor force needs on the other hand. The Serbian Plan goes on to mention the potential contribution of migrant workers to filling some of these gaps, though it seems the intent may be more one of encouraging the return of Serbs from abroad. Croatia's quota scheme is designed to meet their labor market needs in the face of a declining and ageing population. This scheme provides the largest numbers of work permits in the shipbuilding, construction, and tourism sectors; the construction and tourism sectors also employ significant numbers of irregular, seasonal migrant workers. Of the documented foreign workers in Croatia in 2006 only about 15 percent possessed a university degree. Together these indications for the two largest countries in the region suggest that current labor market demands are not for the highly educated but rather for skilled workers in such fields as construction and shipbuilding.

There is always a temptation for states to consider filling perceived skill gaps by importing migrant workers. This can indeed be a productive strategy in the short run. However, reliance on manpower planning techniques to forecast future shortages is generally very risky. If economies prove at all dynamic then the patterns of future demands will prove volatile, demanding fluid responses on behalf of skilled workers. Designing current migration quotas on the basis of immediate needs, and then proving incapable of reallocating these workers or encouraging their onward or return migration, can result in a cumulative problem.

The Distribution of Benefits and Costs

Although there may be efficiency gains from expanded migration, the net benefits will not be evenly divided, either between countries or across households.

Scale economies might evoke an image of each country specializing in particular activities, with migration sorting out the required allocation of workers. In reality the higher income countries within the free labor movement agreement will no doubt experience net immigration while lower income signatories will serve as migrant sources. The impacts on the two types of states are, to some extent, mirror images of each other.

For competing, indigenous workers in countries of immigration, wages and the chances employment are likely to diminish, and the opposite tends to be true in countries of origin. There are, however, potentially important off-setting effects. First, the agglomeration of activities in the migrant host countries can actually serve to enhance productivity of prior inhabitants to the extent that scale economies prove important. The potential attractions for direct foreign investment can then actually serve to expand job offerings, rather than displacing domestic workers. Second, not all migrant workers compete with domestic workers: some indeed complement domestic labor. For instance, access to foreign skilled workers can alleviate production bottlenecks, expanding opportunities for the domestic labor force; even availability of low skill service workers can free the time of local professionals, cheapening the cost of enjoying the services provided.

The effects of expanded migration on labor in countries of immigration are, thus, quite mixed. The effects on employers and migrants are, however, clearer. From the perspective of employers, immigration can offer a source of relatively cheap labor, possibly keep down the costs of domestic labor, and provide access to specific skills. Hence it is typically presumed that employers and the migrants themselves are the big winners in the expansion of migration.

From the perspective of the countries of emigration, particularly in the face of significant unemployment of low skill workers, the biggest concern is frequently that of intellectual emigration; the so-called brain-drain. The costs imposed by the emigration of highly skilled professionals hinges on at least two key elements. First is the manner in which their education has been financed. Second is the issue of how effectively professionals are deployed if they remain at home. If highly skilled workers remain unemployed at home, or under-employed in activities that do not utilize their training, or are employed in activities offering little social benefit, then their departure will impose minimal cost.

Vying with brain drain concerns has been a good deal of recent discussion of the potential for brain gain, which refers to the advantages of having a highly educated diaspora. At least four types of benefit have been discussed: the transfer of technologies from professional citizens abroad; a stimulus to trade through improved information about trading opportunities with the home country and easier contract enforcement with friends and relatives at home; return migration with freshly acquired skills; and the inducement for those remaining at home to extend their educational experience (Lucas, 2005).

On one hand, a number of programs exist in the CEFTA states to support study abroad, which frequently accelerates departure of the highly skilled, while nonetheless providing important opportunities for nationals. On the other hand, attempts have been made in most of the CEFTA states to encourage interaction with and return of skilled nationals through such efforts as the Temporary Return of Qualified Nationals program in Kosovo and the Brain Gain Program in Albania.[1] Just how successful such programs are, in promoting return, remains unclear. Moreover, the merits of such programs are often questionable on the grounds that the skills acquired abroad are of limited relevance in the lower technology setting of countries of origin.

There are, however, at least three studies in Southeast Europe that indicate a gain in productivity among workers who return from abroad. Each of these contributions adjusts for the fact that those emigrating are self-selected and, hence, possibly more enterprising than non-migrants. Co *et al.* (2000) find that Hungarian women who have worked abroad earn a premium for having done so, though men do not. De Coulon and Piracha (2005) compare migrants returned to Albania with those who never migrated. The migrants receive higher wages as a result of their experience. However, the non-migrants would have gained even more had they migrated. De Coulon and Piracha suggest that the non-migrants are generally more highly skilled in the first place: to emigrate would require greater adjustment costs for them, such as learning a foreign language to access skilled jobs, and this additional cost discourages their emigration. Iara (forthcoming) looks at earnings of returned, young, male migrants in thirteen countries of Central and Eastern Europe. Her results demonstrate a substantial gain in earnings among those who migrated to Western Europe. Iara also draws attention to the fact that these migrants to Western Europe are generally from better-off households in the first place, so the substantial rewards to migrating exacerbate income inequality at home.

Albania, Bosnia and Herzegovina, Serbia, and most likely FYR Macedonia are all highly dependent on remittances. But who benefits from these remittances and what are their consequences? The migrants from Albania have been drawn disproportionately from poor, rural areas and the ensuing remittances have consequently been quite critical in poverty alleviation. Remittances appear to have financed significant movement out of rural areas and into Tirana, and also to have spawned start-up small-scale enterprises, though the employment generated by these enterprises has been largely confined to family members (Konica and Filer, 2003). On the other hand, in Albania the infusion of remittances may have propped up the real exchange rate, thus limiting export expansion and hence employment creation (Lucas, 1985). In the context of Serbia, Jovicic and Mitrovic (2007) note that remittances have moved counter-cyclically with consumption, suggesting a poverty alleviating role. However, this study also notes that much of the supported consumption has resulted in additional imports of consumer goods, limiting any multiplier benefits.

The Transition to EU Requirements

As in most contexts, a good deal of irregular migration is occurring amongst the CEFTA states. Formalizing these movements should offer better protection to the migrants. It may also serve to reinforce national autonomy. Yet this may come at a cost. Granting better rights to migrants often comes at the expense of reduced numbers; formalizing existing irregular patterns may actually restrict the prevailing volume of migration and its associated benefits. Moreover, free labor mobility provisions will induce some degree of dependence upon this movement, both by workers and employers. Subsequent attempts to restrict these movements, such as imposing EU external visa requirements, may result in exacerbated, irregular migrations.

Perhaps most importantly, as accession to the EU is achieved among the various CEFTA members, the labor mobility provisions of the EU will come into force (though possibly with a lag). Implementing mobility within CEFTA will therefore take place against this background. Reviewing labor mobility provisions within CEFTA, presumably in conformity with EU requirements, should therefore prove beneficial in preparation for EU entry.

Note

[1] http://www.braingain.gov.al/.

CHAPTER 10

Implementing Mobility in CEFTA

Migration Management: Alignment with the EU

Each of the current CEFTA countries has aspirations to follow their predecessors in joining the EU, which means they must bring their immigration and asylum laws into conformity with the EU *acquis*. CEFTA countries in the Balkans are developing migration laws and policies with the help of EU-based facilitators. The Vienna-based ICMPD outlined the migration and asylum systems in the CEFTA countries, and summarized them in a publication concluding the two-year Aeneas project (Regional Guidelines, 2008).

The Aeneas project, which involved seminars that allowed migration-related agencies in the Balkans to learn about EU migration policies, aimed to set the stage for increased cooperation between migration agencies in the various countries.

Croatian law requires visas of its southern Balkan neighbors, as per the EU *acquis*, but has implemented these visa requirements only for Albanians. After EU entry, Croatia will have to implement EU-visa requirements, and they may exempt nationals of some non-EU Balkan states from obtaining visas for tourist visits. For example, The European Commission in July 2009 proposed that citizens of Macedonia and Serbia and Montenegro have visa-free access to EU member nations for tourist visits beginning January 1, 2010.

Table 10.1 sets out the matrix of visa requirements among the remaining SEE states. The requirements clearly vary both by host and by country of origin, though all countries except FYR Macedonia and Montenegro require visas of Albanians.

Table 10.1. Intra-SEE Visa Requirements

	Host Country					
Source Country	Albania	Bosnia and Herzegovina	Croatia	FYR Macedonia	Montenegro	Serbia
Albania		Yes	Yes	No (1)	No (1)	Yes
Bosnia and Herzegovina	Yes		No (1)	No (1)	No (1)	No
Croatia	No (1)	No (1)		No (1)	No (1)	No
FYR Macedonia	No (1)	No	No (1)		No (2)	No
Montenegro	No (1)	No	Yes (3)	No(2)		No
Serbia	Yes	No (4)	Yes (3)	No (2)	No	

Source: MARRI: Overview of the Visa Regimes Among and Between SEECP Countries, 2008.
Notes: 1. No visa required for entry up to 90 days; 2. No visa required for entry up to 60 days; 3. Temporary suspension of the visa regime until 31 December 2009. Holders of national passports, temporarily do not require visas to enter Croatia, for tourist visits up to 90 days; 4. Holders of UNMIK Passports need a visa.

The IOM reported (IOM, 2008b, 38) that Albania was developing a "centralized IT system to administer visas." In turn, Albania reached a Visa Facilitation Agreement with the EU in 2008. A border police cooperation agreement was signed with FYR Macedonia, Montenegro, and Kosovo in 2007, and on February 19, 2008, Albania and FYR Macedonia eliminated border-crossing fees for nationals of the two countries. Registered suitcase traders from one country may enter the other twice a month (Regional Guidelines, 2008, 70). At a much earlier stage, bilateral labor agreements on seasonal employment were signed with Germany (1991), Greece (1996), and Italy (1997), though again no such agreements seem to have been reached with any CEFTA countries.

In FYR Macedonia "A permanent stay permit is issued to a foreign national who has, prior to applying for a permanent stay permit and on the basis of a temporary stay permit, resided in the territory of the Republic of Macedonia for at least five years without interruption.... According to the situation reported on October 15, 2008, the total number of foreign nationals with granted temporary and permanent residence in the Republic of Macedonia amounts to 7,673 persons. Out of them, 7,148 are foreigners with temporary stay, while 355 are foreigners with granted permanent residence." (Government of FYR Macedonia, 2009, 8–9). The report goes on to explain that some 58 percent of those granted temporary residence in 2008 had arrived for marriage to a Macedonian citizen and another 15 percent were family members joining foreigners residing in FYR Macedonia to work. FYR Macedonia (2009, 9) distinguishes two types of temporary stay: "Foreign nationals with temporary stay are persons residing in the country from 3 to 12 months, while foreign nationals with extended temporary stay are persons residing in the country for longer than 12 months." During 2006 and 2007, of the 4,543 temporary stays granted to aliens, 58 percent were for extended temporary stays.

IOM (2008a) reports no bilateral labor agreements in place for Serbia, though ongoing negotiations are noted with Algeria, Belarus, Germany, Hungary, Libya, and Romania. Meanwhile, Serbia is revising its immigration and asylum laws to bring them into conformity with the EU *acquis*. Many of these laws were in preparation in 2008, including a law on the employment of foreigners (Aeneas, Serbia, 2008, 14); the goal is to have revised migration laws reflect the EU *acquis*.

Perhaps the most important institutional development has been the creation of the Migration, Asylum, Refugees, Regional Initiative (MARRI) in Skopje, Macedonia in 2003. The six major CEFTA members are also members of MARRI, whose responsibilities include promoting regional cooperation on migration issues, including labor migration.[1] MARRI, which promotes the development of orderly labor migration in the region, held a workshop on labor migration in Zagreb in February 2006.

MARRI staff have been providing advice to member-country governments on how to develop migration management systems. However, most of this advice is general rather than specific. For example, Medved (2007, 5) advises governments to "synthesize migration policy goals with the economic as well as demographic policy goals [and] balance between the interests of the State, business and individual migrants." Medved (2007, 6–7) goes on to advise governments to "work towards providing a single application procedure leading to one combined title, encompassing both residence and work permit within one administrative act and improve the recognition of qualification and professional skills prior and after admission in order to attract high skilled migrants."

Medved (2007, 42) summarized the status of MARRI-member integration with the EU as of December 2006. However, many MARRI-EU discussions center on issues such as returns and re-admission, not the benefits of increasing labor mobility within the region.

Specific labor agreements among the SEE states thus do not appear to have been established to date. Nonetheless bilateral agreements have been struck on a wide range of cross-border issues. Although there are, thus, signs of progress in terms of easing movement between some of the SEE states, extensive visa and residence permit requirements remain in place. On the other hand, it should be noted that many nationals of SEE countries are dual nationals, making visa requirements less of a barrier to mobility.

Croatia and Serbia made liberal provision for persons outside their borders to acquire nationality if they wish. Others, such as Bosnia and Herzegovina allow dual citizenship only on a bilateral basis, so that, under the Bosnia and Herzegovina 1997 citizenship law, refugees who acquire another citizenship from particular states automatically lose Bosnia and Herzegovina citizenship. Serbs in the Republic Srpska part of Bosnia and Herzegovina are eligible for Serbian citizenship, helping to explain why many young people from Republic Srpska study in Serbia.[2] Similarly, many of the Croats in the Federation part of Bosnia and Herzegovina are eligible for Croatian citizenship.

In addition, although attempts are underway to tighten enforcement of the commensurate border controls and, in particular, to bring these into line with EU standards, it is clear that the borders remain quite porous. Irregular migration is extensive, both en route to the EU and with the more prosperous SEE countries as targets in their own right.

Informal Economies and Work Permits

Several CEFTA members possess substantial shadow economies, offering unregulated employment to both domestic and undocumented alien workers in "grey" labor markets. In Serbia, for instance, "It is estimated that the informal economy comprises up to 30 per cent of GDP, which means that the actual number of working persons is much larger than the official number of employed persons ... [with] the highest number of illegally hired foreign workers in agricultural, construction and catering in bordering areas."[3] Schneider (2006) estimates the size of Serbia's shadow economy to be even larger, though this is not out of line with his estimates for the remaining CEFTA members[4] (table 10.2).

Table 10.2. Shadow Economy, 2002–03 (Percent of GDP)

Albania	35.3
Bosnia and Herzegovina	36.7
Croatia	35.4
FYR Macedonia	36.3
Serbia and Montenegro	39.1

Source: Schneider (2006).

Access to formal labor markets requires work permits for foreign workers. In Croatia, the 2003 Aliens Act exempted 23 categories or migrant workers from the work permit requirement, including permanent foreign residents, foreign spouses of Croatian nationals, key staff of companies, university professors, scientists and researchers, athletes and artists. Croatia in 2004 introduced a quota system allowing foreign workers to be employed in shipbuilding, construction, tourism, culture, science and education, transport and health care, but only half of the permits were requested in the first three years of operation: "Low utilization of quotas shows that improvements could be made in the quota system which should be more flexible and able to promptly respond to actual labor market needs." (IOM, 2007, 32). Instead of using the quota system to obtain work permits, employers in construction and tourism appear to employ substantial numbers of irregular foreign workers. In addition to the work permit scheme, Croatia's Alien Act also provides for business permits to facilitate foreign investment and business transactions.

In moving toward conformity with EU policy, FYR Macedonia also introduced a quota system in February 2008, issuing 3,500 work permits in the course of 2008. The Government of FYR Macedonia (2009, 10) notes, however, that "Most of the employed foreign nationals have secondary or higher education and fall into the category of administration staff." In view of the massive unemployment rates in FYR Macedonia this is not surprising. Unlike Croatia, FYR Macedonia still issues a Business Visa, though the number of such remains tiny (170 in 2008).

Montenegro's Strategy for Migration, (Government of Montenegro, 2008), envisages three categories of work permits: A Personal Work Permit would render a foreigner, holding such a permit, equal to a Montenegrin citizen in terms of labor and unemployment rights; an Employment Permit would permit local employers to hire foreign workers to fill a job that is permanent in character but only for a limited period; and a Work Permit which would encompass temporary jobs, including seasonal work.

The Aeneas Regional Guidelines advise that Serbia's national migration laws should distinguish between foreigners arriving to work for wages and those who are self employed, a distinction found in EU law (2008, 36). Moreover, the new Serbian legislation is to permit management personnel of foreign companies to enter without the need to obtain a work permit.

Credential Recognition, Social Security, Other Issues

Besides the barriers already outlined to mobility between the CEFTA states, some additional economic and non-economic barriers may be mentioned.

First, enhanced mutual recognition of credentials obtained in other CEFTA countries would undoubtedly ease the movement of skilled workers. This is true not only at a professional level and with respect to college qualifications, but also with respect to the various trades. Moving toward such recognition is not simple, in part because skilled groups naturally attempt to prevent entry of competitors. (The American Medical Association is a prime example). It is made more difficult by the potential to recognize qualifications in principle but not in practice, requiring some process of arbitration.

Second, the lack of portability of social benefits can serve to limit migration in both directions. First, the prospect of not being able to return home and enjoy the benefits accumulated while away may well discourage initial movement. Second, for those who do migrate, inability to transfer benefits to the home country will deter return migration. Portability of benefits raises some complex questions that have not been entirely resolved within the EU. The SEE countries already possess a number of bilateral agreements amongst themselves with respect to social insurance, but further negotiations on these may need to address the issue of portability of benefits more explicitly.

Third, as noted in the course of discussing EU labor mobility, people are naturally reluctant to relocate in unfamiliar circumstances, and differences in ethnicity, languages, and religions commonly contribute to this reluctance, even among the Balkan states. Comparisons of opinion surveys for 2006 and 2008 indicate that: "All countries in the Western Balkan region have seen a decrease in their residents' willingness to leave. This reduction is especially pronounced in the countries that recently proclaimed independence: Montenegro and Kosovo. Here, the percentage of people willing to leave has almost halved…. Results from the survey further suggest that migration from the Western Balkans is not likely to be of a permanent nature: of respondents that mentioned a desire to migrate, 60% stated that they intended to return after a couple of years at the most" (Gallup, 2009, 3).

Fourth, in all free trade areas enhancing labor mobility meets resistance from those who believe they will be hurt economically by legal admission. One might suspect that, at both a political and perhaps personal level, the history of conflict among some of the CEFTA member states make acceptance of migration even more difficult. Interestingly, however, Gallup (2009, 7) reports "Across the Western Balkans, people are convinced that the free circulation of people and goods will help the region to have a peaceful and prosperous future. Asked what is needed for peace and development, the free movement of people and free trade within the region came second only to putting an end to corruption. Unrestricted travel and free trade between countries were both said to be important by more than 8 in 10 respondents across the region. The desire for free movement of people between countries was particularly strong in Macedonia and Serbia, where more than 9 in 10 respondents thought there would be no peace and development without it."

Notes

[1] Marri (www.marri-rc.org) officially opened in September 2004 and was recognized as an inter-governmental organization a year later.

[2] Interview with Alenka Prvinsek, ICMPD, June 18, 2009.

[3] IOM (2008a) p.49.

[4] In revising GDP data in January 2009, Croatian Statistics estimated a much smaller role for their informal sector at an average rate of about 8.4 percent of GDP from 1995 to 2005.

CHAPTER 11

Conclusions

This report examined the potential gains from the increased mobility of skilled workers between the eight members of the Central European Free Trade Agreement (CEFTA). All CEFTA member countries have experience with the "3 Rs" of recruitment, remittances, and returns, and all have significant diasporas that can promote trade and investment and development in their countries of origin.

The purpose of this report is to review policies that could promote especially skilled worker migration between these neighboring SEE countries that aim to join the EU. The fact that six of the eight CEFTA countries were part of the Socialist Federal Republic of Yugoslavia and thus have similar education and credential systems should facilitate migration. On the other hand, lingering effects from 1990s armed conflicts, persisting high unemployment, and new migration systems that in some cases erect barriers to labor mobility, justify government intervention to promote labor mobility.

Moving toward freedom of movement within CEFTA could be expedited by:

- Beginning with skilled workers and agreeing on the mutual recognition of credentials earned in CEFTA member states throughout CEFTA, as in CARICOM, to recognize that small countries are unable to each support specialized universities and training institutions
- Promoting intra-company transfers by allowing firms with branches in several CEFTA countries to transfer workers between them with minimal formalities, the part of the GATS trade-in-services negotiations that has received the most liberalizing offers.[1]
- Allowing CEFTA employers to offer jobs that normally require a university degree to CEFTA nationals with at least one university degree without a labor market test, as in NAFTA, where such a job offer and proof of citizenship and university credentials allows issuance of an indefinitely renewable work and residence visa.
- Encouraging student migration, allowing foreign students to work while studying and graduates to seek employment with minimal bureaucracy, as in the EU
- Speeding up the adoption and incorporation of the migration provisions of the EU *acquis* into national law. Currently, CEFTA member states are focused on facilitating travel to the EU, which normally requires signing of re-admission agreements that oblige countries to accept the return of apprehended nationals[2]abroad instead of preparing for EU accession.

- Creating and expanding guest worker programs that allow the admission of seasonal CEFTA workers to fill seasonal jobs in other CEFTA member states, and expanding such programs to encompass a wider range of workers and jobs over time
- Recognizing the migration that is already occurring as dual nationals move,[3] and encouraging more bilateral labor migration agreements.[4]

Encouraging more labor migration within the CEFTA region may not be easy. Employment rates are generally low, especially for women and older workers, unemployment rates are high, especially for women and youth, and there is a significant informal economy that makes it difficult to accurately assess labor supply and demand. As CEFTA governments formalize their labor markets and raise employment and lower unemployment rates, labor market vacancies are likely to appear. Indeed, the studies in Kathuria (2008) find that many of the countries in the region face skill gaps in certain sectors, despite the high overall unemployment. Filling these gaps with nationals of neighboring CEFTA countries can promote both economic efficiency and economic integration.

EU accession will, in any case, eventually require development of such mechanisms. It may therefore behoove the CEFTA states to focus on bringing their migration and permit systems into line with the EU standards, implementing these among themselves initially, either on a multilateral or bilateral basis.

Notes

[1] Under GATS Mode 4, intra-company transfers are often limited to managers, workers with specialized skills, and sometimes trainees who have been employed by the multinational firm at least a year.

[2] For example, the EU-Serbia agreement was signed April 29, 2008 and ratified by the Serbian Parliament in September 2008.

[3] Up to 10 percent of Balkan residents may be dual nationals, as with Kosovars who are Serbs as well as Slovenes or Croats. Interview with Alenka Prvinsek, ICMPD, June 18, 2009.

[4] For example, Montenegro allowed the entry of up to 40,000 migrant workers from Serbia and Bosnia and Herzegovina in 2008 to fill jobs in agriculture and tourism. Interview with Alenka Prvinsek, ICMPD, June 18, 2009.

Part III

The Impact of Establishing a Virtual Customs Union between Southeast Europe and the European Union

Selen Sarisoy Guerin[*]

[*] The author would like to acknowledge excellent research assistance by Emre Tuncalp and Tilman Anger.

Abstract

In this study we analyze the costs and benefits of implementing EU's common external tariff in Southeast Europe (SEE). A detailed examination at 6-digit product level indicates that each country requires a different level of adjustment. Furthermore, we carried out a partial equilibrium analysis to estimate trade diversion and trade creation effect. The overall trade creation effect is positive for the region, as imports increase by 4.3 percent after reform. There is a negative impact on intra-regional exports; however, the loss in exports amounts to only 0.1 percent of GDP.

CHAPTER 12

Introduction

The aim of this report is to provide an in-depth analysis of the potential impact of adopting EU's common external tariff (CET) covering industrial goods hence forming a virtual customs union between the EU and the CEFTA region.[1] Several studies indicated that although exports of the region have grown steadily, they remain below potential (World Bank, 2008a, 2008b). The economic integration of the region significantly accelerated as all countries have been offered Stabilization and Association Agreements (SAA) with the EU. Currently all have duty and quotas free access to the EU, their largest trading partner due to the autonomous trade preferences granted in 2000.[2] The Council of the EU have granted Southeast Europe[3] asymmetric trade liberalization preceding the SAAs, in order to contribute to the process of economic and political stabilization in the region. In this sense, *"the granting of autonomous trade preferences is linked to respect for fundamental principles of democracy and human rights and to the readiness of the countries concerned to develop economic relations between themselves"* (EC no 2007/2000). As part of the regional dimension of the SAA, these countries have also signed a series of bilateral FTAs with each other and these bilateral agreements have been brought under one agreement, CEFTA that entered into force in 2007.

So far the impact of preferential access to the EU has not produced the desired effect of boosting the competitiveness of the region through increased exports to the EU nor its intra-regional trade that is much needed for the sustainable growth of Southeast Europe. In a recent report Handjiski (2009) concludes that growth in intra-regional trade in 2008 has been significant after the entry into force of CEFTA, however in comparison to EU-10 the intra-industry trade is still low and trade is largely dependent on commodities. In terms of extra-regional trade, deepening integration for the region revealed itself in the form of large current account deficits: all five countries within the region have started running wide current account deficits that are concern for macroeconomic stability.[4] The current account deficits in the region were all in excess of 10 percent, reaching at 40 percent of GDP in Montenegro, 18 percent in Serbia, and 15 percent in Bosnia and Herzegovina (2008). A closer examination of the balance of payment statistics reveals that several countries in the region have trade deficit in goods and services (and income) larger than their current account deficits. The large trade deficits are typically characterized by large imports of goods and low exports, whereas they tend have trade surplus in services. The poor performance of merchandise exports is especially disappointing as small open economies depend largely on trade to boost growth. In a recent World Bank report (2008), the sustainability of future growth in Southeast Europe (SEE) was raised as an issue of concern as much of the transition-driven growth has already been achieved. In the report, it is suggested that in order to reduce their still high poverty rates and to fulfill their EU aspirations the SEE countries need to increase their growth rate through increases in total factor productivity (TFP).

Classic international trade theory argues that trade liberalization help countries specialize in the production of those products where they have a comparative advantage, as a result of which the country benefits from static productivity gains. Several empirical studies test the relationship between trade openness and growth such as Sachs and Warner, 1995, Frankel and Romer 1999 and Dollar and Kraay 2004. Even though empirical results are inconclusive about the relationship between trade openness and growth, theoretical models have evolved to explain how trade can boost growth. According to endogenous growth models and new trade theories the interaction between trade openness and growth is no longer static and the gains from trade liberalization come from accumulation and/or transfer of technology or a concentration on innovation. Hence new trade theories foresee the gains from trade liberalization to be dynamic as countries accumulate more technology and carry out more innovation which is the key to long-term growth. Other channels through which trade openness might improve productivity growth are: (i) the disciplining effect of imports, and (ii) the increasing variety of available inputs. An inspection of the evolution of total factor productivity over time suggests that, during periods of the most rapid decline in protection rates, productivity gains are largest. In an empirical analysis of the impact of customs union on Turkish manufacturing sector productivity Taymaz and Yilmaz (2007) find that the gains in productivity of Turkish firms are higher if they are import-competing.

FDI is also another channel through which new technology transfer can be achieved, hence a positive impact on productivity. For example, Blalock and Gertler (2008) find theoretically and empirically that multinational firms in emerging markets transfer technology to local suppliers to increase their productivity and lower input prices.[5] They argue that this is welfare improving not only for those sectors that attract FDI but also those sectors downstream who are suppliers.

The main motivation of this study is to identify potential sources of export-led growth for the region. As exports have not yet reached their full potential, they represent a channel to growth that is largely untapped. Forming a virtual customs union will have three significant effects on the SEEs: (i) reducing tariff dispersion, that is, by reducing or abolishing tariff peaks; (ii) reducing the trade diverting effects of existing preferential agreements, such as the SAAs and CEFTA and hence improving welfare; and (iii) boosting intra-regional trade. The SEE countries' tariff profiles present several tariff peaks much higher and more frequent than the EU's CET. Although there are some tariff peaks in EU's CET as well, a virtual customs union would amount to unilateral trade liberalization for the countries in the region.[6] All preferential agreements, for example, FTAs, such as SAA's Interim Agreement on trade have trade diverting effect (as well as trade creation). As tariffs are fully abolished in the CEFTA region, goods originating within the EU will have a cost advantage over other countries that have to pay the full tariff. If EU is a less efficient producer of a particular good and due to its preferential access to CEFTA region it may replace a more efficient trade partner, hence reducing welfare. As trade will be already diverted toward the EU (when tariff liberalization schedules are completed) adopting the CET will reduce trade diversion that is caused by the SAAs. In addition, the implementation of CEFTA is another source of trade diversion, as trade may be diverted within the members: When an FTA is created parties to the agreement offer each other tariff free access to each other's market, however, they continue to apply their previously established tariffs to third countries. If one partner has lower tariffs than the other, then extra-FTA trade will be diverted towards the partner with lower tariffs as once the good enters the FTA area it can be freely shipped to the higher-tariff partner. This effect of an FTA does not exist in the case of a customs union. Finally, as EU's average MFN rates are lower than SEE countries' rates, adopting CET will amount to a unilateral tariff reduction in relation to third parties, hence it will also have trade creating effects.

Our results indicate that after such a reform, the region's simple average tariffs would be reduced from 5.1 percent to 2.3 percent, trade-weighted average tariff would be reduced from 4.7 percent to 2.2 percent. Among the SEE countries, Serbia is to go through the most ambitious adjustment process due to its higher average tariffs and tariff dispersions. On the other extreme, Croatia requires the least effort to adopt EU's CET thanks to its advanced status as an EU candidate country. In the second part of this study, we estimate quantitatively the costs and benefits of adopting EU's CET by making use of traditional concepts of trade diversion and creation. As our estimation tools we use partial equilibrium model of SMART developed by UNCTAD and the World Bank. The results indicate that the impact of this trade reform is going to be positive with net trade creation in the magnitude of US$998.9 million for the region, an increase of 4.3 percent from pre-reform import levels. Even though imports will increase significantly, the net effect of adopting EU's CET will result in revenue loss roughly half of the gains from trade creation, that is, US$459.7 million. The consumer surplus, which will result from reducing the deadweight loss from tariffs, is a modest US$51.7 million. The overall net effect of CET amounts thus to US$590.9 million, roughly 1 percent of SEE's combined GDP. The impact of adopting CET is going to have a negative effect on intra-regional exports. Nevertheless, the decrease in intra-regional exports (that is, trade diversion) is a readjustment and only amounts to 0.1 percent of GDP. China is going to increase its exports by 8 percent to the region and is going to be the main extra-EU beneficiary of this trade reform.

In chapter 13 we describe in detail how a virtual customs union differs from a customs union and also present theoretical and empirical evidence on customs union literature. In chapter 14, we present the tariff profiles for the region and the level of adjustment required for each country: Albania, Bosnia and Herzegovina, Croatia, FYR Macedonia, Montenegro, Serbia, and Kosovo. In chapter 15, we present results from a partial equilibrium analysis. In chapter 16, we conclude with policy recommendations.

Note

[1] The CEFTA region is comprised of Albania, Bosnia, and Herzegovina, Croatia, the Former Yugoslav Republic of Macedonia (FYR Macedonia), Montenegro, Serbia, and Kosovo. Moldova is excluded as it is not interlinked with the rest of countries in the region, nor it has a clear EU perspective.
[2] With some exceptions like sugar, wine, baby beef, and so forth.

[3] In this paper we will use the terms "CEFTA region" and "Southeast Europe" interchangeably.
[4] IMF estimates, WEO April 2009.
[5] Blalock, G. and P. Gertler (2008), "Welfare Gains from FDI through Technology Transfer to Local Suppliers," *Journal of International Economics* (74).
[6] See Kaminski (2008) for a case study of Albania.

CHAPTER 13

Customs Union versus a Virtual Customs Union

A customs union is a free trade area where parties adopt a common external tariff against the third parties. Since the coming into force of CEFTA in 2007, the SEE countries have become a free trade area where common rules of origin is the most important instrument. As CEFTA was formed from a network of 32 bilateral FTAs, the removal of the quotas and customs duties that existed in the bilateral FTAs is still being negotiated.[1] If the seven SEE countries adopt EU's CET the countries in the region will become part of a customs union. As adopting the common customs tariff of the EU is only one element of a complete customs union with the EU, this unilateral action is envisaged as forming a "virtual" customs union.

Indeed joining the common market and becoming part of EU's common customs requires much more than adopting the CET. All candidate states that joined the EU had to adopt the part of the *acquis communautaire*, namely "Chapter 25: Customs Union." As the borders of the candidate states become the new borders of the EC it is important to assure that the customs aquis is implemented in a harmonious way at all the points of the border of the EU. Hence the customs *acquis* includes the Community's Customs Code and its implementing provisions, the Combined Nomenclature, the Common Customs Tariff with preferences tariff quotas and tariff suspensions, and other customs-related legislation outside the scope of the customs code, as for example the legislation on counterfeit and pirated goods, drug precursors and export of cultural goods (EC, DG TAXUD). Currently, the only non-EU members who have a customs union with the EU are Turkey, Andorra, and San Marino. For example, as part of its customs union, Turkey had to adopt not only the EU's CET but also EU's preferential tariffs with third countries by signing free trade agreements (FTAs) with them.[2] Turkey's approximation of other laws such as intellectual property rights, competition, and taxation are still not fully completed. Turkey also has to implement EU's trade defense instruments such as any anti-dumping rulings against a country.

The difference between a customs union and a preferential agreement (for example, FTA) is that the movement of goods within customs unions is not based on their originating status but on the fact that they comply with provisions on free circulation.[3] This means that any good that is wholly produced or imported from a third party once they are granted free circulation can move freely within the community and/or for example, Turkey, Andorra and San Marino. As goods can circulate freely within the customs borders of the EU from one member state to another, this reduces all costs related to obtaining a certificate of origin once the goods enter a customs union.[4] But of course, administration of a customs union requires several additional measures to be taken, such as the customs administrations must guarantee the accurate development and implementation of a revenue collection and management strategy. This requires the candidate countries to develop policies, systems, procedures, technologies, and instruments compatible with the EU requirements and standards.

The theoretical analysis on customs union dates back to classical analysis of Viner (1950). In his classical analysis of the impact of customs union on the trade between member states, he utilized two competing concepts: trade diversion and trade creation. Trade creation signifies increase of imports from the partner due to tariff elimination that were previously domestically produced. If indeed the imports replaces domestic produce that were more inefficiently produced, trade creation is seen as a positive effect as it allows freeing up of resources that were previously inefficiently used to be diverted to the production of goods where home country has a comparative advantage. Trade diversion, however, implies lower cost trade from a third country be diverted towards a higher-cost producer within the customs union, therefore it is welfare reducing. The subsequent works of Meade and Lipsey have built on Viner's analysis of a customs union. The overall impact of a customs union depends on net effect from trade diversion versus trade creation. In a more recent study, Kruger (1997) argues that basic arguments of trade creation-diversion for customs unions can be expanded in several ways. One of the arguments is that customs unions may promote increased competition and this may stimulate searches for static and dynamic productivity gains. The author also argues that a customs union between developing and developed countries are likely to bring more welfare gains as there is wide divergences between the comparative advantage of one compared to the other.

There are currently in force 14 customs unions around the world that are notified to the WTO. The oldest customs union (CU) is the one established between the then nine member states of the European Community (EC) under the EC Treaty in 1958. Since then there has been a steady increase in numbers of CU where the majority of the agreements have taken place in Africa (for example, East African Community (2000); Economic Community of West African States (1993); West African Economic and Monetary Union (2000); South African Customs Union (2004); Economic and Monetary Community of Central Africa (1999)) and Central and Latin America (Andean Community (1988); Central American Common Market (1961); MERCOSUR (1991); CARICOM (1973). Besides EC's customs union with non-member states there are only two other in force: Gulf Cooperation Countries (2003) and Eurasian Economic Community (1997) established among CIS.

There are several empirical studies on impact of a customs union on member states. Due to differences in methodology used it is difficult to reach a consensus on the outcome of forming a customs union. Overall, an examination of the literature reveals that each case if different and there are no comparative studies available to the best of our knowledge. For the main motivation of this study, we choose to concentrate on the EU-Turkey customs union and Turkey's experience. As EU-Turkey customs union covers only industrial goods and has been in force since 1996, it provides a perfect comparator.[5] Several studies find that EU-Turkey customs union has increased considerably import penetration in manufacturing while not significantly affecting the share of EU in Turkey's trade (Erzan et al. 2002). Although the share of EU in Turkey's trade have remained stable before and after the customs union several studies indicate that there has been significant gains in the manufacturing sector of Turkey in terms of productivity gains. Taymaz and Yilmaz (2007) find that even though growth in productivity of manufacturing sectors slowed down substantially after 1996, productivity actually increased in the manufacturing sectors especially in those sectors with increased import penetration rates. Akkoyunlu et al. (2007) also find that manufacturing imports from EU countries cause total factor productivity increase in Turkish manufacturing industry. The results of Lohrrman (2001) support the "catching-up" hypothesis not the "Hecksher-Ohlin trap" for Turkey because the Turkish trade pattern has shifted towards intra-industry trade. In fact, one of the most important effects of the customs union has been Turkey's increasing intra-industry with the EU. Kocyigit (2007) show that growth of intra-industry trade between Turkey and the EU indicates that Turkey's industrial base is dramatically changing from low technology products group to high technology industries, since the customs union agreement with the EU has been put into effect in 1996. This in return has a positive impact on Turkey's development and growth.

Some of the results discussed are readily observable from export and import data of Turkey (figure 13.1). When one compares Turkey's exports to the EU versus the rest of the world, one can see that they have been increasing in unison with the exception of the impact of the current financial crisis in 2008. This is in line with finding that EU's share in Turkey's exports to the world has remained the same after the customs union. The sharp increase in both exports and imports come much later in 2002.[6] It is interesting to note that after 2003 imports from the rest of the world have increased faster than imports from the EU, hence the larger trade deficit with the rest of the world. This can be partially explained by the fact that adjustment to EU's CET was only completed in 2006. This may also explain the concomitant increase in exports.

In the case of SEE countries, the free trade area is already in place and the Interim Agreements covering trade have entered into force for all countries except Kosovo (table 13.1). As Croatia is in the process of membership negotiations, it is the most advanced in terms of its tariff liberalization with the EU. Tariffs were fully liberalized on industrial goods originating within the EU by 2007. Among the rest, FYR Macedonia also has a more advanced status in terms of implementation of its Interim Agreement: tariff liberalization on EU's industrial goods was to be completed in 10 years, that is, by 2011. On the other hand, Albania, Bosnia and Herzegovina, and Montenegro have just started implementing the Interim Agreement on trade and they are to be completed over 5 years, that is, by 2014 in Albania and 2013 in Bosnia and Herzegovina and Montenegro. Serbia has ratified its SAA but the implementation is on hold due to political reasons.

Figure 13.1. Turkey's Exports and Imports 1986–2008 (US$ millions)

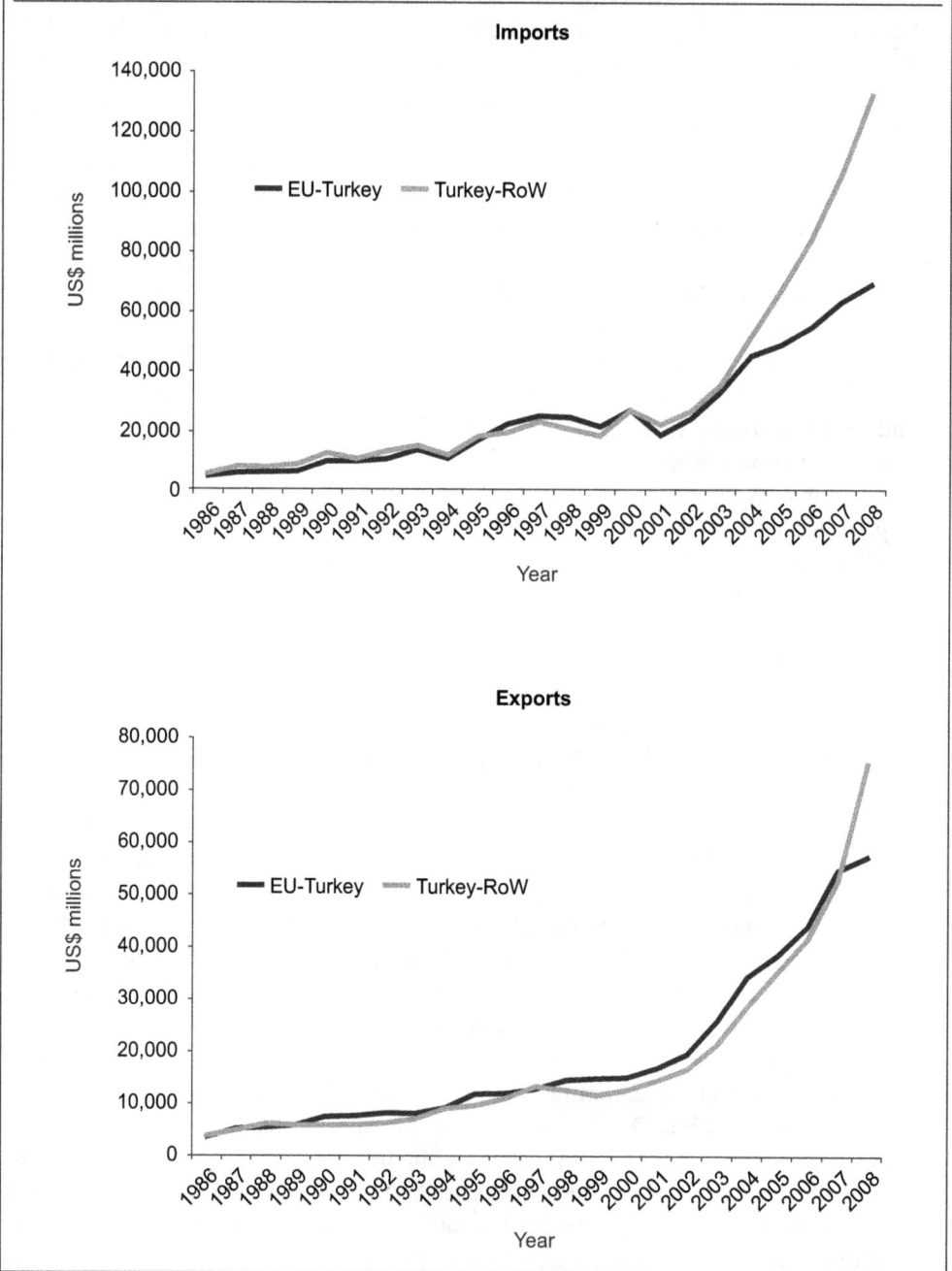

Source: UN COMTRADE database.

Table 13.1. Southeast Europe and Stabilization and Association Agreements

	SAA Signature	Interim Agreement on trade-date of entry into force
Albania	June 12, 2006	December 1, 2006
Bosnia and Herzegovina	June 16, 2008	July 1, 2008
Croatia	October 29, 2001	February 1, 2005
FYR Macedonia	April 9, 2001	June 1, 2001
Montenegro	October 15, 2007	January 1, 2008
Serbia	April 29, 2008	January 1, 2009 (ratified by Serbia, on hold in EU)
Kosovo	Not started	—

Source: European Commission.

When all tariff liberalization is completed in the region with the EU, and with the removal of all intra-regional quotas and customs duties, adopting the CET will amount to forming a 'virtual' customs union without the implementation of other institutional and regulatory requirements. The next section examines tariff profiles of SEE in detail in order to assess the adjustment that would be necessary to apply the CET.

Notes

[1] Center for European Perspective, 2008 December.

[2] Although Turkey's MFN tariff rates are fully in line with EU's CET, there are a few discrepancies due to EU's preferential rates. So far Turkey has signed FTAs with several EU bilateral preferential partners; however, this falls short of the full list as mostly there is no incentives for some of the third countries to sign FTAs with Turkey. This is at times a controversial issue.

[3] Some products, such as agriculture, coal and steel, in trade with the countries concerned do not fall within the scope of the customs union but remain subject to a preferential treatment based on origin.

[4] According to the responses to a survey (CEPS and CASE report for DG Trade) on Euro-Mediterranean economic integration, the Mediterranean exporters to the EU reported the cost of obtaining certificates of origin to be negligible but the process to be very complex, bureaucratic, and time-consuming.

[5] Although Turkey is expected to align with the *acquis* in several supporting aspects of the customs union (for example, IPR and elimination of state subsidies) progress lacks behind to this day.

[6] This may be explained by effect of the stabilization program introduced by IMF following the 2001 financial crisis.

CHAPTER 14

Tariff Profile of
Southeast Europe

Southeast Europe is comprised of a diverse group of countries not only in terms of their macroeconomic performances but also in their trade policies. Within the region Albania (2000), Croatia (2000) and FYR Macedonia (2003) are already members of the WTO. Bosnia and Herzegovina started negotiations in 1999 and it is at an advanced stage whereas Serbia and Montenegro both applied in 2004.[1]

Table 14.1 compares EU's simple average and trade-weighted average MFN rates for non-agricultural goods to those of SEE in the upper part of the table. As can be clearly seen the EU's simple average MFN rate of 3.8 percent and trade-weighted average MFN rate of 2.4 percent are considerably lower than those of SEE.

Table 14.1. Summary of MFN Applied Tariff Profiles of the Western Balkans and the EU, Non-agricultural Goods (Percent of Tariff Lines), 2007

MFN applied on non-agricultural goods	Simple average MFN applied		Trade-weighted average			
EU	3.8		2.4			
Albania	5.0		6.1			
Bosnia and Herzegovina	6.2		6.5			
Croatia	4.0		3.7			
FYR Macedonia	6.8		6.3			
Montenegro	4.0		—			
Serbia	6.4		5.4			
Frequency distribution	**Duty-free**	**0<=5**	**5<=10**	**10<=15**	**15<=25**	**>25**
EU	31.0	36.6	24.7	6.7	0.9	0
Albania	30.7	33.7	19.8	15.9	0	0
Bosnia and Herzegovina	26.9	31.8	31.9	9.4	0	0
Croatia	52.4	15.7	20.6	11.0	0.3	0
FYR Macedonia	37.2	18.7	19.4	15.9	8.7	0
Montenegro	2.2	74.8	20.5	1.6	0.7	0.1
Serbia	1.2	61.1	23.9	4.5	8.9	0.4

Source: WTO tariff profile 2008.

Among the countries in the region only Croatia and Montenegro come close to the EU average MFN rate with a simple average rate of 4 percent each. Albania, Bosnia and Herzegovina, FYR Macedonia, and Serbia have both simple and trade-weighted rates that are significantly higher than that of the EU. Among all, FYR Macedonia has the highest simple and trade-weighted average MFN rates, even though it is now officially a candidate country. Although simple averages are informative, a more detailed examination of the distribution of tariffs over tariff lines reveals wider differences (the second part of table 14.1). Table 14.1 presents the percent of tariff lines that are duty-free in the first column followed by the share of tariff lines in increasing range, that is, 0–5 percent, 5–10 percent, 10–15 percent, and 15–25 percent.

In comparison to the EU, Croatia and FYR Macedonia have more tariff lines that are duty-free. In contrast, Serbia and Montenegro have only 1.2 and 2.2 percent of tariff lines that are duty-free respectively. If one can generalize, EU's MFN is skewed to the left with few tariff peaks. For example, the EU has only 6.7 percent tariff lines in the tariff range of 10–15 percent and 0.9 percent in 15–25 range. This is exactly where the countries within the region begin to differ. With the exception of Montenegro, all countries have larger percent of tariff lines in excess of 10 percent tariffs. Serbia and Montenegro have tariff in excess of 25 percent even though only a few exist. Although this table shows the tariff profiles of each country it does not give information where the adjustment has to take place. For example, one can see that Albania has similar tariff structure for the range below 5 percent but needs to reduce the percent of its tariff lines that fall in the category of 10–15 from 15.9 percent to 6.7. This line of reasoning is misleading as the table below does not indicate whether a tariff line with 15 percent tariff has to be reduced to below 10 percent or to zero percent. Hence in the section we will examine tariff structure of each country and its distribution among different products. The adjustment is to be more severe for those countries which have a higher percent of tariff lines in the range 10 percent and more, especially if they differ from EU's sensitive products. The following section gives a precise idea about the level of adjustment required in the tariff profiles of SEE.

The Level of Adjustment

In this section we analyze in detail how much adjustment would be required for each country in the region. The analysis is carried out at 6-digit product level using UNCOMTRADE TRAINS database. With the exception of Albania and Serbia, all countries report their tariff structure according to HS07 classifications as the EU. Albania and Serbia use HS02 classification. The HS07 classification renders a total of 4330 products and tariffs and HS02 classification has more product categories than HS07 classification. In order to be able to compare EU's MFN rate at HS 6-digit level we only used the products that matched on both side for Albania and Serbia[2]. Before introducing a country-by-country analysis of the level of adjustment required, in table 14.2 we present the average level of adjustment required to adopt the CET by examining pre- and after-reform simple and trade-weighted average tariffs.

Among the six countries, Serbia has to undertake the most dramatic change to its tariff structure by nature of its high protectionism. Currently in Serbia simple average tariffs on industrial products are 8.8 percent, with a trade-weighted average of 8.0 percent.

Table 14.2. Pre-Reform and After Reform Average and Weighted Tariffs

	Old simple average tariff	New simple average tariff	Old weighted tariff	New weighted tariff
SEE average	5.1	2.3	4.7	2.2
Albania	4.0	1.8	4.1	1.9
Bosnia and Herzegovina	6.4	2.8	5.9	2.7
Croatia	3.6	2.1	2.9	1.7
FYR Macedonia	5.9	2.7	5.7	2.7
Montenegro	2.0	0.7	1.4	0.5
Serbia	8.8	3.8	8.0	3.5

Source: Author's calculations.
Note: Average tariffs include preferential tariffs as well as MFN tariffs.

After the adoption of EU's CET, Serbia's simple average tariffs will be reduced to 3.8 percent and a trade-weighted average of 3.5 percent. However, even after the adjustment Serbia's average tariffs (both simple and trade-weighted) will remain to be the highest within the region. This is simply because other countries have a considerably higher number of tariff lines that are duty-free, hence do not require adjustment. On average Bosnia and Herzegovina's simple average tariffs will decline to 2.8 percent from 6.4 percent and trade-weighted tariffs to 2.7 percent from 5.9 percent. In order of the level of adjustment required Bosnia and Herzegovina will be followed by FYR Macedonia, Albania, and Croatia. On the other extreme, Montenegro has the lowest average tariffs (2.0 percent of simple average and 1.4 percent trade-weighted average) and will further achieve even lower average tariff rates that are close to one percent. The after-reform weighted tariffs will be lowest in Montenegro, followed by Croatia, Albania. Bosnia and Herzegovina and FYR Macedonia will have an after-reform trade-weighted average tariff similar to the EU's MFN rate, while Serbia's average tariffs will remain above EU average.

In the remainder of this section a detailed analysis of the level of adjustment will be discussed for each country in the region. Starting with Albania, there are 4098 products categories that matched with the EU's tariff profile.[3] In the first column of the table below, to give an idea about the extent of adjustment needed, we report the number of tariff headings that have be zeroed (that is, 100 percent reduction), headings where tariffs have to be reduced by more than 75 percent, 50–74 percent, 25–49 percent, 0–24 percent. We also report the number of headings that require no change, and the number of tariff heading where EU's MFN rates are higher than in the SEE country. Due to concern on WTO compatibility, especially for those countries that are WTO members (but also others as they are in the process of negotiation) we propose that the tariff headings with tariff rates lower than EU's MFN rates be left unchanged. According to a WTO ruling on customs union, in the particular case of Turkey, the appellate body concluded that any customs union, to be WTO compatible, has to respect GATT Art. XXIV and should especially ensure that it is not erected against third parties. The report of the Appellate body stated: "According to paragraph 4, the purpose of a customs union is "to facilitate trade" between the constituent members and "not to raise barriers to the trade" with third countries. This objective demands that a balance be struck by the constituent members of a customs union. A customs union should facilitate trade within the customs union, but it should not do so in a way that raises barriers to trade with third countries" (WT/DS34/AB/R).

Table 14.3 summarizes the adjustment requirement of Albania's tariff structure. Out of Albania's 4,098 tariff headings, 2,230 of them are lower than EU's MFN rate. Since there is very little overlap between Albania's and EU's rate (only 16 tariff lines), together with the 2,230 tariff headings that are lower than EU's MFN rate, the remaining tariff headings that require some level of adjustment is less than 50 percent. Among those tariff headings that need to be zeroed (542 tariff headings), the majority (429) of them are already in the low tariff bracket ranging between non-zero and 5 percent. On the other hand, there are 60 tariff headings that are in the range of 5–10 percent and 53 in the range of 10–15 that need to be brought down to zero. When the table is examined by columns, one can see that there are more numbers of headings that require reduction in the higher tariff categories. For example, among the tariff range 10–15 percent (column 6), 53 heading tariffs need to be abolished, 253 need to be reduced by more than 75 percent, 113 need to be reduced by more than 50 percent (but less than 75 percent), 40 needs to be reduced by more than 25 percent (but less than 50 percent), and 180 need to be reduced by less than 25 percent. In summary, Albania's external tariff structure need to be reduced significantly, as 761 tariff headings require more than 50 percent reduction fall into the 5+ percent category.

Table 14.3. Albania: Adjustment to EU's CET

	Total tariff lines	0<=5	5<=10	10<=15	15<=25	>25
100 percent reduction	542	429	60	53	0	0
75–99 percent reduction	332	0	79	253	0	0
50–74 percent reduction	331	15	203	113	0	0
25–49 percent reduction	163	28	95	40	0	0
0–24 percent reduction	484	17	287	180	0	0
no reduction	16	14	2	0	0	0
No. heading where EU MFN is higher	2,230					
Total	4,098					

Source: Own calculations, UN COMTRADE TRAINS.

Bosnia and Herzegovina uses HS07 classification as the EU, hence the adjustment will cover full 4330 tariff headings. There are 1507 tariff headings that do not require adjustment as they are already lower than EU's MFN rates, plus the 29 that are the same as the EU. Unlike in Albania, the tariff headings in the range 10–15 require less of an adjustment: only 8 of them need to be reduced to zero, 41 of them need to be reduced by more than 75 percent, 43 need to be reduced by more than 50 percent, but the majority (almost 300) need to be reduced by less than 50 percent (table 14.4). The weight of adjustment in Bosnia and Herzegovina will largely fall on the tariff heading that are in the range of 5–10: more than half of a total of 1264 headings have to be reduced by more than 50 percent. On the other hand, in the 0–5 percent tariff range there is also significant reduction within the range.

Table 14.4. Bosnia and Herzegovina: Adjustment to EU's CET

	Total tariff lines	0<=5	5<=10	10<=15	15<=25	>25
100 percent reduction	616	398	210	8	0	
75–99 percent reduction	206	19	146	41	0	
50–74 percent reduction	785	283	459	43	0	
25–49 percent reduction	494	238	184	72	0	
0–24 percent reduction	693	205	263	225	0	
no reduction	29	27	2	0	0	
No. heading where EU MFN is higher	1,507					
Total	4,330					

Source: Own calculations, UN COMTRADE TRAINS.

Croatia, as a country that is at an advanced stage of negotiations for EU membership, needs to make more minor adjustments to its external tariff structure (table 14.5). First of all, out of 4330 tariff headings, 2515 are less than EU's MFN rate and 407 are exactly the same. As can be seen, Croatia has already been making preparations for membership and aligning its tariff profile towards EU. Among the 407 tariff heading that are the same as EU's, 76 are in the range 0–5, 310 are in the range 5–10 and 21 are in the range 10–15. The tariff headings that need to be abolished are mostly in the category 0–5 range, however there are still 199 tariff headings in the range 10–15 that have to be reduced by more than 50 percent. But in summary the majority of the adjustment that has to take place is within the lower tariff ranges and by about 25–75 percent.

Table 14.5. Croatia: Adjustment to EU's CET

	Total tariff lines	0<=5	5<=10	10<=15	15<=25	>25
100 percent reduction	240	145	81	13	1	
75–99 percent reduction	239	8	89	137	5	
50–74 percent reduction	414	114	238	62	0	
25–49 percent reduction	220	112	64	44	0	
0–24 percent reduction	295	48	54	193	0	
no reduction	407	76	310	21	0	
No. heading where EU MFN is higher	2,515					
Total	4,330	503	836	470	6	

Source: Own calculations, UN COMTRADE TRAINS.

As the other countries in the region, Macedonia also has a large number of tariffs that are less than EU's MFN rate (1969) and also those that are the same (56). In contrast with the countries examined above, Macedonia has a large number of tariffs (376) in the range 15–25 percent (that others did not have) that all have to be reduced (table 14.6). However, the heavy weight of adjustment will fall on the two tariff categories, that is, 5–10 percent with 801 tariff heading and 10–15 percent with 685 tariff headings. In total, there are 316 tariffs that have to be reduced to zero, 553 have to be reduced by more than 75 percent and 699 have to be reduced by more than 50 percent.

Table 14.6. Macedonia: Adjustment to EU's CET

	Total tariff lines	0<=5	5<=10	10<=15	15<=25	>25
100 percent reduction	316	93	115	98	10	–
75–99 percent reduction	553	4	88	394	67	
50–74 percent reduction	699	100	207	123	269	
25–49 percent reduction	290	130	79	52	29	
0–24 percent reduction	447	159	269	18	1	
no reduction	56	13	43	0	0	
No. heading where EU MFN is higher	1,969					
Total	4,330	499	801	685	376	

Source: Own calculations, UN COMTRADE TRAINS.

Montenegro in general has lower incidence of tariff peaks compared to Serbia and to Macedonia. There are only 30 tariff headings with tariffs in the range of 15–25 percent, out of which 13 have to be completely abolished and the remaining 17 have to be reduced by 75 percent. This indicates that those tariffs of Montenegro were not the same sensitive products as EU's. In fact, Montenegro has only 98 tariff headings that are the same as EU's and 29 of them are in the range 0–5 range and 67 are in 5–10 range (table 14.7). Unlike other countries, Montenegro has large number of tariff headings that have to be reduced to zero: out of 1046 heading that have to be reduced to zero, 890 fall in the range of 0–5 percent, 109 into 5–10 range, 34 in 10–15 range and 13 in 15–25 range.

Table 14.7. Montenegro: Adjustment to EU's CET

	Total tariff lines	0<=5	5<=10	10<=15	15<=25	>25
100 percent reduction	1,046	890	109	34	13	–
75–99 percent reduction	103	10	62	14	17	
50–74 percent reduction	348	126	206	16	0	
25–49 percent reduction	314	220	91	3	0	
0–24 percent reduction	239	162	77	0	0	
no reduction	98	29	67	0	0	
No. heading where EU MFN is higher	2,182					
Total	4,330	1437	612	67	30	

Source: Own calculations, UN COMTRADE TRAINS.

In general the majority of adjustment is going to take place in the 0–5 percent range: 1,408 tariff headings have to be reduced at various degrees. There are also 545 tariff headings in the range 5–10 percent that have to be reduced as well. The weight of adjustment in Montenegro will fall largely on these two tariff categories, that is, 0–5 and 5–10 percent and they will have to be reduced by more than 25 percent mostly (with the exception of 999 headings that have to be brought down to zero).

Serbia uses the HS02 classification for its tariff headings and a similar adjustment as was done before for Albania to make it comparable to the EU's CET (table 14.8). Hence we ended up with somewhat less than 4,330 headings for our analysis (that is, 4,098). Serbia stands out among the SEE countries as having the most protectionist tariff structure: it has in total 529 tariff headings in access of 10 percent, with 350 falling in the category 15–25 percent and 13 in excess of 25 percent. Across all categories in Serbia, 1,001 tariff headings will have to be abolished to adopt EU's CET. As the majority of tariff headings are in the 0–5 and 5–10 percent range there are significant adjustment required in the lower percentages as well.

Table 14.8. Serbia: Adjustment to EU's CET

	Total tariff lines	0<=5	5<=10	10<=15	15<=25	>25
100 percent reduction	1,001	783	172	31	15	0
75–99 percent reduction	239	7	119	54	47	12
50–74 percent reduction	560	114	346	50	49	1
25–49 percent reduction	500	159	66	42	233	0
0–24 percent reduction	505	214	271	14	6	0
no reduction	28	22	6	0	0	0
No. heading where EU MFN is higher	1,265					
Total	4,098					

Source: Own calculations, UN COMTRADE TRAINS.

Table 14.9 shows which product categories are more protected in Albania. Clothing, leather, footwear, etc. and textiles are the most protected sectors where for example the average MFN rate for clothing is 15 percent, with no lines that are duty–free. Leather, footwear, etc. and textiles have average MFN applied duties of 10.8 percent and 7.8 percent with only 3.3 percent and 0.3 percent of tariff lines duty-free, respectively. Petroleum is also a protected sector with 9.2 percent average MFN (with maximum of 10 percent) and no lines duty-free. Manufactures, n.e.s. and minerals and metals are also relatively protected sectors. In fact one can see that all product categories have tariff peaks ranging between 10 and 18 percent. As one would expect, those products that have a lower average MFN tariff constitute a larger percent of total imports: chemicals, non-electrical and electrical machinery. Minerals and metals are an exception.

Table 14.9. Albania: Tariffs and Imports by Product Groups

Product groups	MFN applied duties			Imports share in %	Duty-free in %
	AVG	Duty-free in %	Max		
Minerals & metals	6.0	16.5	18	21.2	15.9
Petroleum	9.2	0	10	6.5	0
Chemicals	1.7	47.8	15	9.4	41.3
Wood, paper, etc.	0.3	95.4	15	4.2	98
Textiles	7.8	0.3	15	5.9	0.4
Clothing	15.0	0	15	5.6	0
Leather, footwear, etc.	10.8	3.3	15	4.1	0.1
Non-electrical machinery	1.6	32.7	10	10.2	31.2
Electrical machinery	3.6	39.9	10	7.4	32.8
Transport equipment	4.1	27.7	15	6.0	2.9
Manufactures, n.e.s.	7.0	34.7	15	3.4	52.0

Source: WTO tariff profile 2008.

In Bosnia and Herzegovina, with the exception of petroleum and chemicals, high tariff rates are pervasive in all product categories (table 14.20). By far the most protected products are textiles and clothing as in Albania. Besides these two product categories average MFN rates range between 5 percent in minerals and metals to 7.9 in leather, footwear, etc., with a tariff peak of 105 percent in minerals and metals.

Table 14.20. Bosnia and Herzegovina: Tariffs and Imports by Product Groups

Product groups	MFN applied duties			Imports Share in %	Duty-free in %
	AVG	Duty-free in %	Max		
Minerals & metals	5.0	35.1	105	18.2	35.2
Petroleum	1.6	83.6	10	8.2	62.1
Chemicals	3.3	50.1	15	12.2	21.6
Wood, paper, etc.	5.6	27.9	15	5.0	19.4
Textiles	9.0	4.5	15	4.5	0.8
Clothing	15.0	0	15	2.1	0
Leather, footwear, etc.	7.9	19.2	15	4.0	3.1
Non-electrical machinery	6.0	12.9	15	11.8	6.3
Electrical machinery	6.7	21.6	15	5.8	10.4
Transport equipment	5.7	25.5	15	7.9	6.5
Manufactures, n.e.s.	6.4	21.6	15	4.2	43.8

Source: WTO tariff profile 2008.

Croatia has a different tariff structure when compared to the countries discussed above (table 14.21). Although it has tariff peaks reaching as high as 18 percent (for example, in minerals and metals and manufactures) it has a higher percent of tariff lines that are duty-free under each product category. As Albania and Bosnia and Herzegovina, the most protected sector in Croatia is also textiles and clothing. Chemicals, wood, paper, etc., non-electrical and electrical machinery, manufactures, n.e.s. and minerals and metals are imported mostly in duty-free lines.

Table 14.21. Croatia: Tariffs and imports by Product Groups

Product groups	MFN applied duties			Imports Share in %	Duty-free in %
	AVG	Duty-free in %	Max		
Minerals & metals	3.7	57.2	18	17.8	61.4
Petroleum	9.8	23.5	14	11.1	79.2
Chemicals	1.3	77.8	7	12.2	57.4
Wood, paper, etc.	1.4	74.4	12	5.7	54.9
Textiles	6.5	16.7	14	3.1	14.5
Clothing	13.2	1.4	14	2.2	1.2
Leather, footwear, etc.	4.6	43.4	15	2.7	37.4
Non-electrical machinery	3.0	61.5	15	12.7	64.5
Electrical machinery	3.6	61.2	15	4.8	62.4
Transport equipment	6.1	28.3	15	13.5	24.6
Manufactures, n.e.s.	3.2	63.8	18	5.1	76.0

Source: WTO tariff profile 2008.

Macedonia has higher average MFN rates in all product categories compared to other WTO members Albania and Croatia (14.22). The average MFN rate in clothing is 25 percent with no lines duty-free. Petroleum, leather, footwear, etc., and textiles are also highly protected. The only product categories that have low tariffs on average are chemicals and wood, paper, etc., minerals and metals and non-electrical machinery.

Table 14.22. FYR Macedonia: Tariffs and Imports by Product Groups

Product groups	MFN applied duties			Imports Share in %	Duty-free in %
	AVG	Duty-free in %	Max		
Minerals & metals	5.6	47.3	23	17.8	66.5
Petroleum	14.1	6.7	20	18.5	96.9
Chemicals	3.5	37.7	25	10.4	29.4
Wood, paper, etc.	2.9	75.7	18	3.5	67.3
Textiles	9.1	11.5	25	11.5	6.9
Clothing	25.0	0.0	25	1.8	0.0
Leather, footwear, etc.	10.4	22.6	25	2.6	7.4
Non-electrical machinery	5.4	44.5	16	8.4	53.9
Electrical machinery	8.0	33.9	25	2.4	23.8
Transport equipment	7.1	23.9	20	7.5	4.4
Manufactures, n.e.s.	7.1	31.6	25	4.0	65.4

Source: WTO tariff profile 2008.

Montenegro is different than the other countries discussed so far. Its average MFN rates are low; however, the number of tariff lines that are duty-free within each product category are also low (table 14.23). Simply put Montenegro has very few tariff lines that are duty-free as was indicated in table 14.1.

Table 14.23. Montenegro: Tariffs and Imports by Product Groups

Product groups	MFN applied duties			Imports Share in %	Duty-free in %
	AVG	Duty-free in %	Max		
Minerals & metals	4.2	2.9	20	No	
Petroleum	2.2	3.4	10	information	
Chemicals	1.3	2.3	3.7	available	
Wood, paper, etc.	4.4	1.2	15		
Textiles	3.6	1.4	15	No	
Clothing	10.0	0	10	information	
Leather, footwear, etc.	6.3	0	15	available	
Non-electrical machinery	2.7	0.5	15		
Electrical machinery	1.9	0.2	7	No	
Transport equipment	2.0	14.8	10	information	
Manufactures, n.e.s.	5.2	0.6	25	available	

Source: WTO tariff profile 2008.

Tariff peaks are highest in manufactures, n.e.s. (25 percent) and petroleum (20 percent) but on average only 5.2 and 4.2 percent respectively. Like the other WB countries, clothing is the most protected product category, and leather, footwear, etc. to a lesser extent. Unlike others, average MFN rates for textiles are only 3.6 percent. Average MFN rates in petroleum, chemicals, wood, paper, etc., textiles, non-electrical, electrical machinery, transport equipment are all below 5 percent.

Serbia as well as others has clothing, textiles and leather, footwear, etc. as its most protected sectors (table 14.24). Besides these three product categories, average MFN rates for minerals and metals, petroleum, chemicals, wood, paper, etc. and non-electrical machinery are all below 5 percent. On the other hand, electrical machinery, transport equipment and manufactures, n.e.s. have tariff above 5 percent. As in Montenegro, Serbia has very few tariff lines that are tariff free.

UNMIK Kosovo has adopted its Integrated Tariff (TARIK) in 2005. It consists of a Goods Nomenclature based on the HS of the World Customs Organization and on the Combined Nomenclature of the EC. The tariffs for each tariff line are either zero or 10 percent. Average MFN applied tariffs on industrial products are 8.2 percent, which is higher than average rate for agricultural goods (7.2 percent). Average tariffs for textiles in Kosovo are 6.31 percent (HS code 11), 9.74 percent for footwear (HS code 12) and 9.54 percent for mineral products (HS 05). Average tariffs are lower for plastics, rubber, etc. (HS code 07), raw hides and skin, etc. (HS code 08), and for pulp and paper (HS code 10).

Table 14.24. Serbia: Tariffs and Imports by Product Groups

| Product groups | MFN applied duties | | | Imports Share in % | Duty-free in % |
	AVG	Duty-free in %	Max		
Minerals & metals	4.9	2.7	30	23.1	1.0
Petroleum	2.1	4.7	10	12.7	2.3
Chemicals	3.3	1.0	30	13.4	2.5
Wood, paper, etc.	4.9	0	20	5.7	0
Textiles	9.2	1.9	30	3.6	1.0
Clothing	20.4	0	22	1.8	0
Leather, footwear, etc.	8.6	0	30	2.9	0
Non-electrical machinery	4.6	0	20	11.7	0
Electrical machinery	6.9	0.2	15	5.6	0
Transport equipment	5.3	5.6	20	8.1	0.1
Manufactures, n.e.s.	5.8	0.2	25	3.9	0

Source: WTO tariff profile 2008.

Finally, examining the EU's tariff profile, one can see that clothing, textiles, footwear are also sensitive product categories (table 14.25). Although average MFN for transport equipment is 4.1, there is a tariff peak of 22 percent in this sector, and only 15.7 percent of tariff lines are tariff-free. Albania will see its largest adjustment in the minerals and metals, petroleum and manufactures n.e.s.; Bosnia and Herzegovina in all except in petroleum and chemicals; Croatia in all except in chemicals, textiles and footwear; Macedonia in almost all with exceptionally high adjustment in petroleum, clothing, leather, footwear, etc., electrical machinery, transport equipment and manufactures, n.e.s.; Montenegro in wood, paper, etc., leather, footwear, etc, and manufactures; Serbia in all except chemicals. Montenegro is the only country in SEE to have a lower average MFN rate in clothing and textiles compared to the EU.

Table 14.25. EU: Tariffs and Imports by Product Groups

Product groups	MFN applied duties			Imports share in %	Duty-free in %
	AVG	Duty-free in %	Max		
Minerals & metals	2.0	49.6	12	17.4	70.8
Petroleum	2.0	50.0	5	21.7	96.4
Chemicals	4.6	20.0	7	9.6	60.5
Wood, paper, etc.	0.9	84.1	10	3.1	90.3
Textiles	6.5	3.4	12	2.4	1.9
Clothing	11.5	0	12	4.8	0
Leather, footwear, etc.	4.2	27.8	17	2.5	19.6
Non-electrical machinery	1.7	26.5	10	13.1	67.6
Electrical machinery	2.4	31.5	14	6.3	39.5
Transport equipment	4.1	15.7	22	6.1	22.9
Manufactures, n.e.s.	2.5	25.9	14	6.3	56.8

Source: WTO tariff profile 2008.

Notes

[1] Montenegro is in the final stage of becoming a member.

[2] The differences in HS07 and HS02 tariff headings were examined carefully. Usually, those tariff headings that exist for Albania or Serbia but not for the EU were the ones where EU trade was negligible. For simplicity we suggest that Albania and Serbia adopt CET only on those products that are commonly traded.

[3] This number corresponds to the number of tariff lines that were matched in different product classifications as mentioned before.

CHAPTER 15

Estimates of Trade Diversion and Trade Creation Due to Adoption of EU's CET

In this section we will present simulation results quantifying the impact of adopting the EU's CET for each country. Using partial equilibrium analysis (that is, the WITS SMART model), we estimate trade diversion and creation, welfare and revenue changes for each country in the region. As will be presented below in greater detail adopting the EU's CET for industrial products (HS 2-digit codes 25–97) and applying these new rates against all countries in the world (with the exception of partners of SEE's preferential agreements) is for all practical purposes a unilateral liberalization. As mentioned above, this move towards trade openness will have two significant effects: one on reducing trade diversion from preferential trade partners of the region to more efficient producers (countries), and a second effect on trade creation from third countries.

The choice of partial equilibrium model of SMART is manifold. Recently computable general equilibrium (CGE) models have become popular in estimating the reaction of an economy to changes in trade policy. Even though CGE models are more comprehensive (since they factor in not only direct effects of a policy change but also secondary/indirect effects such as inter-industry effects and macroeconomic adjustment) than partial equilibrium models, they suffer from data availability as they are more data demanding. As such the required data to run CGE models only exist for Albania and Croatia in the GTAP database. Although CGE models estimate impact on output, employment, as well as exports and imports at a sectoral level, they have been heavily criticized on theoretical grounds. On the other hand, partial equilibrium models such as SMART can deliver estimates of trade diversion and creation, as well as change in revenue and consumer welfare at a highly disaggregate level that may be more useful for policy makers.

The partial equilibrium model of SMART which was developed by UNCTAD and the World Bank relies on several assumptions. First, SMART assumes a perfect competition model; hence a tariff cut is fully reflected in the price paid by consumers. The simulations are then based on estimates of supply elasticity, import substitution elasticity and import demand elasticity. In the model,

- Supply elasticities are assumed to be infinite (=99). This means that an increase in demand for a given good will always be matched by the producers and exporters of that good without any impact on the price of the good. This assumption is reasonable when the importer is a small country, for example, like the SEE countries, and the exporter is rest of the world (that is, large).

- Import substitution elasticity is the rate of substitution between two of the same good from different origins. The Armington assumption is incorporated in SMART, meaning that similar goods from different countries are imperfectly substitutable. In SMART the import substitution elasticity is considered to be 1.5 for each good. As tastes and preferences also play a significant role in international trade this assumption is reasonable.

- Import demand elasticity measures the demand response to a shift in import price. In SMART, the import demand elasticity varies at the HS-4 level and is based on a survey by Stern in "price elasticities in international trade."

As indicated above, all countries in the SEE region were offered SAA and they all signed and started implementing the Interim Agreement on trade, with the exception of Kosovo and Serbia. As Kosovo is not yet signed its SAA, it will be left out of further analysis. Since the latest data available on tariffs in WITS is from 2008,[1] for Albania, Bosnia and Herzegovina, Montenegro and Serbia the tariffs have not yet been adjusted for the first phase of tariff reductions with the EU. Hence, much of the analysis involves not only the impact of adopting EU's CET but also tariff liberalization towards the EU. As all SEE countries in the region have signed preferential agreements with the EU and within the region (CEFTA), this indicates that most of the trade is duty-free. Hence the trade creation effects of EU's CET can be expected to be only moderate, whereas some trade diversion may be expected away from preferential trade partners to more efficient producers in the world. Such trade diversion may be considered a positive outcome as consumers can access the same goods and pay less. This kind of trade diversion in fact corrects for the negative trade diversion that is usually created when an FTA is established.

Table 15.1 summarizes the effects of adopting EU's CET on the region and for each of the countries in the region and divides them into its effect on total trade, revenue and the consumer surplus. The total trade effect is the net effect from trade diversion, trade creation and price effect (that is, terms of trade). Trade diversion effect refers to trade diverted towards the FTA partners. In this case, as the adoption of EU's CET is applied to all countries in the world (less any FTA partners of the region), the beneficiaries of this unilateral move are practically all countries in the world minus the EU and CEFTA (for them the new tariffs are zero for all industrial goods).[2] Hence the simulation results have all the features of a virtual customs union with the EU, as they include the impact of completion of tariff liberalization schedules with the EU plus the implementation of the CET.[3] Since trade liberalization will apply to all countries the overall trade diversion effects cancels out as there are some losers and some winners. In other words, when Albania reduces its tariffs on a given product from 15 percent to 1.7 percent (EU's MFN), Albania's preferential partners observe a preference erosion as more efficient non-preferential partners gain access to Albania. Trade creation in this model refers to trade creation for both the SEE countries and the partners (that is, all countries). The price effect is the effect of the change in term of trade due to the change in the tariff of a given country. In this simulation the price effect is zero since we use export supply elasticity equal to infinity. This translates into claiming that the SEE countries are price takers, or in other words too small to have any impact on the world unit price of a product.[4] In summary the total trade effect for a given country in this simulation is the net effect of trade creation and trade diversion across all product categories.

Table 15.1. Summary of Simulation Results (US$ millions)

	Pre-reform Imports	Total Trade Creation	Change in Revenue	Consumer Surplus	Net effect of CET
SEE Total	23,442.7	998.9	−459.7	51.7	590.9
Albania	2,106.8	50.2	−26.2	0.9	24.9
Bosnia and Herzegovina	4,446.6	253.7	−120.8	12.7	145.6
Croatia	7,703.6	93.3	−46.4	2.7	49.6
FYR Macedonia	2,067.9	81.6	−67.0	3.6	18.2
Montenegro	694.9	10.2	−5.1	0.2	5.3
Serbia	6,422.9	509.9	−194.2	31.6	347.3

Source: Various country sources, WDI.

The above table shows in the first column the total imports of SEE from the world before the implementation of the EU's CET.[5] The second column of the table shows simulation results of total trade effect which comes from trade creation, the third column returns the total reduction in revenue from trade liberalization and the fourth column gives estimates of consumer surplus and the final column is the net effect of CET (that is, addition of total trade creation plus change in revenue and consumer surplus). Consumer surplus in this model refers to the change in deadweight loss: as the economy looses in terms of welfare by imposing a tariff on the imported good, it incurs a deadweight loss. When the tariff is reduced the economy as a whole gains from additional tariff revenue from increased imports and/or from additional consumer surplus by increased imports.

As can be seen the total trade creation in the region is positive and it represents an increase of US$998.9 million in imports to the region, and an average increase of 4.2 percent from pre-reform levels. As total pre-reform imports into the region constitutes 40 percent of the region's GDP, this increase is rather significant and represents an increase of 1.7 percent of GDP.[6] Implementing CET will increase most dramatically imports into Serbia, by US$509.9 million, an increase of 7.9 percent from pre-reform level. Trade creation effect is also high for Bosnia and Herzegovina, with an increase of US$253.7 million, a 5.7 percent increase. In order of significance, imports into Croatia will increase by US$93.3 million, FYR Macedonia by 81.6 million, Albania by US$50.2 million and by US$10.2 million to Montenegro. These results are in line with expectations as the most protectionist country in the region will benefit the most from trade liberalization (that is, Serbia) and the least protectionist will benefit the least (that is, Montenegro).

Naturally, tariff liberalization is going to reduce revenue from customs duties in the region. This effect amounts to a decrease of US$459.7 million SEE countries as a whole, that is, 53 percent reduction on pre-reform levels (roughly 1 percent of GDP). The tariff revenue change is the net effect from two opposite effects: (i) the tariff revenue lost at constant import value, which correspond to a transfer from State to consumers (ii) a tariff revenue gain through the increase in imports which enlarges the tax base. As the model assumes an import demand elasticity that implies that gains are less than losses SMART returns negative values in most cases. The largest revenue loss, as can be expected, will be in Serbia (US$194.2 million), followed by Bosnia and Herzegovina (US$120.8 million), then by FYR Macedonia (US$67 million), Croatia (US$46.4 million), Albania (US$26.2 million) and Montenegro (US$5.1 million). However, the overall fiscal impact of the revenue loss for each country differs in line with the level of dependency on customs duties for revenue. As table 15.2 shows, Bosnia and Herzegovina has the highest rate of customs and other duty to taxes (18 percent), followed by Albania (10 percent), Montenegro (9.7 percent), FYR Macedonia (9.2 percent), Serbia (6.5 percent) and Croatia (2.7 percent). Clearly, Croatia will be the least affected country in the region as its tax base is well diversified even though the reduction in revenue amounts to 37 percent of pre-reform levels. On the other hand, both Albania and Bosnia and Herzegovina will face a 52 percent reduction in revenue and therefore these two countries will be the largest hit if they cannot take measures to diversify their tax base. FYR Macedonia and Montenegro are also going to be facing significant losses as the change in revenue amounts to a 67 percent cut in revenue for both. Although Serbia is going to lose the largest amount in dollar terms, in relative terms it will be less affected when compared to the four SEE countries mentioned. These results are based on observations of the latest years data are available for a breakdown of government revenue, and hence do not take into account the volatility of the ratios. For example, WDI data indicate that Serbia has generated 11 percent of its taxes from import tariffs in 2007, as opposed to 6.5 percent in 2008. This adds uncertainty into our analysis and hence these results may only be interpreted with caution.

Table 15.2. Tariff Revenue in SEE (LCU million)

Country	Revenues	Taxes	Customs and other import duties	TR/Taxes (%)
Albania			13,871.7	10.0
Bosnia and Herzegovina			546.5	18.0
Croatia	120,036.7	69,572.7	1,900.9	2.7
Serbia (in billion RSD)	1,145.9	1,000.3	64.8	6.5
FYR Macedonia	144,705.0	80,639.0	7,420.0	9.2
Montenegro (€ million) [a]	774,718,974.0	690,880,722.1	67,151,545.3	9.7
Kosovo	1,033,145.0	805,030.0	604,196.0	75.1

Source: various country sources, WDI.
a. figures are extrapolated from based on 10-month figures to annual (2007). Albania and Bosnia and Herzegovina figures are from 2004, others are from 2008.

Finally the total consumer surplus that will be generated after the reform will amount to US$51.7 million, equivalent to 0.1 percent of GDP. The consumer surplus is modest indicating that for several of the main trade partners of SEE countries FTAs are already in place and hence trade is conducted duty-free. Serbia is to receive the largest share in consumer surplus, 61 percent of the total, followed by Bosnia and Herzegovina that will receive 25 percent. The rest will gain only small shares of the total consumer surplus in the region, ranging from a zero percent for Montenegro to 7 percent for FYR Macedonia. The simulation results provide a 6-digit breakdown of consumer surplus for each country. Since the overall effect of the gains from consumer surplus is low, we refer the reader to Appendix 1 for details.

The net effect of adopting EU's CET is the cumulative effect from trade creation, revenue change and consumer surplus. This net effect amounts to US$590.9 million (approximately 1 percent of GDP) for the SEE countries as a region. Individually, the net effect is going to be higher for Serbia and reach 2.8 percent of GDP. The overall net effect of the customs union is also going to be significant for Bosnia and Herzegovina, and will amount to 1.9 percent of GDP. On the other hand, Croatia is going to gain 0.2 percent of GDP, FYR Macedonia, and Montenegro 0.4 percent of GDP each and Albania is going to gain only 0.5 percent of GDP.

Breakdown of Trade Diversion and Creation among Trade Partners

In this section we will examine in detail the impact of adopting EU's CET on exports of SEE trade partners. As discussed above, the theoretical implication of such a trade reform would mean that some trade partners will export more to SEE (that is, trade creation) due to increased market accessibility, while some trade partners will export less due to preference erosion. Theoretically, trade creation is seen as a positive outcome of trade liberalization as more efficiently produced goods gain access to the domestic market. Some of the new trade created may replace domestic production. This can also be seen as a positive aspect of the preferential agreement as domestic resources are free-up to be used in a more productive way (that is, efficiency gains). On the other hand, there are two types of trade diversion. First trade may be diverted in favour of a FTA partner, even though the goods may be produced more efficiently somewhere else. The second type of trade diversion happens when the trade is diverted from an existing FTA partner to an third party due to preference erosion. This type of trade diversion is considered positive. In the case of EU-SEE customs union, we may expect to see trade creation and trade diversion that is positive. As the SEE countries have already signed FTA with the EU, and with other parties, adopting CET will erode these countries' privileged access to the SEE. In summary, a priori, one would expect all preferential trading partners to lose out in exports, in a manner of correction/reduction to trade diversion caused initially due to the FTAs signed.

Table 15.3 ranks the top 10 trading partners and their exports to the SEE region. Italy and Germany are the two most important exporters to the region and they stand to gain the maximum amount in export revenues, as exports increase by 13 and 10 percent respectively. Other EU member states, such as Slovenia, Austria, Bulgaria, and the Czech Republic are among the top 10 beneficiaries. However, these countries gain not due to the adoption of CET but rather the completion of the implementation of the SAA's interim agreements on trade. This result is significant: it indicates that even when the

SEE's common external tariffs are reduced to EU's MFN rates, the gains from completing the FTAs will be larger and hence accrue a net positive effect for these countries.

Table 15.3. Top Exporting Countries to the Region (US$ millions)

	Pre-reform exports	After reform exports	Change
Italy	1,334.66	1,503.39	168.73
Germany	1,264.18	1,391.18	127.00
China	1,234.47	1,333.79	99.32
Slovenia	868.83	952.51	83.68
Russia	768.74	819.60	50.86
Austria	407.24	453.00	45.76
Turkey	334.14	363.40	29.26
United States	310.06	364.83	31.08
Bulgaria	278.35	228.26	34.03
Czech Republic	259.45	292.68	33.23

Source: Various country sources, WDI.

On the other hand, there are also a few extra-EU countries among the top 10 trading partners of the SEE that will benefit from increased export revenues. China, Russia, the United States, and Turkey may expect to achieve strong export growth to the region under such a scenario. China already ranks number three among the region's export partners, as its export reach US$1.2 billion. According to the simulations its exports to the region are to be expected to increase by 8 percent. The United States, ranked eigth among export partner is to increase its exports by 10 percent, Turkey by 9 percent and Russia by 7 percent.

In table 15.4 we present the top five countries that benefit from an increase in their exports to each SEE country following the adoption of CET. In this table, we aim to separate out the impact of CET (from the final implementation of EU FTAs) hence we concentrate on those countries that are extra-EU. For example, Switzerland is the number one beneficiary in Albania and Bosnia and Herzegovina. Switzerland also gains significant increase in exports revenues in Montenegro and Serbia. As seen above, China is the overall winner. The CET can be said to induce a secondary positive impact on some of the countries in the region as new export partners gain market share, such as Korea in Bosnia and Herzegovina; Taiwan, China and Hong Kong, China in Croatia; Pakistan in FYR Macedonia; and Hong Kong, China in Montenegro.

Table 15.4. Trade Creation

Albania	Bosnia and Herzegovina	Croatia	Macedonia	Montenegro	Serbia
Switzerland	Switzerland	China	Russia	China	China
China	China	United States	China	Switzerland	United States
Russia	Korea, Rep. of	Japan	United States	Turkey	Ukraine
Ukraine	United States	Taiwan, China	Pakistan	United States	Turkey
Turkey	Russia	Hong Kong, China	Japan	Hong Kong, China	Switzerland

Source: Author.

On the other hand, there are several countries that will experience a decrease in their exports to the SEE countries. Among all the trade partners of Albania, Italy, Serbia, FYR Macedonia, Greece, and Spain will experience the largest decrease in their exports (table 15.5). In line with expectation, many of the countries that will experience a loss of revenue due to reduced exports are other CEFTA members or EU member states.

Table 15.5. Trade Diversion

Albania	Bosnia and Herzegovina	Croatia	Macedonia	Montenegro	Serbia
Italy	Croatia	Italy	Serbia	Serbia	Croatia
Serbia	Serbia	Germany	Turkey	Croatia	Bosnia and Herzegovina
FYR Macedonia	Turkey	Slovenia	Croatia	Macedonia	Russia
Greece	FYR Macedonia	Austria	Albania	Russia	Macedonia
Spain		Hungary	Switzerland		Moldova

Source: Author.

Due to the CET, intra-regional exports are also expected to decrease. According to simulation results, the pre-reform intra-regional exports of US$2.9 billion are to be reduced by US$70.5 million, that is, by 2.4 percent. Among the SEE countries, Albania's exports to the region will decrease by 3.8 percent, followed by FYR Macedonia's exports by 3.0 percent, Croatia's exports by 2.9 percent, Serbia by 2.1 percent, Bosnia and Herzegovina by 1.5 percent and Montenegro by 0.9 percent (table 15.6).[7]

Table 15.6 Impact of EU-SEE Customs Union on Intra-regional Exports (US$ million)

	Pre-reform intra-region exports	After reform intra-region exports	Change	(%)
Total SEE	2,979.8	2,909.3	–70.5	–2.4
Albania	11.3	10.8	–0.4	–3.8
Bosnia and Herzegovina	521.8	513.9	–8.0	–1.5
Croatia	1,043.8	1,013.6	–30.2	–2.9
FYR Macedonia	238.1	230.9	–7.2	–3.0
Montenegro	7.2	7.1	–0.1	–0.9
Serbia	1,157.6	1,133.0	–24.6	–2.1

Source: Author.

It is important to remember again that these results are to be interpreted with caution. As mentioned earlier, partial equilibrium models can only estimate single country equations and hence the results do not factor in secondary interactions between countries and sectors.

Notes

[1] In some cases WITS uses earlier years as reference hence the tariff data are not up to date. In such a case, the data are corrected by the author to fully incorporate all the preferential agreements of SEEs as of today.
[2] Most countries have also signed FTA with Turkey and some with Russia.

[3] In the case of tariffs with regards to the EU27, all tariff data are up to date including first stages of reduction in Albania, Montenegro, and Bosnia and Herzegovina. In the simulations the new tariffs vis a vis EU's industrial products are taken to be zero, hence a scenario which has the impact of completion of SEE tariff liberalizations schedules with the EU.

[4] This is a standard assumption of the SMART model.

[5] These trade statistics are taken from UNCOMTRADE database and are the latest data available, usually for the year 2008.

[6] The GDP of SEE countries as a region is calculated by using the World Bank's WDI database and is the total of average GDPs over the last five years.

[7] The low level of decrease in Montenegro's exports may reflect some data availability problems. For some reporting countries the exports from Montenegro were not available in WITS.

CHAPTER 16

Summary and Policy Recommendations

By now SEE countries' low export potential is well established in literature. Even though exports have been increasing steadily, both intra- and extra-regional exports remain below potential. In addition to this they remain fragile as they heavily depend on a few items, mainly commodities. The aim of this study is to establish the costs and benefits of adopting EU's CET in order to identify whether this can be the right policy option for SEE countries in order to encourage export-led growth.

In the first part of the study, the tariff structure of each SEE country was examined in detail and compared to that of EU. After such a reform, the region's simple average tariffs would be reduced from 5.1 percent to 2.3 percent, trade-weighted average tariff would be reduced from 4.7 percent to 2.2 percent. Among the SEE countries, Serbia is to go through the most ambitious adjustment process due to its higher average tariffs and tariff dispersions. On the other extreme, Croatia requires the least effort to adopt EU's CET thanks to its advanced status as an EU candidate country. Montenegro is a unique case: its simple average tariffs are much lower than the regional average and EU's rates. With the adoption of CET, Montenegro's new rates will be less than 1 percent. Despite the fact FYR Macedonia is a WTO member and an EU candidate country, it require considerable amount of adjustment in its tariff structure. Albania and Bosnia and Herzegovina require a moderate level of adjustment compared to the extreme cases mentioned. In terms of sensitive sectors, textiles, clothing, and footwear are also highly protected in SEE countries as in the EU. Only in Montenegro, textiles MFN tariffs are lower than EU average. Otherwise, there are several sensitive products and sectors in each country and it is hard to generalize.

In the second part of this study, we estimate quantitatively the costs and benefits of adopting EU's CET by making use of traditional concepts of trade diversion and creation. As our estimation tools we use partial equilibrium model of SMART developed by UNCTAD and the World Bank. One has to keep in mind that the results of our analysis present only the direct effect of this trade reform as partial equilibrium models cannot take into account additional effects from inter-industry and macroeconomic adjustments. These secondary effects can be better modeled by computable general equilibrium (CGE) model.[1] Despite this shortcoming, partial equilibrium models have the advantage of presenting the trade diversion and creation as well as revenue and welfare effects of a trade reform on a highly disaggregated level (that is, 6-digit in this study). One of the strengths of our analysis is to show in great detail the sectors (products) and the partner countries that will be impacted by the adoption of EU's CET. Having this in mind, for countries in the region that have already liberalized their trade against the EU, this measure will erode EU member states preference with the SEE. On the other hand, market access of third party countries (that is, extra-EU and non-CEFTA countries) will improve in the SEE market.

The results indicate that the impact of this trade reform is going to be positive with net trade creation in the magnitude of US$998.9 million for the region, an increase of 4.3 percent from pre-reform import levels. Even though imports will increase significantly, the net effect of adopting EU's CET will result in revenue loss roughly half of the gains from trade creation, that is, US$459.7 million. The consumer surplus, which will result from reducing the deadweight loss from tariffs, is a modest US$51.7 million. The overall net effect of CET amounts thus to US$590.9 million, roughly 1 percent of SEE's combined GDP.

Another observation one can make based on the simulation results is that all countries will be able to diversify their trade to other countries outside the region. Although several EU member states are among the top 10 export partners, China, Russia, the United States, and Turkey are set to gain significant market share in the SEE market as a results of trade creation. The exports from China to the region are to increase by 8 percent and reach US$1.3 billion. The next largest beneficiary of this trade reform is Russia: its exports are to increase by 7 percent and reach US$819.6 million. Exports from the United States and Turkey are also going to increase by 10 percent and 9 percent respectively. On the other hand, trade diversion is going reduce exports mostly from existing preferential trade partners as expected. The impact of adopting CET is going to have a negative effect on intra-regional exports. Intra-regional exports will be reduced by US$70.5 million, that is, by 2.4 percent. Albania's exports are going to suffer by far the most. Nevertheless, the decrease in intra-regional exports (that is, trade diversion) is a re-adjustment and hence lessens the negative effect of trade diversion that was caused by the bilateral FTAs that are now brought under the CEFTA umbrella.

As these results are obtained by single-country simulations they do not take into effect indirect (secondary) results and interactions between regions and industries. As such these results may be taken as a conservative minimum impact. For example, one such indirect effect of adopting the EU's CET is increased FDI attractiveness from outside the region. After joining the EU, the 10 new member states have enjoyed increased FDI inflows from outside, such as Southeast Asia for example. This is an additional positive effect of adopting EU's CET. Currently different tariff structures allow for divergences in prices across the region. Hence it brings additional costs to doing business in an economically segmented market. If the SEE adopt EU's CET, this would make the region more attractive to the multinational companies.

If the SEE countries decide to proceed with adopting EU's CET unilaterally and individually, political resistance may arise against such a measure in those countries where the tariff revenue loss is the highest. Ideally a committee should be established to compensate those countries that are most dependent on customs import duties as revenue, for a temporary period of adjustment (for example, five years). Needless to say, this would prove difficult in practice in the case of a virtual customs union with no harmonization of customs regulation within the SEE. This adjustment period should be fixed for all, for example, to be achieved over five years, however, with country-specific tariff liberalization schedules. Each country should be allowed to decide its sensitive sectors. There may be 2-speed for tariff liberalization: one for sensitive products, one for non-sensitive products.

Although it may be difficult for the six SEE countries to pool their sovereignty over "most" of their trade policy, it should be politically easier to adopt EU's CET, an external benchmark, than any other CET. As all countries in the region have a clear EU vocation, adopting the EU's CET would bring them closer to EU membership.

Note

[1] However, CGE models are often very data intensive and hence it is not possible to use them due data limitations.

Consumer Surplus by Product and Country

Albania

Tariff line	Imports before (US$ millions)	Imports, change in (US$ millions)	Product	Consumer surplus (US$ million)
TOTAL	2,106.80	50.22		0.93
270112	18.17	4.79	Bituminous coal, whether or not pulverized, non-agglomerated	0.14
271019	366.83	5.22	Medium oils and preparations, of petroleum or bituminous minerals, n.e.s.	0.11
271600	309.00	19.89	Electrical energy	0.07
721420	100.39	2.94	Bars and rods, of iron or non-alloy steel, with indentations, ribs, groves or other deformations produced during the rolling process	0.04
690890	33.98	0.49	Glazed ceramic flags and paving, hearth or wall tiles (excl. of siliceous fossil meals or similar siliceous earths, refractory ceramic goods, tiles made into stands, ornamental articles and tiles specifically manufactured for stoves)	0.03
841510	11.69	0.54	Window or wall air conditioning machines, self-contained or "split-system"	0.03
691010	7.91	0.36	Ceramic sinks, washbasins, washbasin pedestals, baths, bidets, water closet pans, flushing cisterns, urinals and similar sanitary fixtures of porcelain or china (excl. soap dishes, sponge holders, tooth-brush holders, towel hooks and toilet paper holders)	0.03
252329	48.84	0.95	Portland cement (excl. white, whether or not artificially colored)	0.02
252390	31.87	0.73	Cement, whether or not colored (excl. aluminous cement and portland cement)	0.02
690810	33.68	0.29	Glazed ceramic tiles, cubes and similar articles, for mosaics, whether or not square or rectangular, the largest surface area of which is capable of being enclosed in a square of side of < 7 cm, whether or not on a backing	0.02

Source: UN COMTRADE database.

Bosnia and Herzegovina

Tariff line	Imports before (US$ millions)	Imports, change in (US$ millions)	Product	Consumer surplus (US$ million)
TOTAL	**4,446.64**	**253.68**		**12.71**
870332	119.55	16.81	Motor cars and other motor vehicles principally designed for the transport of persons, incl. station wagons and racing cars, with compression-ignition internal combustion piston engine "diesel or semi-diesel engine" of a cylinder capacity > 1.500 cm³ but <= 2.500 cm³ (excl. vehicles for the transport of persons on snow and other specially designed vehicles of subheading 8703.10)	1.73
640620	21.20	14.03	Outer soles and heels, of rubber or plastics	1.24
830241	16.29	8.31	Base metal mountings and fittings suitable for buildings (excl. locks with keys and hinges)	0.43
840310	13.39	10.76	Central heating boilers, non-electric (excl. vapor generating boilers and superheated water boilers of heading 8402)	0.35
611790	1.98	2.61	Parts of garments or clothing accessories, knitted or crocheted, n.e.s.	0.35
640699	60.81	4.75	Parts of footwear (excl. outer soles and heels of rubber or plastics, uppers and parts thereof, and general parts made of wood or asbestos)	0.31
570320	3.00	2.75	Carpets and other floor coverings, of nylon or other polyamides, tufted "needle punched", whether or not made up	0.30
840991	15.42	3.32	Parts suitable for use solely or principally with spark-ignition internal combustion piston engine, n.e.s.	0.21
350691	7.71	3.68	Adhesives based on polymers of heading 3901 to 3913 or on rubber (excl. products suitable for use as glues or adhesives put up for retail sale as glues or adhesives, with a net weight of <= 1 kg)	0.20
722790	4.89	3.32	Bars and rods of alloy steel other than stainless, hot-rolled, in irregularly wound coils (excl. products of high-speed steel or silicon-electrical steel)	0.17

Source: UN COMTRADE database.

Croatia

Tariff line	Imports before (US$ millions)	Imports, change in (US$ millions)	Product	Consumer surplus (US$ million)
TOTAL	7,703.57	93.32		2.67
271011	184.22	40.40	Light oils and preparations, of petroleum or bituminous minerals which >= 90% by volume "incl. losses" distil at 210°C "ASTM D 86 method"	1.22
271019	586.47	8.57	Medium oils and preparations, of petroleum or bituminous minerals, n.e.s.	0.11
640399	105.14	1.34	Footwear with outer soles of rubber, plastics or composition leather, with uppers of leather (excl. covering the ankle, incorporating a protective metal toecap, sports footwear, orthopedic footwear and toy footwear)	0.07
610910	71.19	0.60	T-shirts, singlets and other vests of cotton, knitted or crocheted	0.05
620342	38.07	0.49	Men's or boys' trousers, bib and brace overalls, breeches and shorts, of cotton (excl. knitted or crocheted, underpants and swimwear)	0.04
420222	10.83	0.42	Handbags, whether or not with shoulder straps, incl. those without handles, with outer surface of plastic sheeting or textile materials	0.03
620462	33.49	0.42	Women's or girls' trousers, bib and brace overalls, breeches and shorts of cotton (excl. knitted or crocheted, panties and swimwear)	0.03
711790	3.71	0.47	Imitation jewelry (excl. jewelry, of base metal, whether or not clad with silver, gold or platinum)	0.03
611020	39.58	0.35	Jerseys, pullovers, cardigans, waistcoats and similar articles, of cotton, knitted or crocheted (excl. wadded waistcoats)	0.03
640510	9.40	0.45	Footwear with uppers of leather or composition leather (excl. with outer soles of rubber, plastics, leather or composition leather and uppers of leather, orthopedic footwear and toy footwear)	0.02

Source: UN COMTRADE database.

FYR Macedonia

Tariff line	Imports before (US$ millions)	Imports, change in (US$ millions)	Product	Consumer surplus (US$ million)
TOTAL	2,067.89	81.56		3.65
270900	570.28	36.67	Petroleum oils and oils obtained from bituminous minerals, crude	1.22
271019	37.26	7.16	Medium oils and preparations, of petroleum or bituminous minerals, n.e.s.	0.50
271011	3.15	3.44	Light oils and preparations, of petroleum or bituminous minerals which >= 90% by volume "incl. losses" distil at 210°C "ASTM D 86 method"	0.35
551339	3.81	1.30	Woven fabrics containing predominantly, but < 85% synthetic staple fibers by weight, mixed principally or solely with cotton and weighing <= 170 g/m², made of yarn of different colors (excl. plain woven fabrics of polyester staple fibers)	0.09
680293	3.99	1.85	Granite, in any form, polished, decorated or otherwise worked (excl. tiles, cubes and similar articles of subheading 6802.10, imitation jewelry, clocks, lamps and lighting fittings and parts thereof, original sculptures and statuary, setts, curbstones and flagstones)	0.09
410711	7.80	3.12	Full grains leather "incl. parchment-dressed leather", unsplit, of the whole hides and skins of bovine "incl. buffalo" or equine animals, further prepared after tanning or crusting, without hair on (excl. chamois leather, patent leather and patent laminated leather, and metalized leather)	0.04
640399	4.47	0.36	Footwear with outer soles of rubber, plastics or composition leather, with uppers of leather (excl. covering the ankle, incorporating a protective metal toecap, sports footwear, orthopedic footwear and toy footwear)	0.04
730830	1.49	0.45	Doors, windows and their frames and thresholds for doors, of iron or steel	0.03
841510	9.79	0.58	Window or wall air conditioning machines, self-contained or "split-system"	0.03
640520	1.35	0.22	Footwear with uppers of textile materials (excl. with outer soles of rubber, plastics, leather or composition leather, orthopedic footwear and toy footwear)	0.03

Source: UN COMTRADE database.

Montenegro

Tariff line	Imports before (US$ millions)	Imports, change in (US$ millions)	Product	Consumer surplus (US$ million)
TOTAL	**694.89**	**10.22**		**0.22**
680293	1.89	2.87	Granite, in any form, polished, decorated or otherwise worked (excl. tiles, cubes and similar articles of subheading 6802.10, imitation jewelry, clocks, lamps and lighting fittings and parts thereof, original sculptures and statuary, setts, curbstones and flagstones)	0.07
841810	2.99	0.50	Combined refrigerator-freezers, with separate external doors	0.02
842211	2.57	0.29	Dishwashing machines of the household type	0.01
851712	37.40	0.85	Telephones for cellular networks "mobile telephones" or for other wireless networks	0.01
441820	4.46	0.62	Doors and their frames and thresholds, of wood	0.01
841581	2.60	0.26	Air conditioning machines incorporating a refrigerating unit and a valve for reversal of the cooling-heat cycle "reversible heat pumps" (excl. of a kind used for persons in motor vehicles and self-contained or "split-system" window or wall air conditioning machines)	0.01
722820	0.18	0.15	Bars and rods of silico-manganese steel (excl. semi-finished products, flat-rolled products and hot-rolled bars and rods in irregularly wound coils)	0.01
481910	1.00	0.34	Cartons, boxes and cases, of corrugated paper or paperboard	0.01
340220	12.73	0.18	Surface-active preparations, washing preparations, auxiliary washing preparations and cleaning preparations put up for retail sale (excl. organic surface-active agents, soap and organic surface-active preparations in the form of bars, cakes, molded pieces or shapes, and products and preparations for washing the skin in the form of liquid or cream)	0.01
845011	6.71	0.11	Fully automatic household or laundry-type washing machines, of a dry linen capacity <= 6 kg	0.00

Source: UN COMTRADE database.

Serbia

Tariff line	Imports before (US$ millions)	Imports, change in (US$ millions)	Product	Consumer surplus (US$ million)
TOTAL	**6,422.92**	**509.92**		**31.16**
870332	127.73	49.36	Motor cars and other motor vehicles principally designed for the transport of persons, incl. station wagons and racing cars, with compression-ignition internal combustion piston engine "diesel or semi-diesel engine" of a cylinder capacity > 1.500 cm³ but <= 2.500 cm³ (excl. vehicles for the transport of persons on snow and other specially designed vehicles of subheading 8703.10)	5.48
840310	14.72	24.52	Central heating boilers, non-electric (excl. vapor generating boilers and superheated water boilers of heading 8402)	1.49
271119	49.114	56.3405	Gaseous hydrocarbons, liquefied, n.e.s. (excl. natural gas, propane, butane, ethylene, propylene, butylene and butadiene)	1.39184
732219	8.24	8.7668	Radiators for central heating, non-electrically heated, and parts thereof, of iron other than cast iron or steel (excl. parts, elsewhere specified or included, and central-heating boilers)	0.980716
611790	2.151	5.61168	Parts of garments or clothing accessories, knitted or crocheted, n.e.s.	0.841752
870210	36.574	6.31626	Motor vehicles for the transport of >= 10 persons, incl. driver, with compression-ignition internal combustion piston engine "diesel or semi-diesel engine"	0.699808
690890	21.853	5.92539	Glazed ceramic flags and paving, hearth or wall tiles (excl. of siliceous fossil meals or similar siliceous earths, refractory ceramic goods, tiles made into stands, ornamental articles and tiles specifically manufactured for stoves)	0.638261
870331	21.76	4.15173	Motor cars and other motor vehicles principally designed for the transport of persons, incl. station wagons and racing cars, with compression-ignition internal combustion piston engine "diesel or semi-diesel engine" of a cylinder capacity <= 1.500 cm³ (excl. vehicles for the transport of persons on snow and other specially designed vehicles of subheading 8703.10)	0.470428
481910	5.514	6.13527	Cartons, boxes and cases, of corrugated paper or paperboard	0.468768
830241	11.113	7.05982	Base metal mountings and fittings suitable for buildings (excl. locks with keys and hinges)	0.445636

Source: UN COMTRADE database.

References

Aeneas. 2008. "Regional Guidelines for Unified Asylum, Migration, and Visa Management in the Western Balkans." ICMPD (www.icmpd.org). October.

————. 2008. "National Reports on Strong Institutions and a Unified Approach in the Asylum, Migration and Visa management in the Western Balkans." ICMPD (www.icmpd.org). September.

Akkoyunlu-Wigley, A., and S. Mihci. 2006. "The Customs Union with the EU and Its Impact on Turkey's Economic Growth." Paper presented at 8th ETSG Annual Conference, Vienna. Albornoz, Facundo, Héctor F. Calvo Pardo, Gregory Corcos and Emanuel Ornelas. 2009. "Sequential Exporting". Preliminary version (forthcoming)

Aminian, Nathalie, K.C. Fung, and Francis Ng. 2008. "Integration of Markets vs. Integration by Agreements." World Bank Policy Research Working Paper 4546. World Bank, Washington, DC.

Anderson, James E., and Eric Van Wincoop. 2004. "Trade Costs." *Journal of Economic Literature* 42(3): 691–751.

Arieti, Samuel. 2006. "The Role of MERCOSUR as a Vehicle for Latin American Integration." *Chicago Journal of International Law* 6: 761–773a.

Augier, Patricia, Michael Gasiorek, and Charles Lai-Tong. 2005. "The Impact of Rules of Origin on Trade Flows." *Economic Policy* 20(43): 567–624.

Besic, Milos. 2009. "Student Mobility in Western Balkan Countries." Research Report. January. King Baudouin Foundation. Available at: www.kbs-frb.be/publication. aspx?id=243444&LangType=1033.

Blalock, G., and P. Gertler. 2008. "Welfare Gains from FDI through Technology Transfer to Local Suppliers." *Journal of International Economics* 74. Bosnia and Herzegovina. 2008. *Migration and Asylum Action Plan: 2008-2011*. Ministry of Security in Cooperation with the International Organization for Migration. November.

Brenton, Paul and Richard Newfarmer. 2007. "Watching More Than The Discovery Channel: Export Cycles and Diversification in Development." World Bank Policy Research Working Paper 4302, Washington DC

CARICOM Secretariat. n.d. "The Free Movement of Skills and Social Security." Available at: the www.caricom.org/jsp/single_market/free_movement.jsp? menu=csme.

Centre for Economic and Social Studies. 2006. "From Brain Drain to Brain Gain: Mobilizing Albania's Skilled Diaspora." Development Research Centre on Migration, Globalization and Poverty. UNDP Policy Paper.

Cerrutti, Marcela. 2009. "Gender and Intra-Regional Migration in South America." HDR Paper 2009/12. Available at: http://hdr.undp.org/en/reports/global/hdr2009/papers/.

Clougherty, Joseph A., and Michal Grajek. 2006. "The Impact of ISO 9000 Diffusion on Trade and FDI: A New Institutional Analysis." CERP Discussion Paper No. 6026.

Co, Catherine Y., Ira N. Gang, and Myeong-Su Yun. 2000. "Returns to Returning." *Journal of Population Economics* 13(1): 57–79.

Coats, David. 2008. "Migration Myths: Employment, Wages and Labour Market Performance." London: The Work Foundation. www.theworkfoundation.com/assets/docs/publications/33_migration%20myths.pdf.

Commission of the European Communities. 2007. "Mobility, an Instrument for More and Better Jobs: The European Job Mobility Action Plan (2007-2010)." Communication from the Commission to the Council, the European Parliament, the European Economic and Social Committee and the Committee of the Regions, COM(2007) 773 final, Brussels, 6.12.2007.

de Coulon, Augustin, and Matloob Piracha. 2005. "Self-selection and the Performance of Return Migrants: The Source Country Perspective." *Journal of Population Economics* 18: 779–807.

Djankov, Simeon, Caroline L. Freund, and Cong S. Pham. 2006. "Trading on Time." World Bank Policy Research Working Paper No. 3909. World Bank, Washington, DC.

Dollar, D., and A. Kraay. 2004. "Trade, Growth and Poverty." *Economic Journal, Royal Economic Society* 114 (493).

Erzan, R. et al. 2002. "Turkey's Customs Union with the EU: A Framework for Evaluating the Impact of Economic Integration." MPRA paper no 382. University Library of Munich, Germany.

European Training Foundation (ETF). 2009. *Country Plans and Labor Market Reviews.* Available at: www.etf.europa.eu/web.nsf/pages/Publications_catalogue_EN?OpenDocument.

Fallon, Peter R. 2008. "Barriers to Labor Mobility in East Africa." Report prepared for the World Bank, June. World Bank, Washington, DC.

Fernandes, Ana M., and Caroline Paunov. 2009. "Does Tougher Import Competition Foster Product Quality Upgrading?" World Bank Policy Research Working Paper 4894. World Bank, Washington, DC.

Fetsi, Anastasia, ed. 2007. "Labour Markets in the Western Balkans: Challenges for the Future." ETF. Available at: www.etf.europa.eu/web.nsf/pages/EmbedPub_EN?OpenDocument&emb=/pubmgmt.nsf/(WebPublications%20by%20yearR)/F624E6A60F073F75C125728F002FFCF0?OpenDocument.

Frankel, J., and D. Romer. 1999. "Does Trade Cause Growth?" *American Economic Review* 89(3): 379–399.

Gallup. 2009. "Focus On: The Impact of Migration." Balkan Monitor.

Gamberoni, Elisa, and Richard Newfarmer. 2009. "Trade Protection: Incipient but Worrisome Trends." *World Bank Trade Note* 37. World Bank, Washington, DC.

Gasiorek, Michael. 2008. "The Impact of the Diagonal Cumulation of Rules of Origin in the Context of Euro-Med Integration." Research n°FEM31-13. CARIS, United Kingdom.

Girvan, Norman. 2007. "Towards a Single Development Vision and the Role of the Single Economy." Paper approved by CARICOM Heads of Government July 1–4. Barbados. Available at: www.caricom.org (accessed June 29, 2009).

Gligorov, Vladimir Anna Iara, Michael Landesmann, Robert Stehrer, and Hermine Vidovic. 2008. "Adjustment Capacity to External Shocks of EU Candidate and Potential EU Candidate Countries of the Western Balkans, with a Focus on Labour Markets." WiiW (Vienna Institute for International Economic Studies). Report 352. December.

Gorodnichenko, Yuriy, Jan Svejnar, and Katherine Terrell. 2009. "Globalization and Innovation in Emerging Markets". World Bank Policy Research Working Paper 4808. World Bank, Washington, DC.

Grecic, Vladimir, ed. 2006. *Visa Policy and the Western Balkans.* Balkan Trust for Democracy. Belgrade. Institute of International Politics and Economics. Available at: www.diplomacy.bg.ac.yu/.

Greene, Edward. 2005. "Free Movement of Persons: The Vision and the Reality." CARICOM Community Secretariat. March 16-17. Available at: www.caricom.org/jsp/single_market/free_movement.jsp?menu=csme.

Grubel, Herbert G., and Peter J. Lloyd. 1975. *Intra-Industry Trade: The Theory and Measurement of International Trade in Differentiated Products.* New York: Wiley.

Government of Albania. 2004. *National Migration Strategy.*

Government of the FYR Macedonia. 2009. *Republic of Macedonia: Migration Profile: 2008.* January.

Government of Montenegro. 2008. *Strategy for Integrated Migration Management in Montenegro: 2008-2013.* Podgorica, September.

Hallaky, Juan Carlos, and Jagadeesh Sivadasanz. 2009. "Exporting Behavior under Quality Constraints." Preliminary version (forthcoming). NBER Working Paper No. 14928.

Hamilton, Pamela Coke. 2000. "Protocol II on Establishment, Services, and Capital." In Sherry Stephenson, ed. *Services Trade in the Western Hemisphere.* Brookings Institution Press: 192–210.

Helpman, Elhanan. 1987. "Imperfect Competition and International Trade: Evidence from Fourteen Industrial Countries." *Journal of the Japanese and International Economies* 1: 62–81.

Helpman, Elhanan, and Paul Krugman. 1985. *Market Structure and Foreign Trade.* Cambridge: MIT Press.

Heston, Alan, Robert Summers, and Bettina Aten. 2006. "Penn World Table Version 6.2." Center for International Comparisons of Production, Income and Prices at the University of Pennsylvania, September.

Hoekman, Bernard, and Simeon Djankov. 1996. "Intra-industry Trade, Foreign Direct Investment, and the Reorientation of Eastern European Exports." Policy Research Working Paper Series 1652. World Bank, Washington, DC.

Iara, Anna. "East to West Europe: Skill Diffusion by Temporary Migration?" In Robert E.B. Lucas, Lyn Squire, and T.N. Srinivsan, eds., *Global Exchanges and Poverty: Trade, Investment and Migration.* Edward Elgar Press, forthcoming.

Iara, Anna, and Hermine Vidovic. 2009. "Employment and Unemployment in the Western Balkans: An Assessment." Monthly Report No. 4/2009. Available at: http://publications.wiiw.ac.at/ ?action=publ&id=details&publ=MR2009-04_1.

International Organization for Migration. 2003. *World Migration Report*. Geneva.

———. 2007. *The Republic of Croatia Migration Profile*, Ministry of Interior, Government of Slovenia, October.

———. 2008a. *Migration in Serbia: A Country Profile*.

———. 2008b. *Migration in Albania: A Country Profile*.

ISEAS. 2009a. "ASEAN Economic Community Blueprint." Institute for Southeast Asian Studies. Available at: http://bookshop.iseas.edu.sg/.

———. 2009b. "Global Financial Crisis: Implications for ASEAN." Institute for Southeast Asian Studies. Available at: http://bookshop.iseas.edu.sg/.

———. 2009c. "MERCOSUR Economic Integration: Lessons for ASEAN." Institute for Southeast Asian Studies. Available at: http://bookshop.iseas.edu.sg/.

Jovicic, Milena, and Radmila Dragutinovic Mitrovic. 2007. "Macroeconomic Analysis of Causes and Effects of Remittances: A Panel Model of the SEE Countries and a Case Study of Serbia." University of Belgrade. Report to GDN.

Kaminski, B. 2008. "Multilateral and Regional Tariff Liberalization in Albania: Gains from Harmonizing MFN Tariffs on Industrial Products with the EU." Mimeo.

Kathuria, Sanjay, ed. 2008. *Western Balkan Integration and the EU: An Agenda for Trade and Growth*. Washington, DC: World Bank.

Katja Zajc Kejžar. 2009. "Ideas for EU Extended Support for Trade Growth in the Western Balkan Countries: Diagonal versus Bilateral Cumulation of Origin." Draft version, February 2009

Kawecka-Wyrykowska Elzbieta. 2009. "Evolving Pattern of Intra-industry Trade Specialization of the New Member States (NMS) of the EU: The Case of the Automotive Industry." Warsaw, January 2009.

Kocyigit, A., and A. Sen. 2007. "The Extent of Intra-industry Trade between Turkey and the EU: The Impact of Customs Unions." *Journal of Economic and Social Research* 9(2): 61–85.

Konica, Nevila, and Randall K. Filer. 2003. "Albanian Emigration: Causes and Consequences." CERGE-EI Working Paper 181. Prague: Center for Economic Research and Graduate Education of Charles University.

Krueger, A. 1997. "Free Trade Agreements versus Customs Unions." *Journal of Development Economics* 54: 169–187.

Lipsey, R. 1957. *The Theory of Customs Union: Trade Diversion and Welfare*. Blackwell Publishing, The London School of Economics and Political Science.

Lohrman, A. 2000. "Development Effects of the Customs Union between Turkey and the EU." *Russian and East European Finance and Trade* 36(4): 26–44.

Lucas, Robert E.B. 2005. *International Migration and Economic Development: Lessons from Low-Income Countries*. Northampton, MA and Cheltenham, UK: Edward Elgar.

———. 2006. "Migration and Economic Development in Africa: A Review of Evidence." *Journal of African Economies* 15 (supplement 2) December: 337–395.

Lucas, Robert E.B., and Laura Chappell. 2009. "Measuring Migration's Development Impacts: Preliminary Evidence from Jamaica." Development on the Move

Working Paper 2, Institute for Public Policy Research and Global Development Network, February.

Lundström, Cecilia. 2009a. Personal communication.

———. 2009b. "Students from the Western Balkans." February 12. King Baudouin Foundation. Available at: www.kbs-frb.be/otheractivity.aspx?id=228446&LangType=1033.

Manning, Chris, and Pradip Bhatnagar. 2004. "Liberalizing and Facilitating the Movement of Individual Service Providers under AFAS: Implications for Labour and Immigration Policies and Procedures in ASEAN." REPSF Project 02/004. March. Available at: www.aseansec.org/16945.htm.

Martin, Philip L. 1993. *Trade and Migration: NAFTA and Agriculture.* Washington: DC: Institute for International Economics, October. Available at: http://www.iie.com.

———. 2005. "Mexico-US Migration," in Gary Hufbauer and Jeffrey Schott (eds.), *NAFTA Revisited: Achievements and Challenges.* Institute for International Economics: 441-486. Available at: http://bookstore.iie.com/merchant.mvc?Screen=PROD&Product_Code=332.

———. 2007. "Guest Workers: New Solution or New Problem." *University of Chicago Legal Forum*: 289-318.

———. 2008. "Low- and Semi-Skilled Workers Abroad." In *World Migration Report. Managing Labour Mobility in the Evolving Global Economy*, IOM: 77-104. Available at: www.iom.ch/jahia/Jahia/cache/offonce/ pid/1674?entryId=20275.

———. 2009. "Recession and Migration: A New Era for Labor Migration." *International Migration Review*. 43(3), Fall: 671–691.

Martin, Philip L. and Manolo Abella. 2009. "Migration and Development: The Elusive Link at the GFMD." *International Migration Review*. 43(2), Summer: 431-439.

Martin, Philip, Manolo Abella, and Christiane Kuptsch. 2006. *Managing Labor Migration in the Twenty-First Century.* Yale University Press. Available at: http://yalepress.yale.edu/yupbooks/book.asp?isbn=0300109040.

Martin, Philip L., and Gottfried Zuercher. 2008. "Managing Migration: The Global Challenge." *Washington D.C. Population Reference Bureau* 63(1), March. Available at: www.prb.org/Publications/PopulationBulletins/2008/managingmigration.aspx.

Meade, J. 1953. *Problems of Economic Union.* Chicago: University Chicago Press.

Medved, Felicita. 2007. Draft MARRI Paper. April. Mimeo.

Mendola, Mariapia, and Gero Carletto. 2009. "International Migration and Gender Differentials in the Home Labor Market: Evidence from Albania." Policy Research Working Paper 4900, Poverty Team, Development Research Group. World Bank, Washington, DC, April.

Micevska, Maja. 2004. "Unemployment and Labour Market Rigidities in Southeast Europe." Global Development Network of Southeast Europe, June.

Njinkeu Dominique, John S. Wilson, and Bruno Powo Fosso. 2008. "Expanding Trade within Africa: The Impact of Trade Facilitation." World Bank Policy Research Working Paper 4790. World Bank, Washington, DC.

Nowak-Lehmann, F., et al. 2007. "The Impact of a Customs Union between Turkey and the EU on Turkey's Exports to the EU." *Journal of Common Market Studies* 45(3): 71–743.

OECD. 2008. "Defining and Strengthening Sector Specific Sources of Competitiveness in the Western Balkans—Recommendation for a Regional Investment Strategy." Presented in Sarajevo on October 9, 2008.

Ratha, Dilip, and William Shaw. 2007. "South-South Migration and Remittances." World Bank Working Paper 102. World Bank, Washington, DC.

Rauch, James. 1999. "Networks versus Markets in International Trade." *Journal of International Economics* 7(35).

Reed, Howard, and Maria Latorre. 2009. "The Economic Impacts of Migration on the UK Labour Market." London: Institute for Public Policy Research. Economics of Migration Working Paper 3, February.

Ruhs, Martin, and Philip Martin. 2008. "Numbers vs. Rights: Trade-offs and Guest Worker Programs." *International Migration Review* 42(1): 249–65.

Sachs, J., and A. Warner. 1995. "Economic Reform and Process of Global Integration." Harvard Institute of Economic Research Working Papers no 1733.

Schneider, Friedrich. 2006. "Shadow Economies of 145 Countries All Over the World: What Do We Really Know?" Working paper. Available at: www3.brookings.edu/metro/umi/events/20060904_schneider.pdf.

Sriskandarajah, Dhananjayan, Laurence Cooley, and Howard Reed. 2005. "Paying Their Way: The Fiscal Contribution of Immigrants in the UK." London: Institute for Public Policy Research. Available at: www.ippr.org/publicationsandreports/publication.asp?id=280.

Taylor, Benjamin J., and John S. Wilson. 2008. "Harmonized International Standards Do Matter to Developing Country Exports." World Bank Trade Issue Brief July 2008. World Bank, Washington, DC.

Taymaz, E., and K. Yilmaz. 2007. "Productivity and Trade Orientation: Turkish Manufacturing Industry Before and After the Customs Union." *The Journal of International Trade and Diplomacy* 1(1): 127–154.

Villarreal, M. Angeles, and Marisabel Cid. 2008. "NAFTA and the Mexican Economy." Congressional Research Service RL34733. November 4.

Viner, J. 1950. "The Customs Union Issue." Carnegie Endowment for International Peace, New York. Available at: wiiw.ac.at/?action=publ&id=searchfulltext&step=2.

Woolcock, Stephen. 2007. "European Union Policy towards Free Trade Agreements." ECIPE Working Paper No. 03/2007.

World Bank. 2008a. *Western Balkan Integration and the EU: An Agenda for Trade and Growth*. Ed. S. Kathuria, World Bank, Washington, DC.

———. 2008b. "Macedonia: Country Report." World Bank, Washington, DC.

———. 2009 (forthcoming). "Albania Country Economic Memorandum." World Bank, Washington, DC.

———. 2009 (forthcoming). "Bosnia and Herzegovina Country Economic Memorandum." World Bank, Washington, DC.

———. 2009 (forthcoming). "Croatia's EU Convergence Report: Reaching and Sustaining Higher Rates of Economic Growth." World Bank, Washington, DC.

———. 2009 (forthcoming). "FYR Macedonia Country Economic Memorandum." World Bank report 44170-MK. World Bank, Washington, DC.

Eco-Audit

Environmental Benefits Statement

The World Bank is committed to preserving Endangered Forests and natural resources. We print World Bank Working Papers and Country Studies on postconsumer recycled paper, processed chlorine free. The World Bank has formally agreed to follow the recommended standards for paper usage set by Green Press Initiative—a nonprofit program supporting publishers in using fiber that is not sourced from Endangered Forests. For more information, visit www.greenpressinitiative.org.

In 2008, the printing of these books on recycled paper saved the following:

Trees*	Solid Waste	Water	Net Greenhouse Gases	Total Energy
289	8,011	131,944	27,396	92 mil.
*40 feet in height and 6–8 inches in diameter	Pounds	Gallons	Pounds CO_2 Equivalent	BTUs

green press INITIATIVE

www.ingramcontent.com/pod-product-compliance
Lightning Source LLC
Chambersburg PA
CBHW080332270326
41927CB00014B/3196